mix&bake

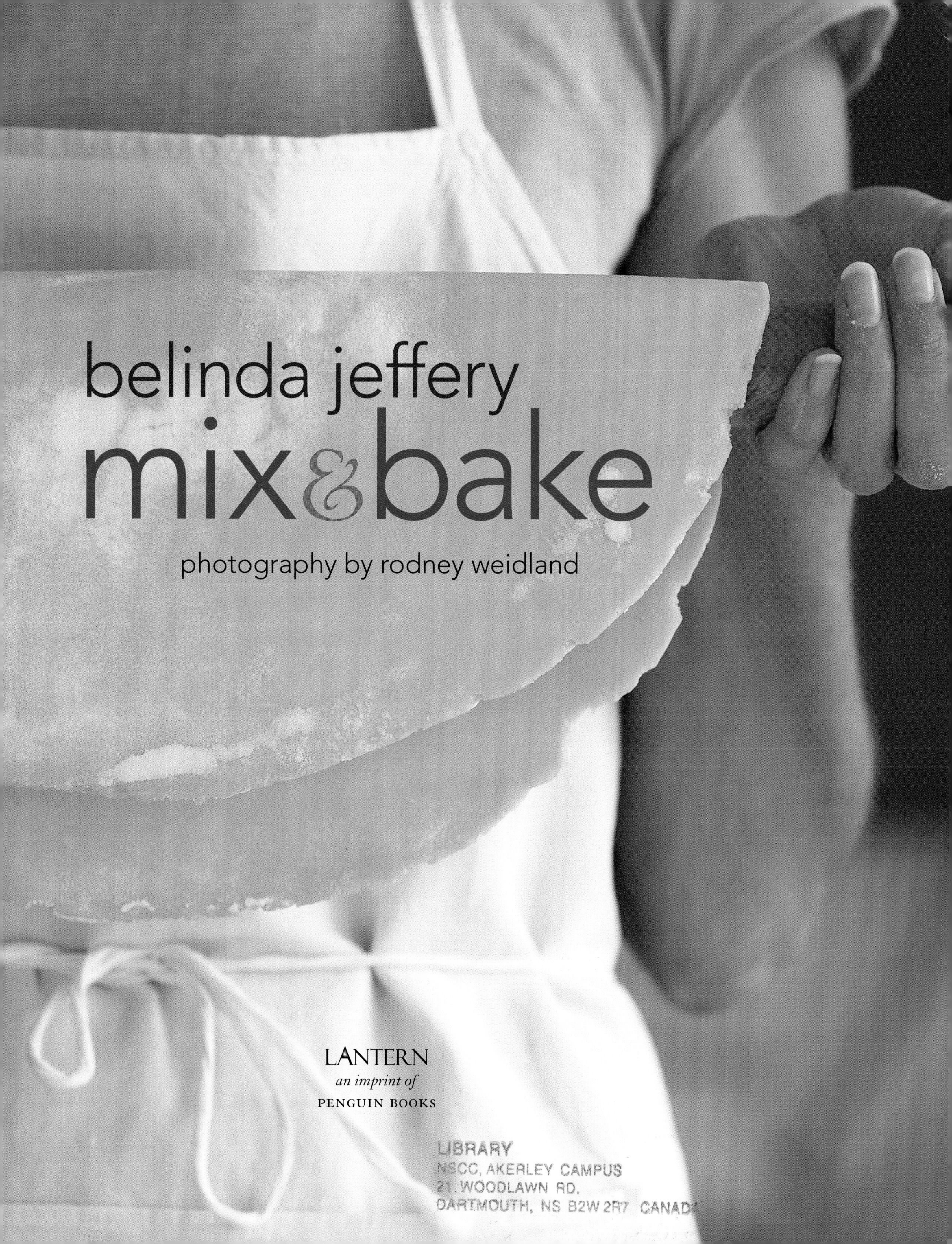

belinda jeffery
mix&bake

photography by rodney weidland

LANTERN
an imprint of
PENGUIN BOOKS

LANTERN

Published by the Penguin Group
Penguin Group (Australia)
250 Camberwell Road, Camberwell, Victoria 3124, Australia
(a division of Pearson Australia Group Pty Ltd)
Penguin Group (USA) Inc.
375 Hudson Street, New York, New York 10014, USA
Penguin Group (Canada)
90 Eglinton Avenue East, Suite 700, Toronto, Canada ON M4P 2Y3
(a division of Pearson Penguin Canada Inc.)
Penguin Books Ltd
80 Strand, London WC2R 0RL England
Penguin Ireland
25 St Stephen's Green, Dublin 2, Ireland
(a division of Penguin Books Ltd)
Penguin Books India Pvt Ltd
11 Community Centre, Panchsheel Park, New Delhi – 110 017, India
Penguin Group (NZ)
67 Apollo Drive, Rosedale, North Shore 0632, New Zealand
(a division of Pearson New Zealand Ltd)
Penguin Books (South Africa) (Pty) Ltd
24 Sturdee Avenue, Rosebank, Johannesburg 2196, South Africa

Penguin Books Ltd, Registered Offices: 80 Strand, London, WC2R 0RL, England

First published by Penguin Group (Australia), 2007

10 9 8 7 6 5 4 3

Design by Debra Billson © Penguin Group (Australia)
Cover photograph by Rodney Weidland
Author photograph by Rodney Weidland
Additional prop sourcing by David Prior

Typeset in 11/15 pt Granjon by Post Pre-Press Group, Brisbane, Queensland
Colour reproduction by Splitting Image, Clayton, Victoria
Printed and bound in China by 1010 Printing International Limited

National Library of Australia
Cataloguing-in-Publication data:

Jeffery, Belinda.
   Mix & bake.

   Includes index.

   ISBN 978 1 920989 53 8.
   1. Baking. 2. Cookery, Australian. I. Weidland, Rodney.
   II. Title.

641.815

penguin.com.au

To the many generous-spirited cooks who, in the
time-honoured tradition of sharing, have handed down
their cherished family recipes – this book is for you,
with heartfelt thanks.

Contents

introduction 1

ingredients 5

utensils and bakeware 9

a few extra tips and practicalities 11

chocolate cakes and brownies 13

all sorts of fruit cakes 49

cakes with lots of nuts 77

muffins 103

biscuits 123

scones 149

pies, tarts and savoury odds and ends 173

slices and bars 205

quick sweet and savoury tea breads and soda breads 227

basics and extras 249

acknowledgements 260

index 261

Introduction

The first thing I ever remember baking was a cake. I can't have been very old at the time, maybe five or six, and my mum stood me next to her on a wooden stool so that I could reach the bench-top to mix everything together. The memory is still crystal-clear – the cake was a small chocolate cake baked in a creamy enamel basin (with a somewhat chipped green rim) which I had taken a shine to and insisted upon using. I can still see and smell that simple cake to this day – the top was a bit cracked but satisfyingly domed and it smelled wonderful – warm and richly chocolate-y. I can also remember the exquisite torture of having to wait for it to cool before I could eat a slice!

Since that time baking has been my 'thing' – I love it and it gives me more pleasure than any other type of cooking. And although, during my years of working in restaurants, I cooked my way around most parts of the menu, it was always baking that I was most passionate about. When I say baking, I don't mean those elaborate, multi-storey cakes and gateaux that you see in shop windows – they're not really my cup of tea – but more the cherished family recipes and heart-and-soul baking that you find in old country cookbooks.

Simple cakes, biscuits and tarts that you just know are going to taste good, and which often have a history to them – as do so many of the recipes in this book. As I bake them, they immediately conjure up images of my family and friends, and tasting them is, for me, like a taste of memories. Be they of my mum, Cooee, making her classic orange cake (I can still see her now, bowl in one hand and wooden spoon in the other, beating the butter and sugar until it was fluffy and always making sure there was plenty of mixture left on the spoon for me to lick), or of my 'Auntie' Beryl wreathed in a cloud of icing sugar as she baked hundreds of her Mexican Wedding Biscuits for my wedding day.

Having said that, I understand that this may well be a somewhat unusual book to write now, when more than ever we seem to be strapped for time and our preoccupation with eating a healthy diet is soaring. However, in a funny way, it is perhaps because of these very two factors that I have written it, for baking can be such a serene and peaceful thing to do, and both the preparation and results can help restore one's body and soul like nothing else I know of in this mad and busy world.

I also realise that, despite the best will in the world, finding the time to make a cake may seem a luxury that few of us can afford these days. In response to this, I have tried to simplify and streamline my favourite recipes as much as I can to make them more suited to hectic modern schedules, so it becomes possible to, say, bake a slice or muffin that only takes twenty minutes or so to make (and, I should add, tastes much more delicious than anything you can buy). And that's the other thing about all of this – homemade cakes, biscuits and pies made with fresh, good-quality ingredients just taste incredibly good.

Now I live in a rural community, I've also noticed that entertaining here tends to be very casual and spontaneous, as so many people are up and working at the crack of dawn and don't have time for planning and preparing elaborate meals. Although we still do manage to get together for simple dinners, an awful lot of 'afternoon tea-ing' goes on in our neck of the woods too. Everybody makes a favourite cake, batch of scones, slice or whatever and it's all put out, either in front of the fire in winter or in the garden in summer. We then proceed to sit and chat and solve the problems of the world in a few hours, all fuelled with cake and tea – nothing could be nicer. (In fact, as I write this, I have just received an invitation to a Mad Hatters' Tea Party where, 'the wearing of hats is mandatory and rabbits are optional'!) It's a wonderful thing to do and such an easy way to catch up when everyone is so busy. I sometimes think that, as life becomes more and more hectic, afternoon tea may well become the new dinner party of the dining world!

As to the health factor, a number of people have said that they feel my writing this book is quite a risky enterprise when there is so much emphasis on obesity concerns these days. However, the words of a dear friend ring in my ears every time I start to wonder if I'm quite sane in doing this. When I told him what I was up to and voiced my concerns, he smiled gently at me and said, 'A slice of homemade cake never made anyone fat, and it certainly made them smile'. And it's true – like everything else in our lives it is all about balance, and I would far rather enjoy eating a piece of cake made with love from good eggs, butter and flour (with no preservatives, food additives or colourings) than something bought any day. I have taken these wise words to heart.

These are the reasons that this book has come about – and so at last I don't have to scrabble through piles of bulging recipe folders to find the ones I love most!

My two greatest wishes in writing this are that it encourages you to make some of these recipes (and in doing so, to enjoy the quiet contentment and pleasure that baking can bring); and, that the recipes themselves, cooked and eaten with great pleasure in my own family for so many years, become favourites of yours too.

Ingredients

BUTTERMILK   Buttermilk is lovely stuff. Although it originally was the thin milky liquid that remained after cream was churned to make butter, in more recent times it's made by adding a culture or cultures to low-fat milk (in much the same way that yoghurt is made). What you end up with is something that looks like slightly thick milk and has a distinctive, and very refreshing, acidity. The reason it's so fabulous in baking is because when mixed with bicarbonate of soda (or anything containing it, such as self-raising flour) it creates lots of bubbles, so the resulting scone, cake or whatever is very light and fluffy with a subtle tang, and in the case of cakes, has a tender, velvety crumb.

CHOCOLATE   I've spoken at length about chocolate in the introduction to the Chocolate Cakes and Brownies chapter (see page 15). Suffice to say here that you should only ever cook with a chocolate that you enjoy eating too.

DOUBLE THICK CREAM   This is another ingredient that is sold under a few names in the supermarket – 'rich, thick cream' or something similar is the norm. It's a beautiful ivory colour, with a satiny sheen and tastes wonderful – it's thicker and richer than regular thickened cream, which has gelatine added to give it body.

DUTCH-PROCESSED COCOA   There are a few types of cocoa powder on the market but I nearly always use brands that have been 'dutch-processed'. This means that the cocoa has gone through a process that removes some of its acidity. It gives the cocoa a softer, smoother flavour, richer colour and it tends to dissolve more easily. This style of 'dutched' cocoa is usually available in good delicatessens and specialty food shops.

EDIBLE RICE PAPER   Not to be confused with the brittle rounds of rice paper used for making Vietnamese rice paper rolls, these sheets are white, flexible and slightly spongy. They are used to bake very sticky things on, such as macaroons, or for lining a tin before baking, for example the panforte on page 99. In both cases, it doesn't matter if the rice paper sticks because you can eat it too.

EGGS   All these recipes were made with 60 g eggs at cool room temperature. As to the eggs themselves, by all means use regular eggs as they'll work just fine. However, I prefer to use free-range eggs for both ethical and taste reasons – the chooks lead a more normal, scratching-about kind of life and the eggs usually have a lot more flavour. You can also buy free-range organic eggs; I really recommend that you give them a try, especially if you're an egg sort of person. You'll find that they're a revelation – they taste wonderful, just how you hope an egg will, and make the best omelettes, poached eggs and simple soft-boiled eggs. (I cooked nearly all these recipes with organic eggs from friends' chooks, and apart from their marvellous flavour, the brilliant orange yolks gave everything the most wonderful colour.)

FLOUR   When I tested all these recipes I made them with regular plain or self-raising flour from the supermarket, although, wherever possible, I used organic flour, which fortunately most places stock as a mainstream item now. I've used some more unusual flours in some of the recipes for cakes and tea breads, and I've discussed these specifically there.

MAPLE SYRUP   Maple syrup is magical stuff, with an intense woody flavour and a fragrance that nothing else can duplicate. The trouble is that there are a lot of syrups around that appear to be maple syrup, but they're not. Check the label to make sure you're getting the real McCoy; you want pure maple syrup, not maple-flavoured syrup. It's also important to remember that once you've opened the syrup it must be stored in the fridge, as it's highly perishable at room temperature.

NIGELLA SEEDS   Also known as kalonji seeds, these are the little angular matte-black seeds you see on top of Turkish and Indian breads. They have a delicious nutty, peppery flavour that is somewhat addictive. If you're a gardener you may well know them as they are a very close relative of love-in-the-mist. They may be a little hard to find but try your luck at a good health food store or delicatessen. If you can't find them, don't worry, as either black or white sesame seeds make an excellent substitute.

NUTS   These are discussed in detail in the introduction to the Cakes With Lots of Nuts chapter (see pages 79–80).

PURE VANILLA EXTRACT   This may be a bit hard to find but it is worth pursuing. It's a gorgeous, dark, sticky syrup made from vanilla beans and has the most wonderfully intense vanilla flavour. It's expensive but you can salve your conscience a bit by knowing that a little goes a long way. It's mainly available from specialty food shops, some delicatessens and cookware stores; a number of these shops also sell it by mail order and are happy to deliver around Australia. But if you can't find it, don't despair – if vanilla essence is all you can get, that will be fine, just increase the quantity by half again from the amount specified in the recipe to help boost the vanilla flavour. As an alternative, you can make a pretty good version yourself. Dissolve 1 tablespoonful of sugar in 1 litre of white rum or brandy. Add 10–12 split vanilla beans, seal the bottle tightly, then leave it for at least three weeks, shaking it now and then, before using it.

SMOKED PAPRIKA   This paprika is particularly delicious as the peppers it is made from are dried over smouldering oak fires for about two weeks before they're cooled and ground. This gives the paprika the most wonderful rich, smoky flavour. It is quite intense so it's a good idea to add a bit less rather than more to a dish initially and then go from there, otherwise its flavour can be overwhelming.

SPELT   The best way to think of spelt is as a cousin of wheat; it's a member of the same family but an entirely different species. An ancient grain that traces its lineage back a very long way, spelt is mentioned in the bible as one of the original seven grains. The flour has a good nutty flavour and is also nutritious as it contains large amounts of B-complex vitamins and is very high in fibre. But perhaps the thing that has brought it most recently to public attention is that although it contains gluten, it's often well tolerated by many people with gluten allergies or sensitivities.

SPICES   Spices are among the most magical things in baking as they can transform a handful of simple ingredients into something much more than the sum of their parts. An apple pie wouldn't be the same without cinnamon; it's hard to contemplate a fruit cake without nutmeg and allspice; and the warm glow of ginger is essential to all sorts of biscuits and cakes. The fresher the spices you use are, the better the resulting flavour, but it is hard to know just how long they've been hanging around both in the shop and in your pantry (dating them helps, although I often forget to do this!). Unless you use your spices regularly, particularly the ground ones, it's a really good idea to taste them after a while to check that they still have a good clear flavour.

There's one spice that I would like to mention in particular and that's nutmeg. There's nothing quite like the flavour of freshly grated nutmeg and I have a little nutmeg grater that I use specifically for this. These graters aren't expensive (although there are some rather grand ones about that are), and really are a worthwhile investment if you like to bake. As to the whole nutmegs themselves, make sure they're plump with a slight sheen, as this means they are full of oil and flavour.

TOASTED HAZELNUT MEAL   You can buy toasted hazelnut meal from health food stores and good nut suppliers, or you can easily make your own. To do this, simply spread the untoasted ground hazelnuts on a baking tray and pop it into a 180°C oven for 5–8 minutes until golden. Keep a close eye on it and every so often stir it around as the edges darken more quickly than the middle. When it's ready, remove it from the oven and leave it to cool. You can do this with almond meal too – it's a simple but very effective way to intensify the flavour of the nuts.

UNSALTED BUTTER   In nearly all these recipes I recommend using unsalted butter. Regular unsalted butter is fine, however, there's another sort of unsalted butter called cultured unsalted or continental butter that's also available. This butter has a culture added to it, in much the same way as milk has to make yoghurt, or cream to make sour cream. It gives the butter a superb, slightly tangy flavour and lovely clean finish that is particularly delicious. There are lots of different versions around, ranging from costly French imports to local supermarket brands. The French ones are divine and look very beautiful in their rather special packaging, but quite honestly, for everyday use I stick with the middle-of-the-road ones and they're very good.

Utensils and bakeware

I'm not going to mention every piece of equipment you could possibly use here, for there seem to be more and more specialised utensils and bakeware coming out every day. Truth be known, I've never had an armoury of kitchenware and certainly don't use anything flash, but there are some really useful, and mainly inexpensive bits and pieces that I wouldn't like to live without as they make baking so much easier.

YOUR HANDS   I think the first thing to remember about utensils is that you have the two best you could possibly use right in front of you – your hands. They've got to be the most versatile 'utensil' of all. There's no piece of kitchen equipment created yet that can strain juice, separate eggs, fold batter, test heat, knead dough, toss, mix, measure – and then rinse clean in a trice! And if you really don't like the thought of dipping your fingers into everything then you can slip on a pair of those tight food preparation gloves that are available just about everywhere and you're set.

OVENS   Aaargh – don't get me started! Ovens would have to be both the most fabulous and vexatious pieces of kitchen equipment ever invented. It seems to me that the more 'bells and whistles' that are added to them the harder they are to use. If only I had a dollar for every time someone has said to me, 'How I just wish they would go back to making a good old-fashioned oven, with a temperature dial, timer and not much else – and please, let it cook evenly.' I heartily agree. The best oven I ever used we inherited in our last home; it was 25 years old and cooked everything beautifully – cakes and biscuits came out looking gorgeous and golden, roasts were evenly browned and the temperature was always accurate. Since then I've battled with no end of whiz-bang ones which at times have driven me to distraction and I only wish we'd had the foresight to bring our old oven with us when we moved.

There's also the question of fan-forced ovens. Like regular ovens, these vary enormously: with some you can switch the fan function off; with others it's a permanent feature; some seem to whirl the air around at a rate of knots; and others are gentler. All of which means it ain't easy to cook in!

If you are baking with the fan on (which many oven manufacturers don't recommend for baking – best check your instruction manual), be aware that everything will cook faster and hotter. This means it has the potential to burn and dry out more quickly, so it's a good idea to reduce the recommended oven temperature in the recipe by 10°C, and to start checking whatever you're cooking a little earlier than the recipe recommends.

MEASURING CUPS AND SPOONS   Cheap and cheerful plastic ones from the supermarket will do just fine and I use mine constantly. When you're buying the spoons just check that the tablespoon measure is for 20 ml. They do vary, depending on where the spoons are made, as many countries, such as the United States, use a 15 ml tablespoon measure.

DIGITAL SCALES   If you're going to do a lot of baking, then a set of these will be invaluable. They're just so much more accurate than mechanical scales. They're not cheap, but I've had mine for 15 years and they're still going strong with just the occasional battery change.

STURDY HEATPROOF MEASURING JUGS   When cooking, these come in really handy, and not just for accurately measuring liquids. They're also great for melting small amounts of butter in the microwave, dissolving gelatine, warming honey and a host of other things. Choose jugs with good, clear calibrations that have both millilitre and cup measures.

STAINLESS STEEL BOWLS   My motto is the more the merrier when it comes to these. I use extra-big ones for mixing batters and doughs so the ingredients don't end up all over the counter when they're whisked or beaten together. Medium-sized and smaller bowls are good as work bowls, used for holding measured ingredients, melting chocolate, storing things and the like. The other big plus with these bowls is that they heat up and cool down rapidly, which is fabulous when you're melting chocolate or whipping cream. The quality of them varies enormously, from top-of-the-range bowls made from high-quality steel to cheapies (that aren't all that good as the steel coating can flake off over time), and plenty of middle-of-the-road ones which are what I use.

BALLOON WHISKS   I use these all the time as they're just so versatile. They come in all sorts of sizes, from tiny ones for whisking small amounts, to enormous affairs that are used for beating maximum air and volume into egg whites for things such as meringues and soufflés.

You'll notice in many of the following recipes that I rarely sift ingredients together, but whisk them with one of these instead; it's just as effective and distributes everything more evenly. They're also useful for folding ingredients into each other as they cause the least amount of volume loss. A good example of this is using a whisk instead of a spatula to fold beaten egg whites into a cake batter – it really does help to keep it light.

SPATULAS   Three or four good solid spatulas of varying sizes are great for everything from getting the very last drops of jam or syrup out of a jar (the baby ones), to mixing batters (middle-size), or folding two mixtures together (the big guns). I find that they need to be replaced every so often as eventually, no matter how well made, they start to perish and become a bit tatty.

NON-STICK AND REGULAR CAKE TINS   I'd have to say that after years of using non-stick tins I have decided I really don't particularly like the cakes they produce and have gone back to searching out regular light-coloured metal tins instead. Yes, it means a bit more buttering and flouring of tins; however the cakes really are much better. No matter how much I adjust the oven temperature and juggle the timing, cakes baked in non-stick tins more often than not form a thicker, darker crust and tend to be drier. Funnily enough this isn't the case with muffins, although I think that's because the baking time is so brief.

Having said that, don't despair if you only have non-stick tins, as most of mine are too, and many of the recipes in this book were baked in just such tins, and despite my gloomy warnings, they worked very well indeed. However, there are a few things you need to do if you are using these tins. First, it's a good idea to set the oven temperature a little (about 10–15°C) lower than the recipe says, and secondly, start checking the cake, loaf or whatever to see if it's done at least 5 minutes or so earlier than you might otherwise.

There's also quite a lot of silicon bakeware appearing on the market, to which virtually nothing sticks. I've had mixed results with these – some brands have baked beautifully and the cake has come effortlessly out of the pan. With others, I've found the outside of the cake hasn't coloured enough and the cake itself has been a bit heavy as it has to cool in the pan.

SPECIALTY CAKE TINS SUCH AS KUGELHOPFS, BUNDTS AND OTHERS   Many people's eyes glaze over when they hear the terms 'bundt', 'kugelhopf' (or gugelhupf if you prefer) and 'fluted ring' tins. They are basically similar in that they're fluted cake tins with a central hole, much like an elaborate deeper version of a regular ring tin. You can quite often swap one for the other when you make big cakes, but a bundt is only ever a large tin while a kugelhopf or fluted ring tin can come in many sizes. If you sit the three of them side by side the kugelhopf is taller with a central funnel and quite an elaborate two-tiered pattern on the outside. The fluted ring tin has long swirling flutes from top to bottom and the bundt has a less elaborate pattern with a wider central tube and broader fluting with alternating wide and small raised ribs. They tend to be measured by the volume of liquid they can hold, that is you can buy 6, 8, 10 and 12 cup kugelhopf tins.

MICROPLANE GRATERS   These graters are terrific. They look just like a regular woodworking file, with a handle and either a broad or narrow stainless-steel 'file', but instead of the file part being solid it's a grater with masses of razor-sharp cutting edges. They can reduce the zest of an orange, lemon or lime to a pile of tiny feather-light strips in moments. (They're also fabulous for grating parmesan.)

PALETTE KNIVES   I love palette knives and use them daily in my cooking, and not just for baking. Nothing works as well as these for spreading butter on bread, fillings on sandwiches or icing on cakes as they're just the right shape. The two sizes I find most useful are medium-sized and small ones. There's also a slightly more unusual palette knife I would recommend, and that's one with an off-set handle. They're especially useful for spreading doughs into baking tins because their shape means they can sit down inside the tin, and so spread everything more easily and evenly.

PASTRY WEIGHTS   These are little metal or ceramic buttons that you can buy in cookware stores and are used to help stop pastry rising when you bake it 'blind' (see page 179).

A few extra tips and practicalities

ACCURACY   With a lot of general cooking, you can do a fair amount of improvising in terms of the quantities of ingredients and substituting a bit of this for that, however, with baking it's not quite so easy. To bake really well and get wonderful results, ingredients do need to be measured, quantities and weights must be accurate and you need to be a bit careful with substitutions. A lot of it is a matter of commonsense – yes, you can substitute one sort of nut or nut meal for another, one similar fruit for another, say nectarines for peaches, or flavour something with vanilla instead of coffee. It's when it comes to mucking about with the actual proportions of ingredients like flour, baking powder and sugar that things get a bit tricky. Probably the best advice I can give on this is to make something once first before you start to change it – that way you know how it should look and taste and you can improvise from there.

BUTTERING AND FLOURING CAKE TINS   There's no big deal to this, however, fluted cake tins like bundt and kugelhopf pans can be a bit fiddlier. The easiest way I've found to do it is to put a little dollop of butter in the tin, then sit the tin in the oven as it's heating up. As soon as the butter has melted, take the tin out and brush a thin film all over the inside. Tip in a good spoonful of flour and rotate the tin to make sure it's coated evenly, then up-end the tin over the sink and give it a good tap to knock out any excess flour.

DIVVYING UP CAKE BATTER EVENLY   I've never been very good at dividing cake batter evenly between cake tins – I always seem to end up with one that is much fuller than the other. So now what I do is to fill the tins as evenly as I can, then weigh them. With a bit of judicial spooning of mixture between the two, they end up the same and cook much more uniformly.

BAKING TIMES   I've tried to be as accurate as I can with baking times, however, truth be known, ovens vary widely in how they function, so it helps if you know the quirks of your oven when you're baking. I always err on the side of caution with timing and start checking at least 5 minutes or so before whatever I'm baking is meant to be ready. It's also difficult to assess the difference using dark non-stick tins or silicone bake-ware makes (see opposite) – things tend to cook more quickly in dark-coloured tins so you need to take this into account too.

WASHING FLOURY THINGS   I must be a slow learner, but it was a revelation to me when I realised that it's much easier and miles more effective to rinse sticky mixing bowls and floury benches and boards with cool water rather than hot. I love swishing about with lots of hot sudsy water for washing up, but in the initial stages of a clean-up this only makes things worse, as it causes the starch in the flour to develop and become gluggy, making it even harder to remove. I love hints like this – so neat and simple.

chocolate cakes
and brownies

Some useful bits
and pieces to do
with chocolate cakes

I'm not going to bombard you with all sorts of rules and regulations for working with chocolate, however, there are just a few things to keep in mind about chocolate in general, and chocolate cakes and brownies in particular, which can be helpful before you launch into baking them.

THE CHOCOLATE ITSELF   Cooking with chocolate is rather like cooking with wine – it's no good using any old one at all, but nor need you use the most expensive on offer. The thing to keep in mind is that the better the chocolate you use, the more delicious the cake or brownie will be. This isn't to say that you have to spend an arm and a leg on some of the beautiful, but very expensive, imported chocolates. There are plenty of good middle-of-the-road ones in most supermarkets, and as long as you choose a chocolate that you enjoy eating, that's the most important criterion. (In case anyone is wondering, I should mention here that as far as I'm concerned, cooking or compound chocolate, as it's also known, is not a goer at all – it tastes terrible and I wouldn't touch it with a barge pole.)

MELTING CHOCOLATE   If I was to give chocolate a personality for a moment, it would be a charismatic mixture of happy-go-lucky sensuality, flamboyance and deep intensity with just a hint of a temperamental edge to it. It's this edge that is good to be aware of when you're baking, and the time you're most likely to strike it is when you're melting chocolate.

It's not rocket science, but there are a few things it helps to know. The first is that once it's melted, or starting to melt, chocolate doesn't like water in any form. If some does get into it at this stage it causes the chocolate to stiffen (the more technical term is seize). You'll know if this happens because the chocolate becomes stiff and awkward to stir. There aren't too many ways of salvaging it at this stage; sometimes a couple of small spoonfuls of oil, melted butter or cream can help, depending on how far gone it is. Funnily enough, if you put a little water in before you start melting the chocolate (see Ganache recipe, page 256), it's not a problem – that's what I mean about temperamental. However, you'll also be pleased to know that not many of the recipes here need straight melted chocolate to start with, so it's not a big issue.

If you're melting chocolate over a saucepan of simmering water, the most likely cause of water getting into the chocolate is steam coming from the pan underneath, so make sure the water doesn't boil. Another surprising source of moisture is not realising that you're stirring the chocolate with a damp wooden spoon. It's best to use a metal spoon or whisk (as long as it's dry!) so you avoid the possibility of it seizing. Also, wooden spoons tend to absorb flavours and there's always a chance that the spoon you used to stir your lovely garlicky pasta sauce last night will also give a garlicky taste to the chocolate today.

While there are a number of ways to melt chocolate, these three are the ones I mainly use.

* I usually melt chocolate over a saucepan of not-quite-simmering water. To do this, put the chopped chocolate into a heatproof bowl over a pan of very hot, but not bubbling, water. Let the chocolate melt, stirring it regularly with a small whisk or spoon until just a few little lumps of chocolate remain. Take the pan off the heat, remove the bowl and whisk the chocolate to melt the last few bits.
* If you've had your oven on and it's still warm, you can put the chocolate into a stainless steel bowl, set the oven temperature to 110°C and pop the bowl in the oven. Check and stir occasionally, until the chocolate has nearly melted, then take it out and whisk it to melt the final few pieces.
* Or you can sit the chocolate, uncovered, in a microwave-proof bowl. Microwave it on medium power, stopping and stirring it occasionally, until it's smooth. (The timing will vary quite a bit depending on how much chocolate you use, so start checking it after about 20 seconds and go from there.)

AN EASY WAY TO SLICE RICH CHOCOLATE CAKES   Chocolate cakes (in fact any cakes with firm icing) can be difficult to cut neatly without mucking up the icing and leaving crumbs on the next slice, which, after going to so much trouble to make it, is about the last thing you want. The best way to get around this is to use a hot dry knife to slice the cake. Just have a tall jug of very hot water nearby and dip the knife blade into the water in between slices. Wipe it dry and make the next cut and so on; the slices will look really sharp and well defined.

HAIR DRYERS ARE WONDERFUL THINGS   I know that most people use a hair dryer for drying their hair, but I have to admit that mine has been known to spend more time in the kitchen than anywhere else. It's fantastic to restore the lustre to chocolate icing that has become too cold and lost its sheen. If you put the dryer on its lowest setting and just whiz it gently (and at a distance) over the icing, it will become rich and glossy again. Just be careful not to let the dryer get too close to the icing as you do this, otherwise it can go to the other extreme and melt it – not quite the desired effect.

If you are making chocolate curls from a chocolate bar but the bar is a bit too hard, again, just run the dryer on its lowest setting over the bar and it will soften it enough to roll the curls effortlessly.

And as I'm convinced that chocolate has some sort of fatal magnetic attraction to any clothing I'm wearing, the dryer is also great for quickly drying a damp patch on a tee shirt where I've yet again sponged off another smudge of chocolate. (I know this is totally off the subject, but while we're talking about hair dryers, I also use mine for drying the skin on chicken before I roast it – it helps make it really crisp and crunchy.)

THE FINAL TOUCH   I've kept decorations to a minimum on all these cakes as I love things to look simple, however, if you do want to tart them up a bit, there are many easy ways.

* A delicate drift of icing sugar or cocoa over a cake iced with ganache looks really elegant.
* Praline or shards of brittle (see the Coffee Bean Brittle on page 31) can look spectacular.
* Chocolate shops are often a treasure trove of yummy things to decorate cakes with – a simple ring of chocolate pralines or chocolate-coated coffee beans can look fabulous.
* Edible 23–24-carat gold leaf (which is available from specialty food stores) can make a simple ganache-iced cake look stunning. The only thing is that it can be a bit tricky to work with, as it's so delicate and flighty. I use a fine, dry artist's paint brush to transfer small pieces of gold leaf onto cakes. For larger pieces, I find the easiest way to handle it is to press the shiny side of the gold leaf against the wet chocolate icing while it's still attached to its backing paper. When that's done, put the cake in the fridge to firm up (see page 256). Once it has, you can carefully peel away the backing paper. It is a bit of an art though, so it may take a while to get the hang of it.

BROWNIES

Unfortunately, all ovens aren't created equal and some definitely cook much faster and hotter than others. With some types of cooking this doesn't matter too much, but when it comes to baking it can cause all sorts of problems, particularly with something like brownies. It's always a good idea to start checking if they're cooked a good few minutes before the actual timing on the recipe, because brownies of all things should be luscious and moist inside.

There's also a trick to testing brownies. Unlike many cake recipes where you're often asked to check that a metal skewer inserted in the centre of the cake comes out clean, for brownies that's not the case. It's best to use a toothpick or fine wooden skewer rather than a metal one, as when you stick it into the middle of the brownie, you want it to come out with moist little crumbs clinging to it. If you use a metal skewer, the crumbs tend to slide off, whereas they will cling to a wooden one.

Chocolate and potato cake

SERVES 8

**YOU CAN BUY ALL
SORTS OF PATTERNED
CAKE TINS...**

*that make even the simplest cake
look a bit swish. As you can see
from the photograph, I baked
this in a tin with a slight dip in
the centre and fluted sides, which
make the cake look surprisingly
elegant. These sorts of tins are
terrific to use as you really need
do nothing more than dust a little
icing sugar over the top of any
cake to make it look gorgeous.*

When I want to make a special cake fast then this is the one I bake, as you basically just whiz everything together in a food processor. I know that potato seems like a rather odd thing to put into a cake but it makes it wonderfully moist (if you think of it as working on the same principle as adding carrots to cakes, it makes a lot more sense). Just so you know, the cake puffs up quite a lot as it bakes, then cracks a little and sinks as it cools, so it's fairly flat but delicious nonetheless.

145 g plain flour, plus 2 teaspoons, extra
¾ teaspoon bicarbonate of soda
¼ teaspoon salt
190 g castor sugar
2 tablespoons Dutch-processed cocoa
   (see Ingredients page 5)
1 small (60 g) potato, peeled
1 cup (250 ml) sour cream
60 g unsalted butter, at room temperature

1 egg
1 teaspoon vanilla extract
165 g good-quality dark chocolate,
   finely chopped (or use top-quality
   chocolate buttons)
Ganache (see page 256)
gold leaf (optional), to serve
   (see page 17)

1 Preheat your oven to 180°C. Butter and flour a 20 cm shallow round cake tin, then set aside.

2 Put the flour, bicarbonate of soda, salt, sugar and cocoa into a food processor and whiz them together for 30 seconds.

3 Grate the potato and add it to the flour mixture in the processor, along with the sour cream, butter, egg and vanilla extract. Whiz everything together for 2½ minutes, stopping and scraping down the sides occasionally with a rubber spatula.

4 In a bowl, toss the chopped chocolate with the extra 2 teaspoons of flour so it is coated in flour, then stir into the batter in the processor. This is a little awkward, I know (I find a rubber spatula works best), but it saves you mucking up yet another bowl.

5 Spoon the batter into the prepared tin and bake for 35–40 minutes or until a fine skewer slipped into the middle comes out clean. Cool the cake in the tin on a wire rack for 20 minutes, then turn it out onto the rack to cool completely.

6 Meanwhile, make the Ganache.

7 When the cake is cool, pour a thin coating of barely warm Ganache over it and leave it to set. (You'll find the easiest way to do this is to pour the Ganache into the middle of the cake, then tilt the wire rack so the Ganache flows evenly over the top. I don't try to make the sides perfect as I rather like the look of the little rivulets of icing running down.) This cake is best eaten within 2 days of baking.

Flourless chocolate and hazelnut cake (gluten-free)

SERVES 8–10

This is one of those terrific flourless middle-European cakes and a beautiful cake it is too – densely chocolate-y and subtly flavoured with roasted hazelnuts, yet not overwhelmingly rich. It's also very moist and the centre is almost fudge-like so it keeps really well in the fridge for a couple of weeks. You don't need to bother with the icing if you don't want to, just dust it with a little icing sugar instead. It looks really pretty and because it's so moist it really doesn't need the extra coating of chocolate (chocoholics will think I've gone crackers saying that, of course!).

By the way, if you do keep this cake in the fridge, it's best to bring it back to room temperature before eating it because the cold tends to dull its flavour and firms up the texture. You can also make this with almond meal.

240 g roasted hazelnuts (see page 139)
120 g unsalted butter
180 g good-quality dark chocolate, cut into chunks
1 cup (220 g) castor sugar
5 eggs, separated
¼ teaspoon salt
Ganache (see page 256)
cocoa powder, for dusting
softly whipped cream and berries (optional), to serve

1 Preheat your oven to 180°C. Butter a 24 cm round cake tin, line the base with buttered baking paper and set aside.

2 Leave the roasted nuts to cool, then grind them in a food processor or chop them very finely.

3 Put the butter, chocolate and sugar into a large heatproof bowl over a saucepan of simmering water. Let them melt, whisking occasionally, until the mixture is smooth. Remove the bowl from the heat and leave it to cool.

4 In a separate bowl, beat the egg yolks lightly to break them up. Pour them into the cooled chocolate mixture, whisking as you go. Stir in the ground hazelnuts.

5 Beat the egg whites and salt in another bowl until soft peaks form. Using a spatula or whisk, stir one-third of the egg whites into the chocolate mixture to lighten it a little, then fold in the remaining egg whites in two batches. Don't over-mix this, it doesn't matter if a skerrick of egg white remains – the cake will be all the lighter for it.

6 Scrape the batter into the prepared tin and bake for 35 minutes or until the centre is firm and springs back when gently pressed. Cool the cake in the tin on a wire rack.

7 Cut out a round of cardboard that's slightly smaller than the bottom of the cake, then cover it with foil and set it aside (I use this as a base for the cake because it makes it much easier to handle when you ice it). When the cake is cool, loosen the sides with a butter knife or fine palette knife and invert it onto the foil-covered cardboard.

8 Meanwhile, make the Ganache.

9 Now you don't have to do the next step, which is known as a crumb coat, but it ensures a lovely smooth finish. With a palette knife, spread a very thin layer of Ganache all over the cake. Sit it on a plate and chill it, uncovered. When the Ganache has set, remove the cake from the fridge and pour more Ganache over it, tilting the cake so it flows evenly over the top (for the smoothest finish, don't use a palette knife for this). I don't worry about the sides so much as I like the look of the Ganache trickling down them. Chill the cake briefly again to set the second layer. (You can cover it once the Ganache sets.)

10 When you're ready to serve the cake, slide it off the cardboard round onto a serving plate and dust it very lightly with cocoa. A splodge of cream and a few berries never go amiss either! This cake keeps well in the fridge for at least 5 days and freezes well for a couple of weeks.

A SHORTCUT . . .

If roasting and skinning the nuts seems all a bit too fiddly, then keep an eye out for roasted skinned hazelnuts – a lot of shops stock them – so all you need do is grind them. Or sometimes, if your luck is really in, you'll find roasted hazelnut meal; just use it quickly as it develops an 'off' taste quite rapidly.

Black-bottom cupcakes

MAKES 10–12 MEDIUM-SIZED CUPCAKES

A COUPLE OF USEFUL
THINGS TO KNOW
* One of the nice things about
these cupcakes is that you can
make them all sorts of sizes, from
extra-large to tiny little bite-sized
ones that look surprisingly swish
to have with after-dinner coffee.
* If you have any leftover
cupcakes (and pigs might fly,
you may well say!) they freeze
well for a couple of weeks.

You're entering serious chocoholics' territory with these appealing cupcakes; originally I made them for kids' parties and then discovered the adults were hoeing into them too. What makes them so special is the topping – it's a bit like cheesecake so you end up with a luscious creamy centre to the rich, deep brown chocolate cake. If you want to make them look more 'grown-up', try baking them in little oval moulds (friand moulds are perfect) and serve them for dessert with lightly sugared strawberries drizzled with a little Grand Marnier or strawberry eau-de-vie.

1½ cups (225 g) plain flour
1 cup (220 g) castor sugar
1 teaspoon bicarbonate of soda
1 teaspoon salt
⅓ cup (35 g) Dutch-processed cocoa
  (see Ingredients page 5)
1 cup (250 ml) warm water
1 teaspoon vanilla extract
⅓ cup (80 ml) light olive oil
1 teaspoon white vinegar

TOPPING
250 g cream cheese, at room temperature
⅓ cup (75 g) castor sugar
1 egg
1 cup (200 g) good-quality dark chocolate
  buttons (I use Callebaut) or 200 g good-
  quality dark chocolate, chopped into
  small chunks

1 Preheat your oven to 180°C. Line a 12-hole muffin tin with paper cupcake cases.

2 For the topping, with an electric mixer on medium speed, beat together the cream cheese and sugar for 2 minutes or until light and fluffy. Add the egg and beat until it's thoroughly mixed in, then stir in the chocolate and set the bowl aside.

3 Tip the flour, sugar, bicarbonate of soda and salt into a bowl, then sift in the cocoa and whisk everything together with a balloon whisk for 1 minute. In another bowl, whisk together the warm water, vanilla extract, oil and vinegar. Make a well in the dry ingredients, pour in the wet ones and stir them thoroughly together (don't overdo this though or the cupcakes will be a bit chewy).

4 Spoon this batter into the cupcake cases, so they're about two-thirds full. This is a bit messy as the batter tends to dribble everywhere as you do it; I find it's easiest to hold the bowl over each cupcake case and spoon it in from above. Scoop a heaped dessertspoonful of the cream cheese mixture on top of each one.

5 Bake the cupcakes for 30–35 minutes or until the dark chocolate part springs back when pressed (or a skewer inserted into this part comes out clean). Cool the muffins in the tin on a wire rack for a couple of minutes, then lift them out and leave them on the rack to cool completely.

White and dark chocolate jaffa swirl cake

SERVES 12–16

My aunt and uncle lived in outback Queensland and every year we would stay with them for a holiday. It was always so exciting for us kids as their way of life was very different to ours. My uncle was the local (read, only) policeman and they lived in an old Queenslander which doubled as the police station and jail too. I remember sleeping out on the enclosed veranda, looking up at the night sky through the mosquito nets that covered our camp beds, and feeling as though I could reach out and touch the stars.

At least once during these holidays, as a treat, we would visit the nearest big town and go to the cinema there. We always sat high up in 'the gods', where my older cousins initiated us into the intricacies of how to roll Jaffas down the aisles to make the maximum amount of noise. Whenever I eat this cake I can feel my fear and excitement at doing this return, as the projectionist would threaten to stop the film if we continued; all of which is a long-winded way of saying that this Jaffa-flavoured cake brings back some very happy memories. And a lovely cake it is too, with its velvety texture, swirls of white and dark chocolate and tang of orange.

55 g good-quality white chocolate, finely chopped

55 g good-quality dark chocolate, finely chopped

290 g unsalted butter, chopped, at room temperature

2½ cups (375 g) plain flour

1 teaspoon baking powder

¾ teaspoon bicarbonate of soda

½ teaspoon salt

4 eggs

2 cups (440 g) castor sugar

1 cup (250 ml) buttermilk

1½ teaspoons vanilla extract

3 teaspoons finely grated orange zest

⅓–½ quantity Ganache (see page 256)

1 Preheat your oven to 180°C. Butter and flour a bundt tin (see page 10) and set aside.

2 Put the white chocolate into a small microwave-proof bowl, then tip the dark chocolate into another. Put 20 g of the butter into each of the 2 bowls. Microwave the white chocolate and butter on high for about 35–40 seconds or until it's melted, stopping to stir it halfway through. Remove it from the microwave and stir it again to make it as smooth as possible (you'll find with white chocolate that it's always a little grainy). Repeat this process with the dark chocolate mixture. Leave both bowls of chocolate to cool to room temperature while you get on with the rest of the recipe. >

3 Put the flour, baking powder, bicarbonate of soda and salt into a food processor. Whiz them together so they're well mixed, then tip them into a bowl. Put the eggs and sugar into the processor and whiz them for 1 minute. Add the remaining butter chunks to the egg mixture and process everything for another minute. Pour in the buttermilk and vanilla extract and whiz together for about 10 seconds to mix them in. Tip in the flour mixture and blend it in with a few quick pulses so the batter is just combined. It's a good idea to stop and scrape down the sides with a rubber spatula at least once when you do this.

4 Transfer half the batter to a bowl, then stir in the dark chocolate mixture. Add the white chocolate mixture and orange zest to the batter in the processor. Blend it in quickly so it's just combined.

5 Spread half the white chocolate batter into the bottom of the bundt tin to form an even layer. Dollop half the dark chocolate batter on top and spread it out as evenly as you can. Repeat this layering with the remaining batters. Run a narrow knife blade right through the batter, moving it around the central tube in a petal or figure-of-eight pattern as you go (this swirls the two mixtures together – it is fun to do but be careful not to get too carried away or they'll blend together).

6 Bake for about 55 minutes or until a fine skewer inserted in the middle of the cake comes out clean. Cool the cake in the tin on a wire rack for 10 minutes. Carefully loosen the edges of the cake and invert it onto the rack. Leave it to cool completely.

7 Meanwhile, make the Ganache.

8 To ice the cake, pour the barely warm Ganache evenly over the cake so it trickles down the sides – I don't cover it completely as I like the look of these rivulets of chocolate. Leave the Ganache to set, then carefully transfer the cake to a serving plate or cake stand. Any leftover cake keeps well for up to 4 days stored in an airtight container in a cool spot.

BUTTERING AND FLOURING BUNDT TINS
Bundt tins make cakes look so beautiful but because of their whorls and swirls they're tricky little blighters to butter. I find the easiest way to do this is to melt the butter and brush it on so that you can get into all the nooks and crannies; then once the butter has firmed up a bit, dust the tin with flour.

Chocolate and coffee crumble cake

SERVES 8–10

The first time I made this cake I did all the things you could possibly do wrong when you're baking something, especially for the first time. I'd promised I'd make a chocolate cake for a friend's afternoon tea and decided it was a good opportunity to experiment with a recipe for this book – wrong move! I kept letting myself be waylaid – phone calls, cups of tea and a potter in the garden as it was a Sunday. By the time I eventually got the cake out of the oven there was no way it would be cool enough to ice before we had to leave. So I did what any self-respecting cook would do and stuck it in the fridge to cool it down first. While it was cooling I also managed to boil the icing, which consequently separated, so that needed some rescuing too (amazing what a spoonful of cream and a fine sieve can do). With ten minutes to spare I poured the still-warm icing over the still-warm cake, crossed my fingers and stuck it back in the fridge to set as best it could. (It was also a 34°C day so icing anything was a bad idea to start with . . .)

Eventually we arrived at the afternoon tea, by which time this poor maltreated cake had also slipped off its plate and skidded across the back seat of the car. I resurrected it as best I could, covered all the dings and dents with a dusting of icing sugar and sat it right at the back of the afternoon tea table in the hope that it wouldn't be noticed. However, that wasn't to be – it seemed that everyone wanted to try a slice of my 'experiment'. I cut it with some trepidation (and my fingers firmly crossed behind my back), but the gods were obviously smiling on me, for somehow, despite all its travails, this cake was so moist, delicious and more-ish that everyone raved about it. I had to laugh and 'fess up' and wondered if I was going to have to re-create the same circumstances to make it work again. However, I'm pleased to say that even made in a more orthodox way, it's still remarkably good.

1½ cups (375 ml) water

1 cup (170 g) raisins

250 g unsalted butter, roughly chopped

1 cup (220 g) castor sugar

1 teaspoon ground cinnamon

3 heaped tablespoons Dutch-processed cocoa (see Ingredients page 5)

¼ teaspoon salt

1 teaspoon bicarbonate of soda

¼ cup (60 ml) boiling water

1½ teaspoons vanilla extract

2 cups (300 g) plain flour, sifted

140 g good-quality dark chocolate, cut into small chunks

½ quantity Ganache (see page 256)

icing sugar (optional), to serve

COFFEE CRUMBLE

¼ cup (55 g) firmly-packed brown sugar

½ cup (60 g) roasted pecans or walnuts (see page 80)

2 teaspoons Dutch-processed cocoa

1½ teaspoons ground cinnamon

1 teaspoon instant coffee powder or granules

40 g good-quality dark chocolate, roughly chopped

1 Put the water, raisins, butter, sugar, cinnamon, cocoa and salt into a large saucepan. Sit it over high heat and bring the mixture to the boil, stirring all the while. As soon as the mixture boils, reduce the heat to low and simmer for 5 minutes, then remove it from the heat and leave it to cool. Meanwhile, dissolve the bicarbonate of soda in the boiling water and let it cool too.

2 Preheat your oven to 180°C. Butter and lightly flour a medium-sized (8 cup) kugelhopf tin (see page 10), then set it aside.

3 While both mixtures are cooling, make the coffee crumble. Combine all the crumble ingredients in a food processor and pulse until the nuts and chocolate are quite finely chopped, then set aside.

4 When the raisin and cocoa mixture is cool, stir the vanilla extract and bicarbonate of soda and water mixture into the saucepan. Mix in all the flour, except for a couple of teaspoons. Toss the chunks of chocolate in the reserved flour, then stir them into the batter (this fine coating of flour helps stop the chocolate from sinking to the bottom of the cake as it bakes). Spoon just under one-third of the batter into the prepared tin and smooth it out. Sprinkle one-third of the crumble evenly over the top, then press it down gently into the batter. Spread just over another third of the cake batter evenly over the crumble layer. Sprinkle this with the remaining crumble, pressing it down into the batter. Dot the remaining cake mixture on top and spread it out evenly.

5 Bake for 50–55 minutes or until a fine skewer inserted in the middle comes out clean. Cool the cake in the tin on a wire rack for 10–15 minutes. Carefully loosen around the sides of the cake with a butter knife or fine palette knife, then invert it onto the rack and leave it to cool completely.

6 Meanwhile, make the Ganache.

7 When the cake is cool, spoon the Ganache over the top (you can coat it completely or leave little trickles running down the sides). Just prior to serving, dust it with a little icing sugar, if using. This cake keeps well for up to 5 days in the fridge – just bring it back to room temperature before eating it. Or, store the cake in the freezer for up to 3 weeks.

SOUR CREAM TO SERVE

More often than not, I serve cakes with sour cream or a half-and-half mixture of regular and sour cream. I love the way its slightly tart edge cuts through the richness of butter or chocolate cakes without being cloying. Funnily enough, and I know it sounds like complete overkill, but often the richer the cake the more it needs cream of some sort to cut its intensity.

One-pan mocha cake with coffee bean brittle

SERVES 8

Some recipes you get asked for over and over again – and this lovely, simple chocolate cake is one of them. I think of this as my little black dress of a cake; a slim, rich chocolate cake that can be dressed up or down at will. It's perfect for afternoon tea with a dollop of cream on top, or can be dolled up with a coating of shiny ganache or shards of chocolate or coffee bean brittle to make a very chi-chi dessert.

It's a somewhat more sophisticated version of the one-pan chocolate cake published in my second book, *Belinda Jeffery's Tried-and-True Recipes* and, of all the recipes in that book, I've had no end of people tell me that they make it over and over again, more so than any other recipe. This mocha version is a little more 'grown-up' than the original and makes a wonderful birthday cake. You certainly don't have to make the coffee bean brittle, but if you want it to be 'dressed to kill' as it were, then give it a go – it looks gorgeous.

⅓ cup (35 g) Dutch-processed cocoa (see Ingredients page 5)
75 g unsalted butter
⅓ cup (80 ml) light olive oil
⅔ cup (160 ml) strong black coffee, cooled (this equals 3 teaspoons instant coffee granules dissolved in ⅔ cup boiling water)
90 g good-quality dark chocolate, finely chopped
250 g castor sugar
1 large egg

1½ teaspoons vanilla extract
1¼ cups (185 g) plain flour
2 teaspoons baking powder
⅓ cup (80 ml) buttermilk (or at a pinch, sour cream or yoghurt)

TOPPING
350 ml double thick cream (see Ingredients page 5), lightly whipped
Coffee Bean Brittle, coarsely crushed (see page 31), or shards of dark chocolate

1 Preheat your oven to 150°C. Butter a 23 or 24 cm round cake tin. Line the base with buttered baking paper, then dust the tin with flour. Shake out the excess flour and set aside.

2 Put the cocoa, butter, oil and coffee into a largish saucepan. Bring them to the boil over medium heat, stirring frequently until the mixture is silky, then take it off the heat. Add the chocolate and sugar and whisk them in until the chocolate has melted and the mixture is smooth.

3 Once the mixture has cooled, add the egg and vanilla extract, whisking them in thoroughly. Sift the flour and baking powder into the mixture and stir them in until they're just combined. Whisk in the buttermilk.

4 Pour the batter into the prepared tin and give it a gentle shake to level it out. Bake for about 50 minutes or until a fine skewer inserted in the middle of the cake comes out clean. Cool the cake in the tin on a wire rack for 5 minutes. Invert the cake onto the rack, remove the paper and leave it to cool completely. >

5 When you're ready to serve, transfer the cake onto a serving plate. You don't see many cake stands these days, but if you have a nice simple one sit the cake on that – it's a great way to make any cake look extra-special. Just before serving the cake, spread the cream on top, then use the back of a spoon to swirl it up a bit. To finish it off, sprinkle some of the Coffee Bean Brittle (see below) or chocolate shards over the cream. This cake keeps well for a couple of days in the fridge, although if it is covered with cream and topped with Coffee Bean Brittle, the brittle will soften. It also freezes well, without the topping, for about 3 weeks.

Coffee bean brittle

Although this makes a bit more brittle than you may need, it keeps indefinitely and is great to have on hand to dress up all sorts of desserts. Even something as simple as scoops of chocolate and coffee ice-cream look fantastic when you scatter them with it, as there's a lovely contrast between the cold, creamy ice-cream, the crunch of the brittle and the slight bitterness of the coffee beans – and the way it sparkles looks really special too.

1 cup (220 g) castor sugar
½ cup (125 ml) water
1 tablespoon roasted coffee beans, coarsely chopped

1 Line a large, shallow baking tray with baking paper or foil and sit it on a chopping board or thick tea towel.

2 Put the sugar and water into a small saucepan over high heat. Stir it constantly until the sugar dissolves, then stop stirring and bring the mixture to the boil. As it boils, wash down the sides occasionally with a pastry brush dipped in water to dissolve any sugar crystals. The mixture will slowly change from being quite liquid to a thicker syrup, with lazy bubbles on the surface.

3 Now is the time to watch it like a hawk as it changes colour quite rapidly. As soon as it turns a light amber colour, add the chopped coffee beans and swirl the pan to mix them in (be careful as it may froth a bit at first). Continue to cook the syrup until it is a deep golden brown, then immediately take it off the heat and carefully pour the mixture into the prepared baking tray. Hold the tray with a thick cloth to protect your hands and tilt it gently to spread the syrup evenly. (Be careful doing this as both the syrup and the baking tray will be very hot.) Leave the brittle to cool and set, then carefully peel away the paper and break it into large shards.

4 To store the brittle, layer the shards in an airtight container between sheets of baking paper to stop them sticking together, then freeze. When you need it, take out as much as you want, crush it coarsely (or leave it in bigger pieces) and return the rest to the freezer. The brittle will keep in the freezer for up to 12 months.

Flourless Chinese five spice chocolate cake (gluten-free)

SERVES 16 – IT'S VERY RICH

I know that this may sound like a rather strange combination, but it's just one of those things that works – and works really well. It's a truly wonderful cake – dense, rich and chocolate-y, with a complex background depth and spiciness from the five spice powder. This cake is probably at its very best when still barely warm – it's amazingly light, almost ethereal, and delicately flavoured, however, it's also a little fragile to handle. Once it's chilled, it firms up considerably and has an altogether denser texture which is equally delicious.

When I want to pull-out-all-stops I make chai-flavoured ice-cream to go with this – a truly spectacular pairing. Having given this cake such a build-up, I have to confess that this is one of the few cakes in this book for which you need an electric mixer to beat the eggs and sugar. However, it's such a fabulous cake I couldn't bear to leave it out – it's well worth it and is still speedy to make.

400 g good-quality dark chocolate, finely chopped
1¼ cups (275 g) castor sugar
½ cup (125 ml) water
5 teaspoons Chinese five spice powder

280 g unsalted butter, at room temperature, cut into small chunks
2 teaspoons vanilla extract
6 eggs (about 340 g total weight)

1 Preheat your oven to 180°C. Butter a 28 cm springform or regular cake tin and line the base with buttered baking paper. If you're using a springform tin, wrap it tightly in extra-wide foil as the cake bakes in a water bath and you don't want any water to leak into the batter through the seals in the tin. Sit the prepared tin in a roasting pan.

2 Put the chocolate into a large stainless steel bowl. Sit a fine sieve over the top of the chocolate and set the bowl aside.

3 Pour ½ cup (110 g) of the sugar, the water and five spice powder into a small saucepan and stir to dissolve the sugar over high heat. Stop stirring and bring the mixture to the boil. As soon as it boils, remove it from the heat and immediately strain it through the sieve into the chocolate. Whisk the mixture constantly with a balloon whisk until the chocolate has pretty much melted. Add the butter and vanilla extract and whisk until the mixture is smooth, then set it aside; you need to work quite quickly during this stage as the five spice syrup needs to be boiling hot to melt the chocolate and incorporate the butter easily. If at any time the mixture becomes a bit too thick and the chocolate or butter haven't melted completely, gently – and very carefully – warm the bowl over low heat or sit it in a bigger bowl of hot water, stirring all the while, to melt the last little pieces.

4 With an electric mixer, beat the eggs and remaining ¾ cup (165 g) sugar together on medium speed until they're light and fluffy, 4–5 minutes maximum. Stir about a quarter of this egg mixture into the chocolate mixture to lighten it a bit, then fold in the remainder thoroughly.

5 Pour the batter into the prepared tin and shake it gently to level it. Pour very hot water (just off the boil) into the roasting pan to come about half-way up the sides of the cake tin. Carefully transfer the whole lot to the oven and bake the cake for 45–50 minutes until the top feels wobbly/firm (see below) and a skewer inserted in the middle comes out with moist but not wet chocolate mixture clinging to it.

6 Remove the roasting pan from the oven. Carefully lift the cake tin out of the water bath and sit it on a wire rack to cool (if you've wrapped the tin in foil, peel it away as some water or condensation may have seeped in). Once the cake is completely cool, gently loosen it around the sides with a palette knife and carefully invert it onto a serving plate. Remove the baking paper; if the cake seems to be sticking to the bottom of the tin, which it can do, especially in cool weather, then warm the base of the tin very gently and carefully over low heat to help loosen it. You can serve the cake upside-down or invert it again onto another plate. Chill it, then cover it loosely with plastic film.

7 When you're ready to serve, cut the cake with a hot, dry knife, dipping the blade into very hot water and wiping it dry between each cut. This cake keeps well in the fridge for up to 10 days and freezes well for up to a month.

WHAT ON EARTH IS 'WOBBLY/FIRM'?
You may well be wondering what on earth 'wobbly/firm' means. I know the term sounds a bit funny, but it's just about the only way to describe what I'm trying to explain. To check for it, rest the palm of your hand on top of the cake when you think it's just about cooked. Use your palm to gently wiggle the cake from side to side – it should feel set but still be a little wobbly, a bit like a jelly – that's what 'wobbly/firm' means.

A wonderful rich chocolate cake
(gluten-free)

SERVES 12–16

THIS CAKE IS ALSO
TERRIFIC AT ROOM
TEMPERATURE OR
EVEN WARM.
*I discovered this the very first
time I made it. I couldn't bear
to wait until it was cool to
taste a bit so I cut a slice while
it was still warm, and it was
sensational – light, airy and
almost mousse-like.*

This is a glorious, sophisticated sort of a cake and perfect as a no-holds-barred dessert for a special dinner. It's dense, rich and very chocolate-y, yet dissolves on your tongue as you eat it, leaving a tantalising hint of dark, bittersweet warmth – all in all, what I think of as a 'grown-up' cake. Although having said that, my young niece sniffed it out (nice to know the chocolate gene runs in the family!), managed to demolish a large slice in record time and still came back for more. I don't usually ice it, however, if you want to, just pour some Ganache (see page 256) over the top, leave it to set and decorate it with roasted pecan halves, or swathe the top in softly whipped cream and sprinkle it with splinters of roasted pecan or chocolate.

250 g unsalted butter

250 g good-quality dark chocolate

85 g sifted Dutch-processed cocoa
  (see Ingredients page 5)

200 g roasted pecans (see page 80)

6 eggs

1½ cups (330 g) castor sugar

⅓ cup (80 ml) brandy *or* Cognac

2 teaspoons vanilla extract

icing sugar (optional), for dusting

lightly sweetened double thick cream
  (see Ingredients page 5), to serve

1 Preheat your oven to 180°C. Butter a 23 cm springform cake tin and line the base with buttered baking paper. Dust the cake tin with flour (or rice flour if you're avoiding wheat completely), and tap out the excess. Set aside.

2 Melt the butter in a medium-sized saucepan over low heat. Add the chocolate and whisk it in until it's melted too. Take the pan off the heat, then add the cocoa, stirring it in until the mixture is thick and smooth. Set aside to cool a little.

3 Meanwhile, whiz the pecans in a food processor to chop them as finely as possible. Stop the machine every so often to check them so they don't become oily and form a paste. Set them aside.

4 In a large bowl, whisk the eggs and sugar with a balloon whisk until they're just blended together, then whisk in the warm chocolate mixture until it's well combined. Mix in the brandy and vanilla extract. Finally, stir in the ground pecans – at this stage the batter looks very loose and sloppy but that's just how it should be.

5 Pour the batter into the prepared tin. Bake the cake for 40–45 minutes or until the side is set but the middle 15 cm or so of the cake is still a bit wobbly when you gently shake the tin.

6 Cool the cake completely in the tin on a wire rack. Once cool, release the sides of the tin and carefully invert the cake onto a plate lined with baking paper. Cover the cake with plastic film and chill it in the fridge, where it keeps well for at least 1 week.

7 When you're ready to eat the cake, slide it off the baking paper onto a serving plate, then dust it with icing sugar, if using. Serve it with cream.

Sticky hazelnut chocolate cake with coffee syrup

SERVES 6–8

This is one of the few cakes in this book that uses the traditional 'creaming' method of making a cake, however, it's such an unusual and delicious dessert that I didn't want to leave it out. It started out life as a simple nut cake; the chocolate came next as chocolate and hazelnuts are one of the great food partnerships, and never better than when they're combined in a cake; and finally came the coffee syrup. Just so you know, it's not the most spectacular cake that you'll ever see – it looks pretty plain in fact. However, taste is what this is all about and it has that in spades – the coffee syrup trickles down into the cake and works its magic with the chocolate and hazelnuts so that everything somehow melds together and becomes incredibly luscious.

50 g plain flour
200 g toasted hazelnut meal (see Ingredients page 6)
1½ teaspoons baking powder
¼ teaspoon salt
250 g unsalted butter, at room temperature
190 g castor sugar
4 eggs, at room temperature
2 teaspoons vanilla extract
100 g good-quality dark chocolate, finely chopped
double thick cream (see Ingredients page 5), to serve

COFFEE SYRUP
3–4 heaped dessertspoons ground coffee beans
2 cups (440 g) castor sugar
2 cups (500 ml) water

1 Preheat your oven to 160°C. Butter a 20 cm square cake tin. Line the base with buttered baking paper, then dust the tin with flour, tap out any excess and set aside.

2 Put the flour (except for 1 tablespoonful), hazelnut meal, baking powder and salt into a bowl and whisk them together with a balloon whisk for 1 minute.

3 Beat the butter and sugar on medium speed using an electric mixer for about 5 minutes or until they're light and fluffy, stopping to scrape down the sides of the bowl occasionally with a rubber spatula.

4 When the butter and sugar are ready, add the eggs, one at a time, beating well after each one is added (the mixture will look a bit curdled at this stage, but don't worry, it will be fine). Add the vanilla extract. Reduce the speed to low and tip in the hazelnut mixture. Mix it in only until it's just combined. >

5 In a separate bowl, toss the finely chopped chocolate in the reserved spoonful of flour, then fold it into the batter. Scrape around the sides of the bowl to make sure everything is well combined, then spread the batter evenly into the prepared tin. Bake for about 1 hour or until a fine skewer inserted in the middle of the cake comes out clean.

6 Meanwhile, make the coffee syrup. First put the ground coffee into the bottom of a medium-sized coffee plunger. Set it aside. Pour the sugar and two-thirds of the water into a medium-sized saucepan over high heat. Stir until the sugar dissolves, then stop stirring and bring it to the boil. Boil the syrup, washing down the sides regularly with a pastry brush dipped in water to remove any sugar crystals. When it's a rich caramel colour take it off the heat, and, using an oven mitt or thick tea towel to protect your hand and arm, pour in the remaining water. It will hiss, bubble and possibly spit furiously, so be careful. Swirl the pan to make sure the caramel has dissolved.

7 Tip the caramel mixture into the coffee plunger and leave it to infuse for a few minutes (longer isn't better in this case, as I discovered when I once somewhat over-enthusiastically let it infuse for 5 minutes thinking the flavour would be more intense, however, it became quite bitter). Push down the plunger and pour the coffee syrup into a heatproof jug. Rinse the plunger immediately.

8 When the cake is ready, cool it in the tin on a wire rack for 10 minutes. Loosen the cake around the edges with a butter knife or fine palette knife and invert it onto the rack. Sit a plate underneath the rack (this is to catch any drips from the coffee syrup) and brush a little of the warm coffee syrup gently over the cake. Reserve the rest of the syrup.

9 When the cake is cool, transfer it to a plate or chopping board and cut it into triangles, diamonds or squares; wipe the knife between each cut so you don't get lots of crumbs on the surface. (I don't usually serve this whole as it looks best if it's sliced and plated up.)

10 To serve the cake, sit a piece on each plate, drizzle a little of the reserved syrup over it and dollop some cream on the side. Serve any remaining syrup and extra cream separately. This cake keeps well for at least 5 days in the fridge and freezes well for up to 3 weeks. Any leftover syrup will keep in the fridge indefinitely and is lovely drizzled over ice-cream.

Luscious white chocolate cheesecake

SERVES 10–12

This is an astonishingly good cake. I know I sound surprised, however, I've never been a great fan of cheesecakes as I find they're often cloyingly rich. So the first time I made this it was with considerable trepidation, especially as it includes white chocolate too, which can also be a bit over the top. Well, I had to eat my words because it's a wonder of a cake, with a glorious satiny texture and surprisingly light, delicate flavour. It's also a blank canvas as far as decorating goes: sometimes I go very Carmen Miranda-ish and festoon the top with all sorts of fruits; other times, it may just be a layer of raspberries, or as I did for a recent birthday, strawberries and unsprayed pink rose petals, which looked so feminine and graceful. I also must tell you that this is a recipe that I've tweaked considerably, however, I can't claim fame for the original, which is from Rose Levy Beranbaum's terrific book *The Cake Bible* (William Morrow & Co.).

BY THE BY

If you want to serve this plain, with just a little something on the side, a tangy, barely sweetened tumble of both whole and puréed raspberries is hard to go past, as it provides a perfect sharp-sweet balance to the luscious cake.

220 g good-quality white chocolate, cut into chunks

450 g cream cheese, at room temperature

¼ cup (55 g) castor sugar

3 teaspoons cornflour

3 eggs

3 teaspoons very finely chopped (or grated) lemon zest

1½ tablespoons lemon juice, strained

1 teaspoon vanilla extract

¼ teaspoon salt

2 cups (500 ml) sour cream

1 cup (250 ml) thickened cream

fruit, for topping (You can use any fruits in season – either a mixture or just one variety. As a guide, if you're using berries, you will need at least 2, and possibly 3, punnets.)

icing sugar, for dusting

1 Put the chocolate in a thick, heatproof china bowl over a saucepan of simmering water, then stir until melted. You need to be particularly careful when you melt white chocolate because it's quite temperamental, so be mindful not to let it get too hot. Remove from the heat and leave it to cool to lukewarm.

2 Preheat your oven to 180°C. Butter a 20 cm springform cake tin and line the base with baking paper. Wrap the outside of the tin tightly in two layers of foil (this prevents any cake mixture seeping out or any water seeping in for that matter, as the cake cooks in a water bath). Sit the cake tin in a large roasting pan and set it aside.

3 Put the cream cheese and sugar into a food processor and whiz them together for 30 seconds or until they're very smooth. Add the cornflour and give the machine a brief burst to mix it in. With the processor going, add the eggs through the feed tube, one at a time, whizzing each one in well before adding the next. At this stage, stop the processor and scrape down the sides with a rubber spatula to ensure everything is mixed in.

4 Sprinkle in the lemon zest, lemon juice, vanilla extract and salt and whiz them in briefly. Add both the sour and thickened cream and pulse them in with on/off turns of the processor, only until they're just blended in. Scrape in the melted chocolate and pulse it in too until the mixture is smooth. (The only slightly tricky bit in this recipe is to make sure that the chocolate is runny enough to mix into the rest of the batter easily; if it seems a bit stiff, re-warm it slightly first.)

5 Scrape the cheesecake mixture into the prepared cake tin. Pour enough hot water into the roasting pan to come about 3 cm up the side of the cake tin. Carefully transfer the whole lot to the oven.

6 Bake for 45 minutes. Turn off the heat and leave the cake in the oven for 1 hour without opening the door.

7 Remove the cake tin from the water bath and unwrap the foil liner. Cool the cake completely in its tin on a wire rack. Once cool, cover the tin with plastic film and refrigerate the cake for at least 6 hours, or preferably overnight. The cake keeps well for up to 1 week in the fridge; however, if you're storing it for any length of time, remove the outer ring of the tin once the cake is firm, to stop any discolouration from the tin.

8 When you're ready to serve the cheesecake, sit the tin on a very hot, damp tea towel to help loosen it a bit and run a fine palette knife around the sides of the cake. Invert it onto your serving plate and remove the tin and paper. If there's a bit of moisture on the surface mop it up gently with kitchen paper. Decorate the top with the fruit – I think it looks best when the fruit tumbles down the sides a bit and looks higgledy-piggledy, rather than carefully placed. Dust with icing sugar just before serving. For clean, sharp slices, cut the cheesecake with a hot, dry knife.

Mars Bar brownies

SERVES 6–8 AS A DESSERT OR MAKES 10–12 BROWNIES

This is the ultimate brownie combination. I know that it probably sounds totally over the top, and it is, but if you love Mars Bars and brownies then this is IT. A dense, chocolate-y brownie studded with little chunks of Mars Bar, the crunch of roasted pecans, and, I have to say it, served either warm or cooled with some good vanilla ice-cream on the side – it's a glorious treat.

¾ cup (105 g) roasted pecans
   or macadamias (see page 80)
¼ cup (35 g) plain flour
¼ teaspoon baking powder
¼ teaspoon salt
225 g good-quality dark chocolate,
   cut into chunks
⅔ cup (150 g) castor sugar

180 g unsalted butter, at room temperature
2 eggs
3 teaspoons vanilla extract
2 × 60 g Mars Bars, cut into small chunks
icing sugar, for dusting
good vanilla ice-cream (optional – well,
   not to me), to serve

1 Preheat your oven to 160°C. Butter a 20 cm square cake tin. Line it with a sheet of buttered foil, then line the base with buttered baking paper. Set aside.

2 Pulse the nuts in a food processor until they're roughly chopped. Tip them into a bowl and toss them with a teaspoon of the flour. Set aside. Whiz the remaining flour, baking powder and salt in the processor until they're just combined, about 10 seconds. Tip them into another bowl.

3 Add the chocolate and sugar to the processor and whiz them together until the chocolate is very finely chopped. Add the butter, eggs and vanilla extract and whiz everything together for 1 minute, stopping to scrape down the sides once or twice with a rubber spatula. Add the flour mixture to the processor and pulse it only until the batter is just combined (don't overdo this or the brownie will be tough). Use a spatula to stir in the nuts and chopped Mars Bars. Smooth the batter into the prepared tin.

4 Bake for 45–50 minutes or until a wooden toothpick inserted in the middle of the brownie comes out with moist, but not wet, crumbs on it. Cool the brownie in the tin on a wire rack.

5 For really neat slices, it's a good idea to chill the brownie in its tin in the fridge before cutting it. Once it's cold, grasp the foil and ease the whole brownie out of the tin. Invert it onto a flat plate and gently peel away the foil and paper, then invert it again onto a chopping board.

6 Slice the brownie into bars with a hot, dry knife. If you're serving the bars straight away, dust them with icing sugar and serve them with ice-cream. Layer the remaining bars between sheets of baking paper in an airtight container. Store them in the fridge for up to 1 week.

Double chocolate pecan brownies

MAKES 12–14 BROWNIES

You can pretty much divide brownie lovers into two camps: the moist but cake-y brownie fan, and the fudge-y, gooey aficionado – or you get someone like me who is terribly fickle, and just loves whichever brownie they happen to be eating at the time. This brownie is definitely of the fudge-y, gooey genre – very rich, dense and thickly-studded with roasted pecans and chunks of chocolate. It also has that translucent, crackled top that really good brownies have.

90 g roasted pecans (see page 80)

¼ cup (35 g) plain flour *or* spelt flour

¼ teaspoon baking powder

¼ teaspoon salt

225 g good-quality dark chocolate,
   cut into chunks

⅔ cup (150 g) castor sugar

180 g unsalted butter, at room temperature

2 × 60 g eggs

3 teaspoons vanilla extract

120 g good-quality milk chocolate,
   cut into small chunks

icing sugar, for dusting

1 Preheat your oven to 160°C. Butter a 22 cm square cake tin. Line it with a sheet of buttered foil, then line the base with buttered baking paper. Set aside.

2 Pulse the pecans in a food processor to chop them coarsely. Tip them into a bowl and toss them with a couple of teaspoons of the flour. Set aside.

3 Whiz the remaining flour, baking powder and salt in the processor until they're just combined, then tip them into another bowl. Add the dark chocolate and sugar to the processor and whiz them together until the chocolate is very finely chopped. Add the butter, eggs and vanilla extract to the chocolate mixture and whiz them together for 1 minute, stopping to scrape down the sides once or twice with a rubber spatula. Add the flour mixture and pulse it in only until everything just combines into a thick batter. Use a spatula to stir in the pecans and milk chocolate chunks. Smooth the batter into the prepared tin.

4 Bake for about 40 minutes or until a wooden toothpick inserted in the middle of the brownie comes out with moist, but not wet, crumbs on it. Cool the brownie in the tin on a wire rack. Once it's cool, pop it in the fridge to chill.

5 When you're ready to cut it, grasp the foil and ease the whole brownie out of the tin. Invert it onto a flat plate and gently peel away the foil and paper, then invert it again onto a chopping board.

6 Slice the brownie into bars with a hot, dry knife. Just before serving the bars, dust with icing sugar to give them pretty snowy tops. Layer the remaining bars between sheets of baking paper in an airtight container. Store them in the fridge for 10 days or so (or freeze them for up to 4 weeks).

One-pan macadamia and chocolate chip brownies

MAKES APPROXIMATELY 20 BARS

A tin of this classic brownie is sitting cooling as I write this, and I can almost feel its fragrant chocolate tendrils weaving their way under my nose, luring me out to the kitchen to try a piece. However, I'm using all my willpower to hold off for a bit, because I know that, good as it will taste now, it will be even better once it's cooled and the flavours have had a chance to meld together. It's a truly delicious brownie which looks very dense but has an astonishingly light, melt-in-the-mouth texture that is beautifully offset by the crisp chunks of macadamia and solid nuggets of dark chocolate.

250 g unsalted butter

180 g good-quality dark chocolate, coarsely chopped

1¾ cups (385 g) castor sugar

1½ teaspoons vanilla extract

4 eggs

1 cup (150 g) plain flour

100 g roasted macadamias (see page 80),
    cut into very large chunks

100 g good-quality dark chocolate buttons *or* chunks

icing sugar (optional), to serve

1 Preheat your oven to 180°C. Butter a 23 cm square cake tin and line it tightly with foil (I find the extra-wide foil is best for this), making sure to push it right down into the corners. Butter the foil lightly, then line the base with baking paper. Set aside.

2 Put the butter and chocolate into a medium-sized heavy-based saucepan over very low heat. Melt them gently, stirring from time to time. Take the pan off the heat when the butter has nearly melted and give it a good stir so the mixture is smooth and shiny. Set it aside to cool for 8 minutes.

3 Add the sugar and vanilla extract to the chocolate mixture and use a balloon whisk to mix them well for 20 seconds or so. Add the eggs, one at a time, beating well after each one is added so it is completely incorporated before you add the next. Just so you know, the mixture may look a bit odd and lumpy after the first couple of eggs are added, however, it thickens and smoothes out after you mix in the last two. Tip in the flour and stir until it's well combined (once the flour is in, don't overdo the mixing or the brownie will toughen as it cooks). Gently fold in the macadamias and chocolate buttons. Scrape the batter into the prepared tin and shake it gently to level the top. >

4 Bake for 40–45 minutes or until a wooden skewer or toothpick inserted in the middle of the brownie comes out with very moist, but not wet, crumbs clinging to it. Another good indicator that it's ready is to rest the palm of your hand lightly on the surface and gently jiggle the brownie from side to side – it should feel wobbly/firm (see page 33).

5 Cool the brownie completely in the tin on a wire rack. The middle may sink a bit; if it does, just gently press down on the sides as it cools to make it a bit more even.

6 Once it's cool, chill the brownie in the fridge for 30 minutes or so to firm it up so it's easier to slice. When you're ready to cut it, grasp the foil and carefully ease the whole brownie out of the tin. Invert it onto a chopping board and gently peel away the foil and paper. Slice the brownie into bars with a hot, dry knife. Dust the bars with icing sugar if liked and line them up on a serving plate.

7 If you're not eating them straight away, you can store the brownies in an airtight container for a day or two at cool room temperature. Otherwise, layer them between sheets of baking paper in an airtight container and store them, tightly sealed, in the fridge for 1 week or freezer for 3 weeks.

I LOVE COLD BROWNIES STRAIGHT OUT OF THE FRIDGE . . .
however, with these particular ones, I think they're best brought to room temperature before you eat them so you can really appreciate their lightness.

Marbled mocha brownies

MAKES 18–24 BROWNIES

This is a more sophisticated brownie than most as it's laced with both coffee and coffee liqueur. It has a superb, slightly bittersweet flavour from the coffee, and a creamy, melt-in-the-mouth texture. The bars look good too, with their marbled tops and ivory and mahogany coloured layers. I also love that they keep really well. I've had bars in the fridge for at least 3 weeks now and they're still going strong – great for unexpected visitors (I seem to have had a lot of those while I've been trying out the recipes for this book – I can't imagine why!), or just when a little morsel of something chocolate-y is the order of the day. I should warn you, though, that they do take a bit longer to make than the other brownies in this chapter, but I really think the results are worth it.

180 g good-quality dark chocolate, coarsely chopped
90 g unsalted butter
3 teaspoons instant coffee granules
4 eggs
1½ cups (330 g) castor sugar
1 cup (150 g) plain flour
¼ cup (25 g) Dutch-processed cocoa (see Ingredients page 5)
½ teaspoon salt
1 teaspoon vanilla extract
1 tablespoon coffee liqueur *or* very strong black coffee

TOPPING
250 g cream cheese, at room temperature
60 g unsalted butter, at room temperature
½ cup (110 g) castor sugar
2 eggs, lightly beaten
1½ tablespoons plain flour
1 tablespoon coffee liqueur *or* very strong black coffee

1 Preheat your oven to 180°C. Butter a 32 × 24 × 5 cm baking tin. Line it with foil, then butter the foil lightly and set aside.

2 In a heavy-based saucepan, warm the chocolate, butter and coffee granules over low heat, stirring constantly for 2–3 minutes until they're melted and smooth. Turn off the heat and leave them to cool slightly.

3 In a large bowl, whisk together the eggs and sugar for 1 minute. Sift the flour, cocoa and salt into this egg mixture. Stir them in lightly. Add the vanilla extract, liqueur and the melted chocolate mixture and stir together until well blended. Set the bowl aside.

4 For the topping, beat the cream cheese, butter and sugar in an electric mixer until they're light and fluffy. Drizzle in the beaten eggs, a little at a time, beating well between each addition, then mix in the flour and liqueur. (The mixture may look a little curdled but it will be fine.)

5 Give the brownie batter a good stir in case it has settled a bit, then pour nearly all of it into the prepared tin, leaving about ½ cup in the bowl. Tilt the tin to spread it evenly. Dollop spoonfuls of the cream cheese topping all over this layer. Drop teaspoonfuls of the reserved brownie batter over this. Use a skewer or knife to swirl the brownie batter on top into the cream cheese mixture. I love doing this swirling as it's a bit like playing mud pies, but I've learnt that it's best not to overdo it or you lose the lovely marbled effect on top.

6 Bake for about 35–40 minutes or until the edges are pale golden and a wooden toothpick inserted in the middle of the brownie comes out with moist, but not wet, crumbs clinging to it. Cool the brownie in the tin on a wire rack. Once it's completely cool, pop it into the freezer for an hour or so to chill.

7 Once it's firm, invert the brownie onto a baking tray and peel away the foil. Sit a chopping board lightly on top and invert the brownie again onto the board. Cut it into slices with a hot, dry knife and serve. Alternatively, layer the slices in an airtight container between sheets of baking paper. Store the brownies, tightly sealed, in the fridge for a fortnight or so. The brownies also freeze really well.

I'VE USED THIS AS A DESSERT . . .
on many occasions, and if I'm doing so, usually cut the brownie into diamonds
so it looks a bit more special – a scoop of coffee ice-cream is absolute heaven
with it, but a spoonful of cream will do very nicely too. However, I should let
you know that if you do cut the brownie into diamonds, you will end up with
lots of rather odd-shaped off-cuts (which I view as an added bonus as they're
perfect pop-in-the-mouth size).

all sorts of
fruit cakes

A few helpful things to know about fruit cakes

This particular chapter is very close to my heart as I adore the combination of cake and fruit. And these recipes cover the spectrum – from glorious, rich, dark fruitcakes and sticky syrup cakes to the enchanting appeal of upside-down cakes with their shimmering cargo of fruit. I remember that upside-down cakes were all the rage when I was little, and it seemed to me that every man and his dog were baking upside-down pineapple cake, as it was considered so very sophisticated. To this day, I still think my mum made the BEST one of all – yes, with rings of canned pineapple and bright pink glacé cherries – I've certainly never bettered it.

CHOOSING AND USING FRUIT   None of these are difficult cakes to make; the only thing to keep in mind is that they all depend on using really good fruit to start with.

* As a general rule of thumb, if you're baking a fresh fruit cake where you want to keep the shape of the fruit, such as the Gooey Butterscotch Peach Cake (see page 64), then it's best not to use absolutely ripe fruit, as it collapses and softens too much once it's cooked. What you want for these cakes is fruit which is on that fine borderline of being ripe and sweet, but still firm.
* When it comes to apple cakes, the variety of apple you use does count as some apples, once they're cooked, collapse, whereas others hold their shape much better. If you keep in mind that the sweeter the apple, the more likely it is to keep its shape, then you can't go too far wrong. I find apples like Pink Lady, Fuji and Royal Gala are particularly good for baking.
* I hate to say it, but of course there are always exceptions to the rule, and on the opposite side of the coin, come bananas. For an upside-down cake, when you're using bananas to make that gorgeous pattern on the bottom of the cake, then they need to be firm. However, if you're using them in cake batter, it will taste much better and more properly banana-ish if they're very ripe and soft.

* The same principle of using really good quality, fresh fruit applies to dried fruit too – use the best quality you can find and the results will pay you back in spades.
* Where cakes are studded with fruit (or nuts and chocolate chunks, for that matter), it's always a good idea to toss the fruit in a little of the flour in the recipe before adding it to the batter. This helps to suspend the chunks of fruit in the batter; otherwise they're likely to sink to the bottom and form a thick, fairly gluggy layer. If this does ever happen to you, just stop calling it a cake and say it's a pudding instead – serve it warm with cream and no one will be any the wiser. Many is the time I've done this when something hasn't quite worked out – it's amazing what a dusting of icing sugar and dollop of cream can do!

THE MIDDLE GROUND IS BEST

The other thing I should mention about baking cakes, and this goes for any kind of cake, is that unless the recipe says otherwise, they are best baked on the middle shelf of the oven. If the cake is baked in two layers, as a few of the recipes are here, either sit the tins side by side on the middle shelf (but make sure they don't touch, otherwise the cakes will dip down where they do) or off-set them on the middle and bottom shelves, so the air can flow around them, allowing them to cook evenly.

Sticky sour cream, golden syrup and ginger cake

SERVES 8–10 (IT COULD SERVE MORE, BUT I FIND NEARLY
EVERYONE COMES BACK FOR SECONDS WITH THIS)

I didn't really know where to put this cake, but I was determined to have it in the book and figured it just sneaks into this chapter because of its quotient of dates. If you were only to make one cake from this book, then this is it. It's a really wonderful cake and so reminds me of the golden syrup and ginger steamed pudding my mum used to make when we were young – in fact, you can actually serve this cake warm as a sort-of pudding. It's really moist but surprisingly light, with a triple-shot of 'oomph' from fresh, ground and glacé ginger. I think it probably lasts quite well, however, so far there has never been enough left to test out the theory.

130 g plain flour, plus 2 teaspoons, extra

130 g self-raising flour

1 tablespoon ground ginger

1 teaspoon baking powder

½ teaspoon salt

2 eggs

170 ml golden syrup, gently warmed

170 ml sour cream

1½ teaspoons finely grated lemon zest

1 tablespoon freshly grated ginger

½ cup (110 g) brown sugar

280 g unsalted butter, melted and cooled

150 g pitted dates, roughly chopped

6 pieces crystallised or glacé ginger,
   very finely sliced

icing sugar (optional), for dusting

1 Preheat your oven to 180°C. Butter a 24 or 25 cm round cake tin (a springform one is fine). Line the base with buttered baking paper and dust with flour. Set aside.

2 Put the 130 g plain flour, self-raising flour, ground ginger, baking powder and salt into a large bowl and whisk them together with a balloon whisk for 1 minute. In a separate bowl, lightly beat the eggs so they are just combined, then add the warmed golden syrup (warming helps it pour more easily), sour cream, lemon zest, fresh ginger, brown sugar and cooled butter. Whisk together only until they are just well mixed.

3 Tip the flour mixture into the egg mixture and stir them together until they're combined. Toss the dates with the extra 2 teaspoons of plain flour and mix them into the batter. Scrape the batter into the prepared tin, then scatter the crystallised ginger slices over the top.

4 Bake for 35–40 minutes or until the cake springs back when gently pressed in the centre or a fine skewer inserted in the middle comes out clean. Cool the cake in the tin on a wire rack for 7–8 minutes. Gently loosen the cake around the edges and invert it onto a flat plate, then remove the tin and paper and invert the cake again onto the wire rack. Leave to cool completely.

5 You can either serve the cake as is or dust it lightly with icing sugar. It keeps well stored at room temperature for 2 days in a tightly sealed container, or in the freezer for a couple of weeks. Left-over pieces are lovely when gently warmed in the microwave.

Apple and pecan crumble cake

SERVES 12–16

BUNDT TINS

Bundt tins look somewhat like a very large, deep ring tin. Sometimes the sides are plain although many are fluted or patterned. There are also some mini-bundt tins on the market which are terrific for individual serves.

I adore apple cakes and am forever making different ones, so it took me ages to decide which recipes to include here. This particular cake was always a given. It looks quite resplendent and is surprisingly light and very moist with a lovely spicy apple flavour and crunchy topping.

2 cups (300 g) plain flour
1½ cups (330 g) castor sugar
1 teaspoon bicarbonate of soda
1 teaspoon salt
1 teaspoon ground cinnamon
4 medium-sized apples (Pink Lady or Gala
   are extra-good in this), peeled, cored and
   cut into small thumbnail-sized chunks
110 g roasted pecans (see page 80),
   roughly chopped
1 cup (250 ml) light olive oil
3 eggs
1½ teaspoons vanilla extract
icing sugar, for dusting

CRUMBLE TOPPING
½ cup (75 g) plain flour
1 teaspoon ground cinnamon
¼ cup (55 g) firmly-packed brown sugar
60 g cold unsalted butter, cut into
   small chunks
45 g coarsely chopped pecans

1 Preheat your oven to 180°C. Butter and flour a 26 cm bundt tin. Set aside.

2 For the crumble, put the flour, cinnamon and brown sugar into a food processor and whiz them together for 10 seconds to mix. Scatter the butter over the top and whiz until the mixture resembles coarse breadcrumbs. Add the pecans and pulse a few times just so they're mixed in. Tip the crumble into a bowl and set aside.

3 Put the flour, sugar, bicarbonate of soda, salt and cinnamon into the processor and whiz them together for 30 seconds. Put the apples and pecans in a large bowl and sprinkle a couple of tablespoons of the flour mixture over them, then toss to coat. Set aside.

4 In another large bowl, whisk together the oil, eggs and vanilla extract. Tip the flour mixture into the egg mixture and stir them together until they're just combined. Mix in the apples and pecans. There will be lots of apples and not much batter to hold them together, but that's fine. Scoop the batter into the prepared tin and spread it out evenly as best you can. Scatter the crumble mixture over the top and give the tin a gentle shake to even it out.

5 Bake for 50–55 minutes or until a fine skewer inserted in the middle of the cake comes out clean. Cool the cake in the tin on a wire rack for 10 minutes. Invert the cake onto a flat plate, then gently invert the cake onto the rack again so the crumble side is up. Leave to cool completely.

6 To serve, dust the cake with icing sugar. This cake keeps well stored at room temperature in a tightly sealed container for a few days, or in the freezer for a couple of weeks.

Almond and lemon syrup cake

SERVES 8

I've never quite figured out what it is about cake batter that makes it taste even better than the cooked cake. To this day, I love to lick the spoon and scrape my finger around the bowl of any cake I make. This golden almond and lemon cake is a particular favourite – cooked as well as raw, I hasten to add. I tend to serve it more as a dessert cake, but it is delicious any-which-way, and I certainly wouldn't say no to a slice of it with a cuppa.

50 g plain flour

200 g almond meal

1½ teaspoons baking powder

¼ teaspoon salt

4 eggs

190 g castor sugar

250 g unsalted butter, at room temperature,
  cut into large chunks

1½ teaspoons vanilla extract

¾ teaspoon almond essence

finely grated zest of 1½ large lemons

double thick cream (see Ingredients
  page 5), to serve

LEMON SYRUP

⅔ cup (150 g) castor sugar

zest of 2 lemons, cut into 1 cm-wide strips

½ cup (125 ml) lemon juice, strained

1 cup (250 ml) water

1 Preheat your oven to 160°C. Butter a 20 cm square cake tin and line the base with buttered baking paper. Dust the tin lightly with flour and set aside. (Actually, after I wrote this, I double-checked the tin size and discovered that the one I use is slightly tapered. The measurements for it are 17 cm square across the base and 19 cm across the top; however a 20 cm one will work just fine.)

2 Put the flour, almond meal, baking powder and salt into a food processor. Whiz them together for 20 seconds, then tip them into a bowl. Add the eggs and sugar to the processor and whiz them together for 1 minute or until they're light and creamy. Scrape in the butter and whiz everything together again for about 40 seconds; the mixture will look a bit curdled at this stage, but it will be fine. Stop the processor and add the vanilla extract, almond essence and lemon zest and blitz them for another 10 seconds.

3 Add the flour mixture to the butter mixture in the food processor and pulse to combine the two until they're just mixed (don't overdo this or the cake will be a bit tough). Scrape around the sides of the processor with a spatula to make sure everything is well mixed. Scoop the batter into the prepared tin and smooth it out evenly with the spatula.

4 Bake for about 1 hour or until a fine skewer inserted in the middle of the cake comes out clean. >

5 Meanwhile, for the lemon syrup, put all the syrup ingredients in a medium-sized saucepan over high heat. Stir them until the sugar dissolves, then stop stirring and bring it to the boil. Let it bubble fairly rapidly for 10–12 minutes or until it looks thicker and more syrupy, then turn off the heat and set aside. Keep warm.

6 When the cake is ready, cool the cake in the tin on a wire rack for 10 minutes. Loosen the cake around the edges with a butter knife or fine palette knife, invert it onto the rack and remove the paper. It's now that you brush the warm syrup over the cake, so it's not a bad idea to sit a plate underneath the rack to catch any drips as it's all a bit messy. Brush between one-third and half of the lemon syrup gently over the cake. Reserve the rest of the syrup, including the zest. Leave the cake to cool completely.

7 To serve, transfer the cake to a plate or chopping board and cut it into diamonds or squares (wipe the knife clean between each cut so you don't get lots of crumbs on the surface). Sit a piece on each plate, drizzle with a little of the reserved lemon syrup and drape a few strips of zest on top. Put any leftover syrup and a bowl of cream on the table and let everyone help themselves.

8 This cake keeps well for about 1 week in the fridge; just return it to room temperature or warm it gently before serving.

Apple, rum and raisin cake

SERVES 12

This cake makes the most wonderful winter dessert and I always think of it as more of a pudding than a cake. It's very moist and redolent with the fragrance of warm, tender apples, plump rum-imbibed raisins and roasted pecans. It's wonderful served with vanilla (or better still, cinnamon) ice-cream that melts into very satisfying puddles around it as you eat. Sometimes I go completely over the top and make the Luscious Homemade Caramel Sauce (see page 257) to go with it – it's totally unnecessary but ever so good.

¼ cup (60 ml) overproof (dark) rum
120 g raisins
2 cups (300 g) plain flour
1½ teaspoons bicarbonate of soda
½ teaspoon salt
¾ teaspoon ground nutmeg
1 teaspoon ground cinnamon
pinch ground cloves
2 cups (440 g) castor sugar
1 cup (250 ml) light olive oil

2 teaspoons vanilla extract
2 eggs
3½ cups peeled, cored and diced Fuji, Gala or Pink Lady apples (roughly 3–4, depending on their size)
100 g roasted pecans or walnuts (see page 80), coarsely chopped
icing sugar, for dusting
Luscious Homemade Caramel Sauce (page 257), (optional), to serve

1 Preheat your oven to 160°C. Butter a 25 or 26 cm round springform or fluted cake tin, line the base with buttered baking paper and dust the tin with flour. Set aside.

2 Stir the rum and raisins together in a small bowl and leave them to sit for at least 30 minutes (better still, do them ahead and leave them overnight so the raisins absorb most of the rum). Put the flour, bicarbonate of soda, salt, nutmeg, cinnamon and cloves into a bowl and whisk them together for 40 seconds with a balloon whisk.

3 I'm afraid you'll have to use an electric mixer or beater for this next bit as it's just a bit too hard to do by hand. Put the sugar and oil into the mixer bowl and beat them on medium–high speed for 5 minutes until they're thick; splash in the vanilla extract towards the end. With the mixer going, add the eggs, one at a time, beating well after each one is added.

4 Turn off the mixer, then use a wooden spoon or spatula to stir the flour mixture into the egg mixture until they're thoroughly combined (the batter will be very thick). Stir in the rum and raisin mixture, chopped apples and nuts. Scrape the batter into the prepared tin and smooth the top.

5 Bake for 1¼–1½ hours or until a fine skewer inserted in the middle of the cake comes out clean. Cool the cake in the tin on a wire rack for 15 minutes. Carefully loosen the cake around the sides, if necessary, with a butter knife or fine palette knife and invert it onto the rack. Leave it to cool completely (or at least until it's warm but not hot).

6 When you're ready to serve the cake, carefully slide it onto a large serving plate or cake stand and dust it with icing sugar. (If it's for a birthday or special occasion I sometimes sit glazed pecan halves around the edge – see below.) Serve the cake with a jug of Luscious Homemade Caramel Sauce, if liked.

7 The cake keeps well for up to 3 days in a tightly sealed container. As my husband and I live in a pretty hot climate, I tend to keep any leftovers in the fridge and just warm them up gently in the oven or microwave when I need them.

TO DECORATE THIS WITH GLAZED PECANS
Whisk ½ cup (160 g) apricot jam or conserve with 2 tablespoons cold water in a small heavy-based saucepan over medium heat. Bring to the boil, reduce the heat a little and let it bubble gently for 5 minutes or so, until it's thick and syrupy. (Just keep an eye on it so it doesn't scorch.) Sit a dozen pecans on a sheet of baking paper and brush them with the hot glaze. Let the glaze set, then dot the pecans around the edge of the cake.

My last-minute Christmas cake

SERVES 16–20

With the best intentions in the world, I never seem to get my Christmas cake made when I hope to (being a cook and food writer I probably shouldn't confess to this!). Every year, come September, I have great plans to get all my Christmas shopping and baking well underway, however, by mid-December little seems to have happened. Last year, having finally accepted that this is just the way things are, I decided a little lateral thinking was in order and started experimenting with all sorts of cakes. The result is this rich, dense fruitcake – it tastes mellow and rounded, just like it's been baked months ahead, and has an irresistible, spicy flavour.

You needn't use exactly the same dried fruits that I mention – I often put in whatever happens to be in the pantry; as long as the quantities are the same, it doesn't matter. However, I always try to include currants as they add a deep wine-y richness to the mixture. As a personal quirk, I never, ever add mixed peel as its one of the best ways I know of to spoil a perfectly delicious cake.

300 g unsalted butter
420 g raw sugar
2¼ cups (380 g) raisins
180 g pitted prunes
1 cup (160 g) sultanas
90 g dried currants
90 g pitted dates
2 teaspoons bicarbonate of soda
½ cup (125 ml) brandy or overproof
   (dark) rum
1½ cups (375 ml) cool water

2 teaspoons freshly grated or ground
   nutmeg
2 teaspoons ground cinnamon
4 eggs, lightly beaten
2½ cups (375 g) stone-ground wholemeal
   plain flour
150 g pecan halves and 120 g whole
   almond kernels, for decorating
½ quantity Apricot Glaze
   (see page 246), (optional)

1 Melt the butter over medium heat in a saucepan large enough to eventually hold all the cake ingredients. Add the sugar and stir to partially dissolve it so it's wet and slushy. Tip in all the dried fruit, the bicarbonate of soda, brandy and water. Increase the heat to high and keep stirring until the sugar has dissolved. Once it has, stop stirring and bring the mixture to the boil, then reduce the heat to low and let it simmer for 4 minutes. You need to keep an eye on it and adjust the heat as it froths up considerably because of the bicarbonate of soda. When it's ready, turn off the heat and leave it to cool in the pan. I often make this in the evening and leave it to cool overnight. However, if you do this, cover it well; I once left the lid slightly askew and woke to find an army of very inebriated ants weaving their way to and from the pan!

2 Preheat your oven to 150°C. Butter a 23 cm springform cake tin and line the base and sides with two layers of buttered baking paper. Set aside.

3 Add the nutmeg, cinnamon and eggs to the dried fruit mixture and stir them in well. Mix in the flour, then leave the batter to sit for a few minutes. Scrape the batter into the prepared tin and give it a gentle shake to level the top. >

4 Now comes one of the most enjoyable things to do – decorating the top of the cake. I love doing this; you can create all sorts of different patterns by marching alternating bands of pecans and almonds across the top, either curving them into waves or creating rings of concentric circles.

5 Bake for 2¼–2½ hours or until the cake feels quite firm in the centre when pressed and a fine skewer inserted in the middle comes out clean. After an hour or so of cooking, it's a good idea to check the top; if it's a good rich brown then cover it loosely with a sheet of foil to stop it getting darker.

6 Leave the cake to cool completely in the tin on a wire rack. When it's cool, remove it from the tin, wrap it tightly in plastic film or foil and store it in the fridge, where it will keep for up to 6 weeks. For a light sheen, brush the top with a little warm Apricot Glaze before serving.

Blueberry and cinnamon crumble cake

SERVES 8–10

Cakes like this epitomise country baking at its best. The house smells divine as it cooks, filling the air with the spicy, sweet fragrance of cinnamon, nutmeg and blueberries. It also has a crunchy crumble topping which I just love on cakes – here the crumble is a basic brown sugar, pecan and spice one, but it really makes a huge difference to what is such a simple cake, adding another dimension of texture and flavour. When you first bite into it you get the satisfying crunch of the nuts and fragrance of the spices, which is quickly followed by sharp-sweet bursts of blueberries and just a hint of lemon. Lovely stuff.

1 cup (150 g) plain flour
¾ cup (110 g) stone-ground wholemeal
   plain flour
1 cup (220 g) castor sugar
2½ teaspoons baking powder
½ teaspoon salt
½ teaspoon ground cinnamon
⅓ cup (80 ml) light olive oil
¾ cup (180 ml) milk
1 egg
1 teaspoon vanilla extract
2 teaspoons finely grated lemon zest
200 g fresh *or* frozen blueberries
icing sugar (optional), for dusting

TOPPING
¼ cup (35 g) plain flour
¼ cup (55 g) brown sugar
½ teaspoon ground cinnamon
½ teaspoon freshly grated *or*
   ground nutmeg
½ cup (70 g) pecans *or* walnuts
30 g cold unsalted butter, cut into
   small chunks
100 g fresh *or* frozen blueberries

1 Preheat your oven to 180°C. Butter a 24 or 25 cm springform cake tin, line the base with buttered baking paper, then dust with flour and set it aside.

2 For the topping, put the flour, brown sugar, cinnamon and nutmeg into a food processor and briefly whiz to combine. Add the nuts and scatter the little chunks of cold butter over the top. Pulse just until the butter is incorporated and the nuts are the size of coarse breadcrumbs. Tip this mixture into a bowl and keep it in a cool spot.

3 Put both the flours, the sugar, baking powder, salt and cinnamon into the food processor and whiz them together for 20 seconds. Tip this dry mixture into a large bowl. Scoop out 1 heaped tablespoon of it into another bowl.

4 Whiz the oil, milk, egg, vanilla extract and lemon zest together in the processor until they're well combined. Make a well in the centre of the flour mixture and pour in this wet mixture. Stir them together until they're well mixed. Toss the blueberries in the bowl with the reserved spoonful of dry mixture, then gently fold them into the cake batter; I always find it fascinating that this fine, floury coating is just enough to help stop the blueberries from sinking to the bottom of the cake as it bakes. Spread the batter evenly into the prepared tin. Sprinkle spoonfuls of the crumble over the top and give the tin a little shake to even it out. Press the blueberries for the topping gently into the crumble.

5 Bake for 50–55 minutes or until a fine skewer inserted in the middle of the cake comes out clean. Cool the cake in the tin on a wire rack for 12 minutes. Release the outer ring of the tin and gently lift it off. Sit another rack (or a flat plate) on top of the cake and carefully invert it onto this. Remove the base and paper, and then invert the cake again onto the rack to cool.

6 Dust with icing sugar just before serving. You'll find that any leftover cake freezes really well for a couple of weeks. I usually just sandwich the slices of cake between sheets of freezer wrap or baking paper. To defrost, you can microwave them gently, warm them in the oven or just let them sit out at room temperature for about 40 minutes (by way of this, I discovered that the cake is terrific served warm, rather like a pudding, with a little cream). Otherwise, it keeps well stored at room temperature in a tightly sealed container for 2 days.

FROZEN BLUEBERRIES

Frozen blueberries work beautifully in this cake. There's no need to defrost them first, in fact it's better not to as they tend to get really mushy and leave purplish streaks through the cake batter – not that it's a drama, but it is rather nice to bite into a whole berry and have it burst in your mouth.

Gooey butterscotch peach cake

SERVES 8

LIKE MOST UPSIDE-DOWN CAKES . . .

this looks and tastes best on the day it's made. I happily eat it a day later but the fruit tends to become a bit mushy and lose its lovely sheen. However, if you want to make it a few hours ahead of when you need it, that's fine. Gently rewarm it in a microwave or a 150°C oven and brush it with the golden syrup just before serving.

I vividly remember the day we photographed this cake – the smell of it baking nearly drove Rodney, my great friend and the photographer for this (and all) my books, and me, absolutely wild. We could hardly wait to get it shot so we could eat a slice – which we both proceeded to do with unseemly haste and great relish. (It's one of the nicest perks about photographing a book like this, and we took full advantage of it, as did a number of friends who seemed to find numerous reasons to 'just happen to drop by' on the days we photographed!) It's a gorgeous cake – golden, moist and gooey with the caramel, and it makes a wonderful summer dessert.

100 g almond meal

90 g self-raising flour

190 g castor sugar

3 eggs

190 g unsalted butter, at room temperature, cut into large chunks

1 teaspoon vanilla extract

golden syrup, for brushing

PEACH AND CARAMEL TOPPING

80 g unsalted butter

½ cup (110 g) firmly-packed brown sugar

¼ teaspoon salt

3–4 largish, just-ripe, freestone peaches

1 Preheat your oven to 180°C. Lightly butter a 24 cm round cake tin, line the base with baking paper and set it aside. The tin I use has slightly flared sides, so it's actually 24 cm across the top and 21 cm across the base. It's best not to use a springform tin for this as the caramel on the base of the cake tends to leak out of the join in the tin while it's cooking and makes a real mess in the bottom of the oven – unfortunately, I learnt this the hard way!

2 For the topping, melt the butter in a small heavy-based saucepan over low heat. Add the sugar and salt and stir until the mixture is smooth; sometimes this can separate, so if it does, don't worry, just spread it in the tin as best you can, the cake will still be fine. Pour it into the prepared tin, tilting it to coat the bottom evenly (you'll need to hold the tin with a tea towel as you do this because it gets really hot).

3 I have to admit I don't always peel the peaches as I don't mind a bit of skin on them. However, if you want to and find the skins are clinging stubbornly to the flesh, put them into boiling water for about 30 seconds, then give them a quick dunk in iced water to cool them down. Peel and cut them into 6 mm-thick slices. Lay the peach slices decoratively over the top of the caramel. Overlap them slightly as you go and fill in any gaps so the base is completely covered with peaches. I find that I always have to fiddle a bit to make the slices sit properly. Set the tin aside.

4 Whiz the almond meal and flour in a food processor for 10 seconds or until they're well combined. Tip them into a bowl. >

5 Put the sugar and eggs into the processor and whiz them together for 1 minute. Add the butter to the processor and whiz together with the egg mixture for 30 seconds or so, stopping the machine and scraping down the sides once or twice with a rubber spatula. Mix in the vanilla extract. Return the almond mixture to the processor and pulse the two together only until they're just combined. Dollop this batter into the prepared tin and spread it out evenly but gently, so you don't disturb the peach slices underneath.

6 Bake for about 45 minutes or until a fine skewer inserted in the middle of the cake comes out clean; just so you know, the top may be quite dark. Leave it to cool for a few minutes then run a blunt knife around the inside of the tin to loosen the cake. Leave it another couple of minutes then invert it onto a serving plate. Carefully ease off the tin and remove the paper if it sticks to the fruit. Brush the peaches gently with golden syrup to give them a sheen, then serve the cake warm with cream (a scoop of vanilla ice-cream is rather fabulous too).

Very quick pear and pecan or walnut cake

SERVES 10–12

I love the spicy aroma that wafts through the house when this simple, homely cake is baking. It has a really 'old-fashioned' flavour, with its fragrant nuggets of pear, warm cinnamon spicing and roasted nuts. You can also make a rather splendid dessert from it by serving it barely warm with really good vanilla bean or cinnamon ice-cream and a jug of Luscious Homemade Caramel Sauce (if you'd like to try the sauce, the recipe is on page 257).

2 cups (300 g) plain flour

2 teaspoons ground cinnamon

½ teaspoon ground nutmeg

1 teaspoon bicarbonate of soda

½ teaspoon salt

1 cup (140 g) roasted pecans or walnuts (see page 80), coarsely chopped

3 eggs

1½ cups (330 g) firmly-packed brown sugar

¼ cup (55 g) castor sugar

½ cup (125 ml) light olive oil

1½ teaspoons vanilla extract

¼ cup (60 ml) water

5 just-ripe small pears, peeled, cored and cut into 1 cm chunks or 10 well-drained canned pear halves in natural juice, chopped

icing sugar, for dusting

> **THIS LOOKS VERY SWISH . . .**
> *if you glaze whole roasted pecans with a little reduced apricot jam to give them a shine and sit about a dozen or so around the top of the cake (see page 59).*

1 Preheat your oven to 150°C. Butter and flour a 26 cm fluted non-stick bundt tin and set aside. In this case, despite my doubts about non-stick cake tins (see page 10), I find that using one here makes it much easier to turn the cake out as it's quite moist.

2 Put the flour, cinnamon, nutmeg, bicarbonate of soda and salt into a large bowl. Whisk them together with a balloon whisk for 1 minute so they're thoroughly mixed. Tip in the nuts and toss them about to coat them in the flour mixture.

3 Crack the eggs into a separate bowl and whisk to break them up. Add the sugars, oil, vanilla extract and water and mix everything thoroughly together until the mixture is smooth. Pour this mixture into the dry ingredients and stir them together until they're just combined. Add the pears and gently fold them in. Dollop the batter into the prepared tin and spread it out evenly with the back of your spoon.

4 Bake for about 1 hour or until a fine skewer inserted in the middle of the cake comes out clean. Cool the cake in the tin on a wire rack for 10 minutes, then invert it onto the rack to cool completely.

5 To finish the cake off, dust it with a little icing sugar just before serving. Although this is such a simple finish it looks really lovely because the sugar settles, like a fine dusting of snow, into the flutes and curves of the cake. Any left-overs will keep for up to 5 days in the fridge and 2 weeks in the freezer. Slices can be gently warmed in a microwave to serve as a pudding.

Sticky caramel and banana upside-down cake

SERVES 6–8

When I was growing up it was pretty much the norm to have a thicket of banana trees growing in your back garden (along with the ubiquitous passionfruit and choko vines that wound their way along the fence and up into the gum trees). I used to think it wonderful to have such an exotic-seeming tree in the garden and would dress myself up in my hula skirt and lei (aged six, I should add) and pretend I was on a tropical island. The great bunches of bananas fascinated me with their extraordinary purple flower buds, and I remember waiting eagerly for my dad to get out his machete and chop one down. The bunch would then hang in the cool under the house and we would eat the tiny, sugary-sweet bananas as they ripened. Invariably we would end up unable to keep pace with the number of bananas that were ready at the same time, so mum would be constantly making banana 'something or other' to use them up – tea breads, puddings, pancakes, and best of all, cakes. My favourite was a gooey upside-down cake which was heavenly. Unfortunately, she never wrote down the recipe and having tried many versions over the years, I think this is the closest I can get. It's a simple combination of buttery caramel, banana and a whiff of cinnamon and nutmeg that has a wonderful flavour.

It's important that the bananas for the caramel topping aren't too ripe otherwise they collapse and become mushy as they bake; mind you the cake still tastes great, it just doesn't look as pretty.

180 g self-raising flour	CARAMEL TOPPING
¼ teaspoon salt	60 g unsalted butter
½ teaspoon ground cinnamon	¾ cup (165 g) brown sugar
¼ teaspoon ground nutmeg	large pinch salt
1 medium-sized very ripe banana	3–4 large just-ripe bananas
2 tablespoons sour cream	
2 eggs	
180 g castor sugar	
90 g unsalted butter, at room temperature, cut into small chunks	
1 teaspoon vanilla extract	
golden syrup, for brushing, and rich cream *or* vanilla ice-cream, to serve	

1 Preheat your oven to 180°C. Butter a 24 or 25 cm round cake tin and set it aside.

2 For the caramel topping, melt the butter in a heavy-based saucepan over medium heat. Add the brown sugar and salt and cook the mixture, stirring it occasionally, for a few minutes. Pour this into the prepared tin and tilt it to coat the bottom evenly. Peel and slice the bananas fairly thickly. Sit the slices in overlapping circles over the base of the tin so they completely cover the caramel. Set the tin aside.

3 Put the flour, salt, cinnamon and nutmeg into a food processor and whiz them together for 10 seconds. Tip them into a bowl. In another bowl, mash the banana then stir in the sour cream. Set both bowls aside.

4 Put the eggs and sugar into the processor, then whiz them together for 1 minute, stopping and scraping down the sides with a rubber spatula occasionally. Add the butter and vanilla extract and whiz again for 40 seconds or so. Scrape the mashed banana and sour cream mixture into this and whiz them together for 10 seconds. The batter may well look a little curdled at this stage, but don't worry, it will be fine. Add the flour mixture to the food processor and pulse them together until they're just combined.

5 Dollop spoonfuls of the cake batter into the tin, over the top of the bananas, and spread it out evenly. Do this fairly carefully so you don't disturb the bananas underneath.

6 Bake for 45–50 minutes or until the cake is golden and springy when you give it a gentle prod in the middle. Remove it from the oven and leave it to settle in the tin for 3 minutes. Carefully loosen the cake around the sides, watching out for your fingers as the tin is very hot. Sit a serving plate on top of the tin and, holding it with a tea towel to protect your hands, flip the tin and plate over. Sit the plate on the bench and leave the tin on top for 20 seconds – this creates a little bit of steam which helps the cake come out more easily. Gently remove the tin. Don't worry if some banana slices stick to the bottom of it, just scrape them off and press them back onto the cake. Leave the cake to cool.

7 Just before serving, brush a little golden syrup over the top. Serve the cake warm or at room temperature with cream or ice-cream. I'd have to say this cake is best eaten on the day it's made.

A really beautiful orange cake

SERVES 12–16

I couldn't write this book without including a recipe for an orange cake. I love them, as much as anything, because they remind me of my mum. When we were small she always baked a cake for the weekend – sometimes it was chocolate, in winter it was more often than not a lovely warm cinnamon and apple teacake, but her standard, most-loved cake was her orange cake. I can still recall the smell of it baking and see the way the orange icing trickled down the sides while we all waited impatiently for it to be cut for afternoon tea. This particular recipe is for a big, bold, gorgeous cake that looks rather grand – it has a beautiful velvety texture and a rich, buttery orange flavour.

3 cups (450 g) plain flour
½ teaspoon salt
½ teaspoon bicarbonate of soda
3 eggs
2 cups (440 g) castor sugar
250 g unsalted butter, at room temperature, cut into chunks
1 cup (250 ml) buttermilk
finely grated zest of 3 oranges
2½ tablespoons concentrated orange juice drink
80 g dried cranberries (sold as craisins), (optional)
icing sugar, for dusting *or* Simple Orange Icing (see page 72)
   and Candied Citrus Zest (see page 258), (optional)

ORANGE GLAZE
1 cup (160 g) icing sugar mixture, sifted
¼ cup (60 ml) concentrated orange juice drink
30 g unsalted butter, melted

1 Preheat your oven to 150°C. Butter and flour a large bundt tin (approximately 26 cm) and set aside.

2 Put the flour, salt and bicarbonate of soda into a food processor and whiz so they're well mixed, then tip them into a bowl. Put the eggs and sugar into the processor and whiz them for 1 minute. Add the chunks of butter and process the mixture for another minute or until it's thick and creamy. Add the buttermilk, orange zest and concentrated orange juice and whiz for 10 seconds. Add all but one small spoonful of the flour mixture and blend it in with on/off pulses until it's just combined. You'll find that you need to scrape down the sides a few times with a rubber spatula while you're doing all this mixing.

3 Toss the dried cranberries with the reserved spoonful of flour so they're lightly coated. Use a rubber spatula to gently stir them into the batter. Spoon the batter into the prepared tin and smooth the surface. >

4 Bake for about 70 minutes or until a fine skewer inserted in the middle of the cake comes out clean. Cool the cake in the tin on a wire rack for 10 minutes.

5 Meanwhile, for the orange glaze, put all the glaze ingredients into a bowl and whisk them together until they're smooth. Using a fine palette knife, carefully loosen around the edges and middle of the cake. Take your time doing this so you don't spoil the swirl marks from the tin. Invert the cake onto the rack and gently ease off the tin. Sit a sheet of newspaper underneath the rack (this is to catch any drips from the glaze). Brush the glaze all over the cake (including the central hollow). Keep brushing the glaze on until there is none left, as the cake will slowly absorb it. Leave the cake to cool completely. The glaze forms a fine crackly coating which is really delicious.

6 When you're ready to serve, sit the cake on a stand or serving plate and dust it with icing sugar or make the Simple Orange Icing (see below). While it's lovely served just as is, a bowl of softly whipped, rich cream doesn't go at all amiss with it either. The cake keeps remarkably well in an airtight container for 5–6 days and freezes well for up to 3 weeks.

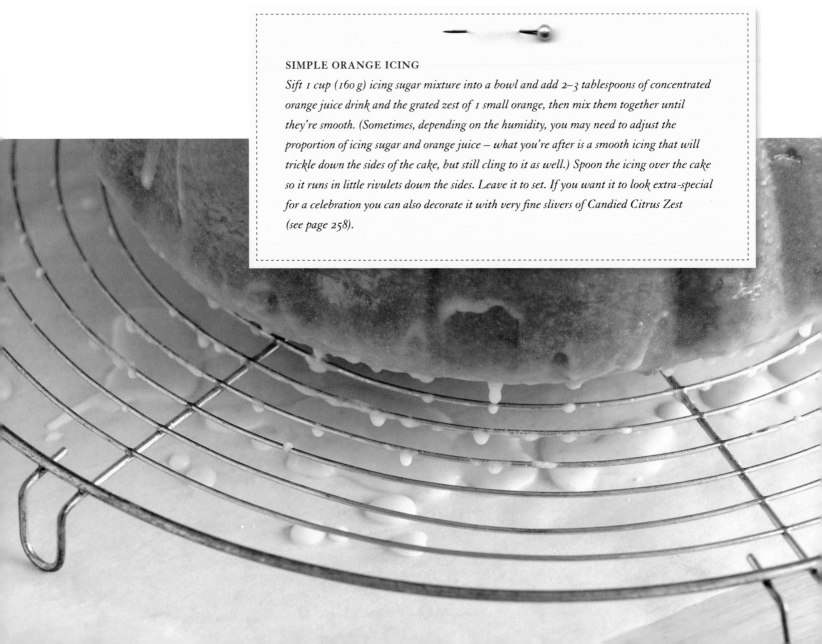

SIMPLE ORANGE ICING

Sift 1 cup (160 g) icing sugar mixture into a bowl and add 2–3 tablespoons of concentrated orange juice drink and the grated zest of 1 small orange, then mix them together until they're smooth. (Sometimes, depending on the humidity, you may need to adjust the proportion of icing sugar and orange juice – what you're after is a smooth icing that will trickle down the sides of the cake, but still cling to it as well.) Spoon the icing over the cake so it runs in little rivulets down the sides. Leave it to set. If you want it to look extra-special for a celebration you can also decorate it with very fine slivers of Candied Citrus Zest (see page 258).

The most fabulous banana cake

SERVES 12

This recipe originally appeared in my first cookbook, *Belinda Jeffery's 100 Favourite Recipes*, and I've included it here, mainly because I don't think I would have lived it down if I hadn't. I'm amazed at the number of people (including my husband, who says this is his all-time favourite cake), who, when they heard I was writing a book on baking, said to me, 'You're going to have your fabulous banana cake recipe in it too, aren't you?' With so much pressure, how could I not? It's a wonderful, moist, dense cake and keeps happily in the fridge for up to one week.

1½ cups (225 g) plain flour

3 teaspoons baking powder

¾ teaspoon salt

½ teaspoon bicarbonate of soda

2–3 large very ripe bananas (to yield 1 cup mashed banana)

1⅔ cups (370 g) castor sugar

2 eggs

125 g unsalted butter, at room temperature, cut into small chunks

100 ml buttermilk

1½ teaspoons vanilla extract

roasted pecans (see page 80), (optional), to serve

ICING

250 g cream cheese, at room temperature, cut into chunks

125 g unsalted butter, at room temperature, cut into chunks

500 g icing sugar mixture, sifted

1½ teaspoons vanilla extract

A NICK IN TIME

Cutting a cake in half evenly is not as simple as it sounds; however, there are a couple of things that make it a bit easier. Firstly, if you mark around the circumference with a line of toothpicks and use them as a guide it helps you slice it into two even layers. Then, before you lift the top off, make a small vertical V-shaped cut in one spot on the sides of both layers, so when you go to put the top back on again all you need do is line up the cuts and the cake will be even.

1 Preheat your oven to 180°C. Butter and flour a deep 26 cm ring tin.

2 Put the flour, baking powder, salt and bicarbonate of soda into a food processor and whiz them together for 15 seconds, then tip them into a bowl.

3 Mash the bananas and measure out 1 cup banana pulp. Scrape this into the processor and purée it until it's smooth. Add the sugar and eggs and whiz together for 1 minute. Add the butter and whiz it for another minute or until the mixture is thick and creamy. Now add the buttermilk and vanilla extract and pulse the processor in quick on/off bursts to just mix them in. Add the reserved flour mixture and again mix it in with quick bursts, scraping down the sides once or twice with a rubber spatula, until it's only just combined (don't overdo it or the cake will be tough). Scoop the batter into the prepared tin and smooth it out evenly.

4 Bake for 30–35 minutes or until a fine skewer inserted in the middle of the cake comes out clean; it won't have risen much as it's quite dense. Don't open the oven any earlier than this or the cake can sink in the middle. Cool the cake in the tin on a wire rack for 7 minutes. Gently loosen the cake around the edges with a butter knife or fine palette knife, then invert it onto the rack and leave it to cool completely. >

5 While the cake is cooling, make the icing. Whiz the cream cheese and butter in the food processor until they're well mixed. Add the icing sugar mixture and vanilla extract and process until the icing is smooth. Scrape it into a bowl and chill it for about 15 minutes to firm it up if it seems a bit too soft (this usually only happens in really hot weather).

6 When the cake is cool, sit it on a serving plate or cake stand and carefully cut through the circumference widthways with a long serrated knife to split it into two even layers. Spread some icing on the bottom layer, then sandwich the two halves back together again. Spread a thick layer of icing all over the top and sides of the cake and smooth it as best you can with a long palette knife.

7 Serve the cake straight away or refrigerate it. It keeps well for up to 1 week – just bring it back to cool room temperature before eating it. Either leave the top plain or decorate it with roasted pecans.

Tropical pineapple crush cake

SERVES 16–20

I've been making this big, beautiful cake since the days when we had our café. It's one of those easy recipes that are such a joy to have in your repertoire as it's perfect for birthday parties or when you need something special for a crowd, without a lot of fuss. It's also a good one for kids' fetes too, as you can bake it in a big slab tin and keep the decoration low-key – it only needs a sprinkle of toasted coconut, or you can really up the ante and sandwich two rounds together with oodles of the creamy icing, then decorate the top with flowers. In summer, it looks very glam garlanded with frangipani blossoms, although I should just say, that while certain flowers are edible, frangipani blossoms aren't among them – in this case, they're purely for decoration.

THE BEAUTY OF THIS RECIPE . . .

is that unlike lots of cakes, you can tweak the recipe quite a bit. I sometimes add tiny chunks of crystallised ginger or pineapple to the batter, then decorate the top with slivers of the same. If you make a layer cake you can sandwich slices of banana, or to make it even more tropical, mango, in the middle; a little passionfruit pulp stirred into the icing is rather fabulous too.

3 cups (450 g) plain flour
2 cups (440 g) castor sugar
1 teaspoon salt
1 teaspoon bicarbonate of soda
1 heaped teaspoon ground cinnamon
¼ teaspoon ground nutmeg
½ cup (75 g) roasted macadamias
   (see page 80), coarsely chopped (optional)
3 eggs
1½ cups (375 ml) light olive oil
1½ teaspoons vanilla extract
1 cup canned crushed pineapple
   (in natural juice), undrained
5–6 medium-sized ripe bananas (to yield
   2 cups roughly mashed banana)

ICING
125 g softened unsalted butter,
   cut into chunks,
250 g softened cream cheese,
   cut into chunks
2 teaspoons vanilla extract
500 g icing sugar mixture, sifted

1 Preheat your oven to 160°C. Butter two 25 cm round cake tins (or for a slab cake, a 32 cm × 24 cm × 5 cm rectangular baking tin). Line the base/s with buttered baking paper and dust the tin/s lightly with flour. Set aside.

2 Put the flour, sugar, salt, bicarbonate of soda, cinnamon and nutmeg into a large bowl. Whisk them together with a balloon whisk for 1 minute. Tip in the macadamias, if using, and toss them about so they're well coated in the flour mixture. Set aside.

3 In a smaller bowl, beat the eggs lightly so they're well mixed but not frothed up. Whisk in the oil and vanilla extract until they're well combined. Add the pineapple and mashed bananas and mix them in thoroughly.

4 Scrape the banana mixture into the flour mixture and stir them together well to form a thickish batter. Divide the batter evenly between the tins or put it all into the slab tin, if using, and smooth the top/s.

5 Bake for 45–50 minutes or until the cakes are golden and springy when gently pressed in the centre and a fine skewer inserted into the middle comes out clean. (If you're baking the cake in a large slab tin it may take a bit longer.) Cool the cakes in their tins on a wire rack for 10 minutes or so. Gently loosen the cakes around the sides and invert them onto the rack – in fact, unless you're using a slab tin, you'll need two racks for the cakes as it's nigh impossible to flip over two at a time onto a single rack without one ending up on the floor (no, I haven't done it, but I've been closer than I care to admit!). Remove the tin and paper if it's stuck to the bottoms and leave the cakes to cool completely. (They keep well at this stage for a couple of days in the fridge if they're tightly wrapped in plastic film; it's handy to know that they also freeze well for up to a month too.)

6 For the icing, put all the ingredients into a food processor and whiz them together, stopping and scraping down the sides with a rubber spatula occasionally, until it looks smooth and creamy. (You can keep the icing in a tightly covered container for a few days in the fridge too. Just return it to cool room temperature to soften a bit before using.)

7 You can finish the cake quite a few hours before you serve it, although if the weather is really warm it is best kept in the fridge. Sit one round on a serving plate (or better still, a cake stand). Spread a bit less than half the icing over the top of it. Centre the other cake on the icing and press down on it gently to stick the two halves together. Spread the remaining icing over the top, then smooth it out with a palette knife – I don't try to get it perfectly smooth as I really like the swirl marks the palette knife leaves behind. Now decorate it as you like (see opposite) – and it's ready to 'rock-and-roll', as they say. Once iced, the cake keeps well in the fridge for up to 5 days.

cakes with
lots of nuts

Roasting nuts and other important things

There is a real liquorice-all-sorts mixture of cakes in this chapter, the distinguishing feature being that they're all made with lots of nuts. Unlike the chocolate cake chapter where there is so much to say about working with chocolate, there's not a whole lot you need to know about nuts. There really is only one golden rule, but boy is it important, and that is (at the risk of stating the obvious) that nuts must be fresh, or it is best not to use them at all. For I don't think there's anything so utterly disappointing as eating what looks to be a delicious slice of cake, only to find the nuts are old and stale. It's a cardinal sin in my book (especially if it happens with a bought cake or in a café or restaurant – it's just not that hard to check if they're fresh, for heaven's sake).

The best way to avoid this is to buy your nuts from somewhere that has a high turnover (it's a bit of a mantra with cookbook writers, I know, but it's the truth of the matter). If you can buy them at a specialty nut shop then you'll have an amazing choice, however, not all that many of us can do that, so a good health food store is often your next best bet.

CHOOSING NUTS Unfortunately, it's a little hard to tell from just looking at them if nuts are fresh – ideally it's great to be able to taste them too, but in many cases I know this isn't possible. However, there are some tell-tale signs to keep an eye out for.

* Pine nuts come in different shapes and sizes (the best I've ever seen were nearly 2 centimetres long and beautiful to eat), but whatever their size, they should all have a soft, creamy lustre. If they're starting to look translucent or oily with a greyish tinge or if they're crumbling, let them be.
* Shelled macadamias and almonds too should have a waxy, ivory colour and not be at all oily-looking or greyish.
* It's harder to tell with nuts that still have their fine skins on, like hazelnuts and brazils, but what you're after are plump, perky nuts – they shouldn't look at all shrivelled or dried out.

＊ If you're buying ground nuts or nut meals, like almond and hazelnut, try to find somewhere that stores these in a fridge. Once ground, nuts deteriorate rapidly and keeping them cool helps stop the oils in them from becoming rancid. So if you find a shop that takes that extra trouble, you can be pretty sure they care about the quality of their nuts.

STORING NUTS   I tend to buy nuts in bulk as we go through them at a rate of knots. Even so, I store all of them, except for those that are still in their hard shells, in the freezer. They never freeze solid because of all the oil they contain, so it's no big deal to defrost them – it only takes a few minutes.

Even with all these precautions, eventually nuts do start to become stale, so before I cook with them I always munch on a couple to make sure that all is well.

ROASTING NUTS   I know you can buy ready-roasted nuts, however, once they're cooked like this they deteriorate more rapidly than normal, so ideally it's best to roast them yourself (plus you get that added bonus of the wonderful aroma as they cook).

To do this, just spread the nuts onto a baking tray lined with baking paper, then pop them into a 180°C oven. While they're cooking, stir them every so often, as the ones around the edge tend to darken more quickly than the ones in the middle. The timing will depend on the quantity and the type of nuts you're using; those with the most oil, like macadamias, tend to brown more rapidly than others. I usually start checking them after about six minutes or so and then every minute or two from there. When they're done, just let them cool on the tray and they're ready to use. When I'm doing this I often roast more than I need and put the extra ones in the freezer, so they're ready to go whenever the baking bug strikes. (They're also lovely to have on hand as an energy booster when you're starting to run out of steam.)

Sticky pineapple, carrot, ginger and macadamia cake

SERVES 12–16

I know this looks like a horribly long list of ingredients, however, I promise you that the cake is remarkably easy to make – and absolutely delicious. It's a sensational cake – just perfect for a birthday cake. It keeps wonderfully well too, although I wouldn't want to lay bets on how long it takes to disappear. I keep 'straightening up the edge' every time I open the fridge – the rest of the family are less subtle and great wedges mysteriously disappear!

2 cups (300 g) plain flour

1 teaspoon baking powder

2 teaspoons bicarbonate of soda

1½ teaspoons ground cinnamon

¼ teaspoon ground nutmeg

¼ teaspoon salt

2 cups (440 g) castor sugar

½ cup (35 g) shredded coconut

120 g roasted macadamias (see opposite),
   roughly chopped

6 pieces crystallised ginger, finely chopped

3 eggs

¼ cup (60 ml) buttermilk

¼ cup (60 ml) macadamia oil
   or light olive oil

2 cups grated carrots (approximately
   4 medium-sized peeled carrots)

1 teaspoon vanilla extract

1 × 440 g can crushed pineapple
   (in natural juice), drained

toasted coconut chips (see page 91),
   to serve

STICKY GLAZE

½ cup (110 g) castor sugar

¼ cup (60 ml) buttermilk

60 g unsalted butter

2 teaspoons golden syrup

1 teaspoon vanilla extract

VANILLA CREAM

1 cup (250 ml) thickened cream

¾ cup (190 ml) sour cream

1½ tablespoons icing sugar, sifted

1 teaspoon vanilla extract

PEELING CARROTS FOR BAKING
I'm not sure why, but if you don't peel them, carrots turn green over time once the cake is baked. The cake still tastes perfectly delicious, but the flecks of green are a bit disconcerting!

1 Preheat your oven to 180°C. Butter two shallow 23 or 24 cm round cake tins. Line the bases with buttered baking paper then dust the tins with flour. Set aside.

2 Sift the flour, baking powder, bicarbonate of soda, cinnamon, nutmeg and salt into a large bowl. Add the sugar and mix everything together with a balloon whisk for 1 minute. Add the shredded coconut, macadamias and ginger and toss them about so they're well coated in the flour mixture.

3 In a separate bowl, lightly whisk the eggs, then whisk in the buttermilk and oil until just combined. Use a spoon or spatula to stir in the carrots, vanilla extract and drained pineapple. Pour this mixture into the dry ingredients and stir them together until just combined. >

4 Divide the batter evenly between the cake tins. Sit them on the middle shelves of the oven and bake them for about 40 minutes or until the centre of each springs back when lightly pressed.

5 Meanwhile, to make the sticky glaze, put all the glaze ingredients except the vanilla extract into a small saucepan over medium–high heat. Stir until the sugar has dissolved, then bring it to the boil. As soon as it boils, reduce the heat to low–medium so the syrup bubbles steadily and cook, stirring, for 4 minutes. Remove from the heat and add the vanilla extract, then set aside in a warm spot.

6 When the cakes are ready, transfer the tins to a wire rack. Leave them in their tins and immediately pour half of the sticky glaze over each cake, tilting them so the tops are evenly coated. Leave them to cool for 30 minutes. Remove the cakes from the tins, discard the baking paper and let them cool completely on wire racks. (This is a bit mucky to do as the cakes will still be sticky from the glaze – I'm forever licking my fingers, then having to wash my hands!) If you're serving the cake immediately you can finish it now, otherwise wrap each layer separately in plastic film and store them in the fridge for 4–5 days.

7 For the vanilla cream, put all the ingredients into a bowl and whisk carefully just until soft peaks form. Gently loosen under one of the cake layers (they tend to stick to the racks a bit) and sit it on a serving plate. Spread about half of the cream evenly over the top, leaving a slight border all around (this is so the cream doesn't squish out the sides when the next layer goes on). Sit the second layer on this. Spread the remaining cream evenly over the top. To finish it off, dot the toasted coconut flakes over the top of the cake. Refrigerate until ready to serve.

Three-nut cake

SERVES 8–10

I tore the recipe for this cake out of an American magazine many years ago and I'm afraid I have no idea who was the originator, but I thank them as it's a terrific cake. When we had our café, this was one of our most requested desserts. It was so popular that some of our regular customers suggested we hang a little banner outside whenever it was on the menu, so if they were driving by they knew to stop and buy a piece. It's a lovely, simple cake, and has a chewy, macaroon-like texture which I adore.

This cake actually freezes well too, so I tend to make two at a time (I'm hopeless at doing anything in small quantities) and stick one in the freezer for down the track. It needs little in the way of decoration except a dusting of icing sugar – although I dressed one up with Chocolate Zig-zags (see opposite) for a friend's birthday and it looked very special. It's very much an 'any time of day cake' and moves seamlessly from being something delish to have with a good cup of coffee to a stylish dessert.

If you have time, it tastes even better if the hazelnuts are roasted in advance.

CRUST
120 g almond meal
2½ tablespoons castor sugar
3½ tablespoons plain flour
75 g very cold unsalted butter,
    cut into small chunks

FILLING
125 g hazelnuts
100 g pecans
½ cup (75 g) plain flour
½ teaspoon baking powder
1 cup (70 g) shredded coconut
2 eggs
1 egg yolk
1 cup (220 g) firmly-packed brown sugar
1 teaspoon vanilla extract
icing sugar, for dusting

1 Preheat your oven to 180°C. Have ready a 23 cm springform cake tin – it doesn't need buttering or lining.

2 To make the crust, put the almond meal, sugar and flour into a food processor and whiz them together for 10 seconds or so. Add the butter and whiz the mixture again until it resembles coarse breadcrumbs. Tip it into the cake tin and press it as evenly as you can over the bottom and about one-third of the way up the side of the tin. Put it in the fridge to chill.

3 For the filling, coarsely grind the hazelnuts, then the pecans, in a food processor and set aside. Tip the flour and baking powder into a medium-sized bowl. Whisk them together with a balloon whisk for 40 seconds. Add the ground hazelnuts, pecans and shredded coconut and whisk them in so everything is well combined. Set aside.

4 I'm afraid that you're going to need an electric beater or mixer for this next part – it's just a bit too hard to do by hand. Put the whole eggs, egg yolk and brown sugar into the mixer bowl and beat them on medium–high speed for about 5 minutes or until they're fluffy. With a wide spatula, fold the flour and nut mixture and vanilla extract into the egg mixture until they're well combined. Pour the mixture into the chilled crust and give it a gentle shake to even it out.

5 Bake for 40 minutes or until the cake is set on the surface but still slightly soft in the centre. To check, carefully insert a fine skewer in the middle; it should come out with a few moist crumbs clinging to it.

6 Cool the cake in the tin on a wire rack. Once it's cool, carefully run a butter knife or fine palette knife around the sides of the cake to loosen it. Release and remove the sides of the tin and invert the cake onto the wire rack. Loosen the base of the tin and gently lift it off. Invert the cake again onto a serving plate. When you're ready to serve it, dust the top lightly with icing sugar. This cake keeps well in the fridge for up to a week or freezer for up to 3 weeks.

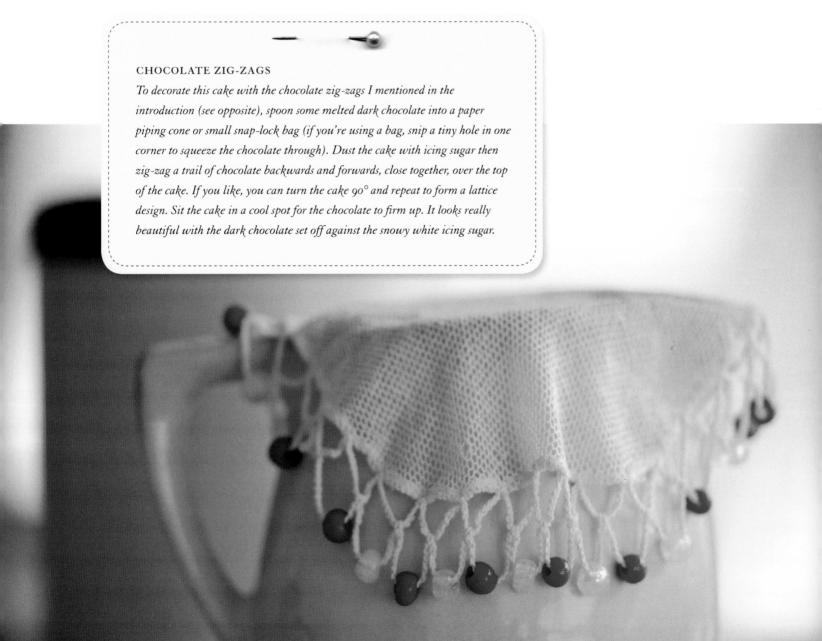

CHOCOLATE ZIG-ZAGS

To decorate this cake with the chocolate zig-zags I mentioned in the introduction (see opposite), spoon some melted dark chocolate into a paper piping cone or small snap-lock bag (if you're using a bag, snip a tiny hole in one corner to squeeze the chocolate through). Dust the cake with icing sugar then zig-zag a trail of chocolate backwards and forwards, close together, over the top of the cake. If you like, you can turn the cake 90° and repeat to form a lattice design. Sit the cake in a cool spot for the chocolate to firm up. It looks really beautiful with the dark chocolate set off against the snowy white icing sugar.

Buttery almond and coconut cake
(gluten-free)

SERVES 8–10

This is from my secret cache of recipes I turn to when I have to whip up something special at very short notice – and it's just fabulous. Although it's an unassuming slim little cake and somewhat wet inside, don't let looks fool you; it has the *best* flavour and there's a lovely contrast between the slightly chewy crust and buttery crumb. What's also appealing is that it only takes about 15 minutes to make and is wonderfully versatile – perfect for afternoon tea, but serve it with poached plums, quince or tamarillos and a dollop of rich cream and it's like waving a magic wand that transforms it into a very elegant dessert.

180 g almond meal	1½ teaspoons vanilla extract
⅔ cup (60 g) desiccated coconut	¼ teaspoon almond essence
¼ teaspoon salt	200 g unsalted butter, melted and cooled
250 g castor sugar	2 tablespoons flaked almonds
4 eggs	icing sugar (optional), for dusting

1 Preheat your oven to 180°C. Butter a 23 or 24 cm shallow springform cake tin and line the base and sides with buttered baking paper. Dust the tin lightly with flour (or rice flour if you're avoiding wheat) and set it aside.

2 Put the almond meal, desiccated coconut, salt and sugar into a medium-sized bowl and whisk them briskly together with a balloon whisk for 1 minute. In a separate bowl, whisk together the eggs, vanilla extract and almond essence until they're thoroughly mixed, then mix in the cooled butter until it is incorporated. Tip the butter mixture into the almond mixture and stir them together (you'll find that it's quite a loose batter). Scrape this into the prepared tin and spread it out evenly, then scatter the flaked almonds over the top.

3 Bake for about 40 minutes or until the top of the cake springs back slowly when you press it gently. Cool the cake in the tin on a wire rack.

4 Once the cake is cool, invert it onto the rack, remove the tin and paper and invert it again onto a serving plate. Dust the top lightly with icing sugar, if liked, and serve. Keep this cake in the fridge for up to a week or freeze for up to 3 weeks.

IT'S HANDY TO KNOW THAT THIS CAKE FREEZES VERY WELL
I usually slice it before I freeze it and defrost (or microwave) it as I need it (frequently in my case!). It also keeps well in the fridge for 5–6 days. Warm it gently or bring it to room temperature before eating it – although it has a rather fabulous 'chewy', almost candy-like texture when it's cold too.

Caramel butter-crunch cake

SERVES 10–12

There's something rather splendid about cakes baked in kugelhopf tins (see page 10) – they look so grand and special. As does this simple European-style coffee cake with its drift of icing sugar that settles like snow in the whorls and curls formed by the tin. Looks aside, the golden, buttery cake is really delicious with its hints of rum and vanilla set off by layers of cinnamon-scented nuts. If it's not all eaten on the day it's made the crumb firms up a little, so before serving it, I gently warm any leftover slices to restore them to their former glory.

1 cup (250 ml) sour cream
½ cup (125 ml) plain yoghurt
1½ teaspoons bicarbonate of soda
75 g roasted walnuts *or* pecans (see page 80)
1¾ cups (385 g) castor sugar
2 teaspoons ground cinnamon
3 cups (450 g) plain flour
2 teaspoons baking powder
1½ teaspoons salt
3 eggs
250 g unsalted butter, at room temperature, cut into chunks
1 tablespoon overproof (dark) rum
2 teaspoons vanilla extract
icing sugar, for dusting
double thick cream (see Ingredients page 5), to serve

1 Preheat your oven to 180°C. Butter and flour a medium-sized (8–10 cup) kugelhopf tin and set aside.

2 Scoop the sour cream and yoghurt into a bowl and thoroughly mix them together. Stir in the bicarbonate of soda, then leave to stand for about 15 minutes; the mixture aerates and puffs up when you do this.

3 Put the nuts, ½ cup (110 g) of the sugar and the cinnamon into a food processor and pulse until the nuts are finely chopped. Pour this mixture into a small bowl. Put the flour, baking powder and salt in the processor and whiz them to combine. Tip them into another bowl. >

4 Put the eggs and the remaining 1¼ cups (275 g) sugar into the processor and whiz them for 1 minute. Add the butter and process everything for another minute. (The mixture may look a bit curdled at this stage, but don't worry, it will be fine.)

5 Stir the rum and vanilla extract into the sour cream mixture; this will cause it to deflate somewhat. Add this to the mixture in the processor and blend it all together with a few quick bursts. Scrape this into a large bowl and stir in the flour mixture until the batter is just combined. (Or you can add the flour straight into the mixture in the processor, if it's big enough to hold everything.)

6 Spoon a 2 cm layer of cake batter into the bottom of the prepared tin and smooth out the surface. Sprinkle about one-third of the nut mixture over the top and shake the tin gently to even it out. Cover this with another thin layer of batter. Sprinkle the rest of the nut mixture over this, even it out again, then spread the remaining cake batter on top.

7 Bake for 50–60 minutes or until a fine skewer inserted in the middle comes out clean. Cool the cake in the tin on a wire rack for 5 minutes. Gently loosen around the sides and central hole (I find a small, narrow palette knife is good for this, as it's a bit awkward to loosen because of the shape of the tin). Invert the cake onto the rack and leave it to cool completely.

8 Just before serving, transfer the cake to a cake stand or plate and dust it with icing sugar. Serve each slice with a big dollop of cream. Keep for up to 3 days at room temperature in a tightly sealed container, or freeze for up to 3 weeks. Leftover slices are also good gently warmed in a microwave.

CAKE STANDS ARE WONDERFUL THINGS . . .
they can make even the plainest, simplest cakes look special. I've gathered quite a few over the years and always keep an eye out for them when I visit our local op and second-hand shops. Fortunately, in more recent years, they've made a bit of a comeback and there are now some terrific modern ones available too – it's hard to beat an elegant white stand, although I do have a soft spot for some of the rather elaborate cut-glass ones as they always remind me of my delightful, and somewhat eccentric, Great-Aunt Moo. Whenever we visited, she would set out her best china and cut glassware and, much to our joy, her cake stand nearly always held a strawberry sponge cake, which was a great treat.

Chewy coconut macaroon cake

SERVES 10–12

If you're a coconut macaroon sort of person (as some of my favourite people are) then this is definitely the cake for you. It has that same moist, chewy centre that good macaroons do and a rich coconut flavour. I had best warn you that this is a somewhat rustic-looking cake (there, that covers a multitude of sins!). The top sinks and cracks as the cake cools, so it's certainly not picture-perfect; however, I don't mind this, as for me, it's part of its charm. And I guess I've always been much more interested in how something tastes, rather than how it looks, and this tastes remarkably good.

CRUST

125 g whole blanched almonds

2 tablespoons castor sugar

2½ tablespoons plain flour

75 g cold unsalted butter,
    cut into small chunks

COCONUT FILLING

4 eggs

1½ cups (330 g) castor sugar

4½ cups (315 g) shredded coconut

1 tablespoon unsalted butter,
    melted and cooled

1½ teaspoons vanilla extract

icing sugar, for dusting

toasted coconut chips (also called coconut
    flakes), (optional), and double thick cream
    (see Ingredients page 5), to serve

TO TOAST THE COCONUT CHIPS TO DECORATE THE TOP . . .

scatter a large handful of coconut flakes onto a baking tray lined with baking paper. Pop the tray into a 180°C oven. After a few minutes, check the coconut and give it a gentle swoosh about to help it cook evenly, as the flakes around the edges colour more quickly than those in the middle. Keep checking and stirring regularly over the next minute or two, as the colour will change rapidly. Once they're speckled with gold, take the tray out of the oven and leave the flakes to cool.

1 Preheat your oven to 180°C. Have ready a 24 cm springform cake tin – it doesn't need buttering or lining.

2 For the crust, put the almonds and sugar into a food processor and whiz them together until the mixture is finely ground (be careful not to let it get to the point where it becomes oily-looking and pasty). Add the flour and whiz the machine again just to blend it in. Scatter the chunks of butter on top and pulse the machine until the mixture resembles coarse breadcrumbs.

3 Tip this mixture into the cake tin, then press it evenly over the bottom and about one-third of the way up the side of the tin. Put the tin in the fridge to chill the crust.

4 Meanwhile, for the coconut filling, put the eggs into the bowl of an electric mixer and beat them on medium–high speed until they're foamy. With the mixer going, gradually trickle in the sugar and keep on beating for about 8 minutes or until the mixture is very light and fluffy. Use a spatula to fold the coconut, melted butter and vanilla extract into the egg mixture. Scrape the filling into the chilled crust.

5 Bake for 55–60 minutes or until the filling has puffed up and the top is a deep beige colour; if you press the cake gently the middle will feel slightly soft. >

6 Cool the cake in the tin on a wire rack. Don't be alarmed when the top starts to sink and crack as this is just what it does. When it's cool, run a fine palette knife around the edge of the tin to loosen the cake, then cover the tin tightly with plastic film and refrigerate it for at least 4 hours or preferably overnight.

7 To serve the cake, loosen around the edges again, remove the sides of the tin and, with the help of a palette knife or butter knife, slide the cake off the base onto a serving platter. Dust it with icing sugar and scatter some toasted coconut chips (see page 91) over it, if liked. Serve it with a bowl of cream. Any leftovers will keep for 5 days at cool room temperature.

Classic flourless orange and almond cake (gluten-free)

SERVES 10–12

I nearly didn't include this cake as many versions of it turn up in books and magazines. However, when I mentioned this to my husband, Clive, he was horrified that I could even consider leaving it out, as it's one of his very-favourite cakes. And he's right; it is truly wonderful and should be included. It's a bit like a cross between a pudding and a cake and is very moist and somewhat dense, with a slightly bittersweet orange tang. The original recipe comes from Claudia Roden's marvellous work, *A Book of Middle Eastern Food* (Penguin). I have altered it somewhat and filled out the detail a bit, but essentially it is her recipe and I'm very grateful for it.

My favourite tin for making this is a torte tin. These tins have slightly sloping sides so the base is a little smaller than the top (mine's 21 cm across the base and 24 cm across the top). When it's turned out the cake has that 'European' look about it that is very elegant.

2 large navel oranges	6 eggs
250 g almond meal	icing sugar *or* apricot glaze and glazed
250 g castor sugar	almonds (see page 94), to serve
1 teaspoon baking powder	

1 Carefully lower the oranges into a large saucepan of boiling water. Keep them bubbling away for 1½–2 hours or until they're very soft and a fine skewer pushes through them easily. You'll need to keep an eye on the water level and top it up from time to time. The oranges tend to bob on the surface, so I spin them around occasionally to make sure they cook evenly.

2 When the oranges are ready, drain off the water and leave them to cool on a plate. (You can do this the day before you bake the cake and store the oranges in the fridge – just bring them back to room temperature before making the cake.) Once they're cool, chop them coarsely, skin and all, then purée them as finely as you can in a food processor. Set the purée aside. >

3 Preheat your oven to 170°C. Butter a 22 cm round cake tin and line the base and side with buttered baking paper. Dust the tin with flour (or almond meal if you want to avoid flour completely). Set aside.

4 In a bowl, use a balloon whisk to thoroughly mix together the almond meal, sugar and baking powder for 40 seconds or so.

5 Put the eggs into the bowl of an electric mixer (or use a hand-held electric beater) and beat them on medium–high speed for 5–6 minutes or until they're very light and fluffy. Turn off the mixer and scrape the orange purée and the almond mixture into them. Mix everything together on low speed until they're just combined.

6 The eggs will deflate a lot, but don't worry as that's just what they do, they're fine. I usually stop the mixer and finish the last bit of stirring with a rubber spatula to make sure everything is scraped up from the bottom of the bowl. Pour the batter into the prepared tin.

7 Bake for about 1 hour or until the top of the cake is just firm when you press on it gently. Cool the cake in the tin on a wire rack. Once it's cool, invert the cake onto a serving plate and peel away the paper.

8 When you're ready to serve the cake, dust it with icing sugar or brush it with a little apricot glaze and decorate the top with coated almonds, if liked (see below). It keeps really well in the fridge for up to 1 week.

APRICOT GLAZE AND GLAZED ALMONDS
To make this cake look very swish, cover it with a glossy apricot glaze. Boil about ¾ cup (240 g) apricot jam or conserve with 2 tablespoons water for about 5 minutes or until the mixture becomes thick and syrupy; keep an eye on it and stir it regularly so it doesn't catch and burn on the bottom of the pan. Pour it through a fine sieve into a bowl to remove any apricot skin. Brush the hot glaze thickly all over the cake (I sometimes pour it on for an even deeper layer) and leave it to set. Brush any leftover glaze over some blanched almonds and dot them around the edge. This makes the cake look awfully professional and the apricot flavour goes beautifully with the almond and orange.

Ever-so-easy pear (or plum) and hazelnut 'cake'

SERVES 6

I'm never quite sure what to call this; it's baked in a ceramic pie or gratin dish so it looks a bit like a tart, especially with the glistening pear slices fanned over the top, and yet the moist, satisfyingly crunchy base underneath has the texture of a cake. It doesn't really matter, what does is that it's a breeze to make, has a lovely, homely flavour and is just the sort of thing to whip up when you want a rather fabulous dessert in a hurry.

100 g roasted hazelnuts (see page 80)
80 g roasted whole blanched almonds (see page 80)
½ cup (110 g) castor sugar, plus 2 teaspoons
⅓ cup (50 g) plain flour
½ teaspoon baking powder
pinch salt
2 eggs
¼ cup (60 ml) milk
1 teaspoon vanilla extract
80 g unsalted butter, melted and cooled
2 medium-sized ripe pears *or* 6–8 plums
20 g cold unsalted butter, cut into small chunks
icing sugar, for dusting
softly whipped cream, to serve

1 Preheat your oven to 180°C. Lightly butter a 25 cm ceramic oven-to-table pie or quiche dish or a 30 cm × 18 cm (at the widest part) gratin dish (you can use square or rectangular dishes too – you'll just find the cooking time varies a bit).

2 Put the hazelnuts, almonds, ½ cup (110 g) of the sugar and 1 tablespoon of the flour in a food processor and whiz them together until the nuts are quite finely ground; be careful not to overdo this or the nuts become oily and start to form a paste. Tip the mixture into a large bowl. Sift the remaining flour, baking powder and salt into this nut mixture and whisk them together with a balloon whisk for 30 seconds.

3 Beat the eggs until they're just frothy, then whisk in the milk, vanilla extract and cooled butter. Pour this egg mixture into the nut mixture and stir them together until they're well combined. Scrape the resulting somewhat runny batter into the prepared dish with a rubber spatula and spread it out evenly. Set the dish aside. >

4 This next bit may sound a bit fiddly, but it's not; it's harder to describe than it is to do! Peel, quarter and core the pears. Cut each quarter into 5 mm-thick slices, starting from the wide base of the pear. Fan the slices slightly by gently pressing down on them with the palm of your hand. Slide a palette knife under one of the fanned quarters and carefully transfer it to the top of the batter. You can form a spoke-like pattern with the pears or make them more higgledy-piggledy. Repeat this with the remaining pear quarters.

5 Sprinkle the remaining sugar over the top of the pears and dot them with the little chunks of butter. (If you're using plums, just halve them, remove the stones and then slice the halves. Sit them skin-side up on the batter.)

6 Bake for 35–40 minutes or until the batter is slightly puffed and golden – the time varies depending on the dish you use. Remove it to a wire rack and sift a thickish layer of icing sugar over the top. Leave it to cool until lukewarm, then dust with a little more icing sugar.

7 Serve the cake directly from the dish, either cut into wedges or just scoop it out with a spoon. Some softly whipped good cream doesn't go astray with this. It is best eaten on the day it is made, as the pears soften a bit and don't look as pretty the next day, although it still tastes wonderful.

Kim's delicious apple, pecan and cinnamon cake

SERVES 8

As far as I'm concerned, you can never have too many good apple cake recipes. This particular one is a beauty – densely studded with apples and nuts held together by a small amount of spicy batter, and blessedly quick to make. It was given to me by a very dear friend, Kim Taylor, and whenever I make it I'm immediately transported back to times we shared sitting around her big old kitchen table, having a cup of tea (she makes the best), and laughing and chatting. I do love the way that a particular dish can bring back memories of such a happy time.

2 large Gala *or* Fuji apples, peeled, cored and cut into 1.5 cm chunks

1 cup (220 g) castor sugar

1 teaspoon bicarbonate of soda

1½ teaspoons ground cinnamon

½ teaspoon ground nutmeg

1½ cups (225 g) plain flour

1 cup (140 g) roasted pecans *or* hazelnuts (see page 80), very coarsely chopped, plus handful extra, for topping

1 egg

1½ teaspoons vanilla extract

125 g unsalted butter, melted and cooled a bit

icing sugar, for dusting

double thick cream (see Ingredients page 5), to serve

1 Preheat your oven to 175°C. Butter a 23 or 24 cm shallow round cake tin and line the base with buttered baking paper. Dust the tin with flour, shake out the excess and set aside.

2 In a large bowl, mix together the apples and sugar – it's easiest to use your hands to do this, so you can toss the apples about and make sure they're well coated in the sugar.

3 Put the bicarbonate of soda, cinnamon, nutmeg and flour into another bowl and mix them together with a balloon whisk for about 1 minute. Tip all but 1 tablespoonful of this mixture into the apples and stir them together well. Toss the nuts in the reserved spoonful of flour and stir them into the apples.

4 Whisk the egg and vanilla extract together, then mix in the cooled butter. Pour this into the apple and nut mixture and stir everything together. Don't worry if the dough is crumbly and only just holds the apples and nuts together, it's meant to look like that. (I often use my hands to mix these, as it's just so much easier.)

5 Press this mixture into the prepared tin as evenly as you can (try to make sure there are no gaps around the sides). Scatter a handful of extra nuts over the top and push them partly into the batter.

6 Bake the cake for 40–45 minutes or until a fine skewer inserted into a cake-y bit in the middle comes out clean. Cool the cake in the tin on a wire rack for 10 minutes. Loosen the cake around the sides with a butter knife or palette knife and turn it out onto the rack. Invert it again onto another rack and leave it to cool completely.

7 When you're ready to serve the cake, put it onto a serving plate and dust it with icing sugar, then serve with lashings of cream. By the way, because of the big chunks of nuts and slightly crunchy crust this cake is a bit difficult to cut – I sort of saw through it using a very sharp serrated knife, which seems to work quite well. This cake keeps well at room temperature for 2 days, stored in a tightly sealed container, or in the freezer for a couple of weeks.

CHOOSING APPLES FOR BAKING

It's a good thing to know that sweeter apples, like Royal Gala, Fuji and Pink Lady, actually keep their shape better when they're cooked than the more traditional cookers like Golden Delicious or Granny Smith, which collapse fairly quickly. Although, I'd have to say, there's nothing quite like Golden Delicious apples in pies, but I fear that nobody makes pies very often any more.

Barbara Lowery's pecan and macadamia panforte

MAKES ABOUT 24 PIECES

My dear friend, wonderful cook and food writer, Barbara Lowery, gave me this recipe for Italy's famous 'strong bread' – it's the best and most easily made panforte I have ever eaten. It has a dense, chewy, almost candy-like texture, but is not so hard that you think you're going to lose a filling when you eat it (some I've tried are more than capable of that). Barb's original recipe used walnuts rather than pecans, but as we live in a pecan-growing area, I substituted them instead. It also included mixed peel, however, it is one of the few things that I'm not too keen on (much to my siblings' amusement, and my mother's horror, as a child I would carefully pick every piece of mixed peel out of her Christmas fruitcake and pudding before eating them – it was such a relief when I was old enough to make them myself and could choose what went in!).

Although panforte is traditionally a Christmas treat, it is so delicious with a cup of tea or coffee and keeps for so long that I always try to have some squirreled away in the fridge.

edible rice paper (see Ingredients page 5) *or* baking paper,
   for lining
½ cup (75 g) plain flour
½ cup (50 g) Dutch-processed cocoa, sifted
1 teaspoon each ground cardamom and cinnamon
½ teaspoon ground nutmeg
¼ teaspoon freshly ground white *or* black pepper
200 g dried figs, coarsely chopped
1 cup coarsely chopped glacé fruits, such as apricots,
   pineapple and cherries
1 cup (140 g) roasted pecans (see page 80),
   coarsely chopped
½ cup (75 g) roasted macadamias (see page 80),
   coarsely chopped
1 cup (160 g) whole blanched almonds
80 g unsalted butter
½ cup (110 g) castor sugar
½ cup (180 g) honey
icing sugar, for dusting >

1 Preheat your oven to 180°C. Butter a shallow 22 cm round cake tin and line the base and sides with edible rice paper or baking paper.

2 In a large bowl, use a balloon whisk to thoroughly mix together the flour, cocoa, cardamom, cinnamon, nutmeg and pepper. Add the figs, glacé fruit, pecans and macadamias and mix them thoroughly together; I do this with clean hands as this way it's much easier to make sure everything is well mixed and any sticky clumps of fruit are separated.

3 Tip the almonds onto a baking tray and roast them for about 5 minutes or until they're pale brown. Timing is important in the next step as the almonds need to be hot when you use them.

4 Meanwhile, put the butter, sugar and honey into a small saucepan over low–medium heat. Warm them gently, stirring until the sugar has dissolved, then stop stirring and bring the mixture just to the boil.

5 Immediately tip the hot roasted almonds and the hot syrup into the fruit and nut mixture. Quickly mix them together until they're well combined. You need to be somewhat speedy here as the syrup and almonds must be hot so that everything mixes together easily; if they're cool the mixture tends to harden and clump together.

6 Scrape the mixture into the prepared tin and use a palette knife or the back of a spoon to press down and flatten it out evenly – I usually use my hands for this final part too, rinsing them in cool water to stop the mixture sticking.

7 Bake for 30 minutes; at this stage it will still appear somewhat soft when pressed (don't worry – this is as it should be, as it firms up considerably once it cools). Cool the panforte in the tin on a wire rack. Once it's cool, turn the panforte out and remove any baking paper (the rice paper is edible and can stay put, just trim it if it sits up above the edge of the panforte).

8 If serving immediately, dust the panforte with icing sugar and cut as much as you want into narrow wedges. Tightly wrap any leftover panforte in plastic film and foil (or put it in an airtight container) and store it in the fridge, where it will keep for weeks.

CARDAMOM
Cardamom seeds have a wonderful haunting flavour, a bit like a cross between citrus and camphor. By all means use ready-ground cardamom – it is fine. However, if you have a mortar and pestle (or an electric grinder that you use for spices) then I'd really recommend grinding your own; when freshly ground, cardamom is incredibly fragrant and almost heady in its intensity. To get the sticky black seeds out of the cardamom pods to grind them, just sit the pods on a chopping board and press down very firmly with the flat side of a heavy knife or sharpening steel to split the pods.

muffins

A few tips for baking really fabulous muffins

If you need a boost to your baking confidence and some almost instant gratification then muffin-making is for you. They have everything going for them – they're good fun to make; the batter is whipped up in no time; there's not a whole lot that can go wrong; they nearly all cook in less than 20 minutes; they taste wonderful; oh, and they freeze well too. It's a pretty hard act to follow!

There's not a whole lot you need to know about muffins; there are just a few useful things to keep in mind that are peculiar to muffin-making and these are easy to remember.

* The most important one of all is to only mix the wet and dry ingredients together until they're just combined. Too much mixing causes the muffins to toughen and form big air holes and tunnels rather than being moist and tender. If anything, it's better to slightly under-mix the batter.
* Generally, it's best to cook muffins in a 190–200°C oven, as they need that big burst of heat to help them rise and give them their characteristic domed tops.
* If you don't have enough batter to fill every muffin hole, pour about a centimetre of water into the empty ones, otherwise the muffins around them can burn.
* A spring-loaded ice-cream scoop is an invaluable thing to have as it makes neatly scooping the batter out of the bowl and into the holes so much easier.
* In the course of writing this book I've made and frozen all the muffins in this chapter. They freeze really well, but after tasting them at regular intervals, I think they're best eaten within about three weeks of freezing.
* As far as reheating muffins goes, a gentle burst in the microwave, just until they feel warm, works really well. Otherwise, wrap them loosely in foil, then warm them up in a 200°C oven for about 10 minutes (frozen ones will take about 20 minutes).
* Many of these muffins are made in a food processor, however, they can easily be made by hand, so don't despair if you don't have one. In general, to do this, mix the 'dry' ingredients thoroughly together in one bowl and the 'wet' ingredients in another, then mix them both together.

Polenta, cheese and chilli muffins

MAKES 10 MUFFINS OR 24 MINI-MUFFINS

We often have soup for dinner in the colder weather and, if I have a little time up my sleeve, I try to make a batch of these fragrant cheese muffins to go with it – they just have a way of making such a simple meal seem special somehow. They're rich and buttery with the kick of the chillies to liven things up a bit, and they go well with all sorts of soups – pumpkin, lentil, potato, pea and ham, to name just a few.

They're terrific as finger food too; just bake them in mini-muffin tins and serve them at room temperature. They look gorgeous lined up on a platter with a tiny basil leaf perched jauntily on top of each one.

120 g fine stone-ground yellow polenta (cornmeal) (see page 130)	225 ml sour cream
1/3 cup (50 g) plain flour	140 g unsalted butter, melted and cooled
2 teaspoons salt	1/4 large red capsicum, seeded and very finely chopped
3 teaspoons baking powder	1/3 cup (55 g) fresh *or* canned corn kernels, drained
1/4 teaspoon dried chilli flakes	
1 cup (120 g) finely grated cheddar	corn kernels, thinly sliced red capsicum and small basil leaves (optional), for topping
2 eggs, lightly beaten	

1 Preheat your oven to 200°C. Lightly butter a 12-hole muffin tin and set it aside. (If you're making mini-muffins, the batter will make about 24.)

2 Put the polenta, flour, salt, baking powder and chilli flakes into a food processor and whiz them for 15 seconds. Tip this mixture into a large bowl. Add the cheese and mix it in well.

3 Thoroughly mix together the eggs, sour cream and melted butter (you can do this in the processor too, or in a separate bowl). Stir in the chopped red capsicum and corn. Pour the egg mixture into the flour mixture and gently stir them together until they're just combined.

4 Divide the batter evenly between 10 of the muffin holes (you can use 12 if you like, but they'll be a bit small as the muffins don't rise all that much). Scatter some corn kernels and thinly sliced red capsicum over the top of each one, if using. Pour a little water (about 1 cm) into any empty muffin holes to stop them from overheating and causing the muffins around them to burn.

5 Bake for about 20 minutes or until the muffins smell mouth-watering and a fine skewer inserted in the middle of one comes out clean (mini-muffins take about 12 minutes). Cool the muffins in the tin on a wire rack for 2 minutes, then carefully loosen them around the edges and turn them out onto the rack. Serve the muffins warm or at room temperature. If you have made mini-muffins, top them with a small basil leaf.

Dill, ricotta and parmesan muffins

MAKES 12 MUFFINS

I'm always a little surprised at just how often friends comment on these aromatic muffins and ask for the recipe. They look really pretty as they're a delicate golden colour speckled with the green herbs, and they have a really lovely fresh taste from the dill. For an easy dinner I serve them warm with soup and a big bowl of salad to follow – it's simple yet so delicious.

However, they can be quite sophisticated too – you can make mini-muffins from the batter and serve them as is with drinks or let them cool a little, split them in half and put a dab of sour cream and sliver of smoked salmon (or if you're really going all-out, a spoonful of salmon roe) in the middle of each. Sit the top back at an angle and press a tiny dill sprig into the sour cream, then line them up in rows on a platter – they look rather fab and are always vacuumed up.

2 cups (300 g) plain flour

3 teaspoons baking powder

1 teaspoon salt

freshly ground black pepper, to taste

30 g freshly grated parmesan

2½ tablespoons finely chopped dill

¼ cup finely chopped chives

1¼ cups (250 g) fresh ricotta

80 g unsalted butter, melted and cooled

1 egg

½ cup (125 ml) milk

½ teaspoon Worcestershire sauce

½ teaspoon Tabasco sauce

½ cup (125 ml) sour cream

tiny dill sprigs, for topping

1 Preheat your oven to 190°C. Lightly butter a 12-hole muffin tin and set it aside.

2 Whiz the flour, baking powder, salt and pepper in a food processor for 15 seconds. Add the parmesan and whiz for another 10 seconds or so. Tip this mixture into a large bowl, then stir in the dill and chives.

3 Put the ricotta, melted butter, egg, milk, Worcestershire and Tabasco sauces into the food processor and whiz together for about 20 seconds or until the mixture looks creamy. Add the sour cream and whiz everything again briefly so the cream is mixed in. Scrape the ricotta mixture into the bowl of dry ingredients and stir them together until they're just combined. (You'll find the mixture is firmer than lots of the muffin batters in this chapter, but that's down to the ricotta, so don't worry as the muffins will still be very moist.)

4 Divide the batter evenly between the muffin holes. Gently press some tiny dill sprigs on top of each one.

5 Bake for about 20 minutes or until the muffins feel springy when you press the tops (mini-muffins will take 10–12 minutes). Cool the muffins on a wire rack in the tin for 1 minute, then gently loosen them around the edges if necessary and lift them out onto the rack. Serve the muffins warm or at room temperature.

Sunflower seed, honey and raisin muffins

MAKES 10 MUFFINS

I have to admit these muffins have kept me going as I've written this book; whenever I've felt my energy flagging one of these with a cup of tea has worked wonders.

   Although they're not the most beautiful muffins to look at, they have a fragrant, nutty, honey sweetness and a terrific, moist, chewy texture from the sunflower seeds that is very more-ish. When you eat them you can almost feel them doing you good because they really are full of good things – olive oil, honey, masses of sunflower seeds, pepitas and sticky-sweet raisins. A real pick-me-up.

1 cup (150 g) plain flour	½ cup (180 g) honey
220 g sunflower seeds	¼ cup (60 ml) light olive oil
1½ teaspoons baking powder	⅔ cup (160 ml) milk
½ teaspoon bicarbonate of soda	1½ teaspoons vanilla extract
½ teaspoon salt	pepitas (pumpkin seeds) and sunflower
½ cup (85 g) firmly-packed raisins	seeds, for sprinkling
2 eggs	

1 Preheat your oven to 190°C. Lightly butter a 12-hole non-stick muffin tin and set it aside (you'll only get 10 muffins from this, so you don't need to butter all the holes).

2 Put the flour, 140 g of the sunflower seeds, baking powder, bicarbonate of soda and salt into a food processor. Whiz them together until the seeds are fairly finely ground (you'll still have some little pieces of broken seed in the mixture). Tip the mixture into a large bowl and stir in the remaining 80 g of sunflower seeds and the raisins. I usually end up finishing this with my hands as the raisins tend to clump together and it's the easiest way to break them up.

3 Put the remaining ingredients into the food processor and whiz them together for about 15 seconds or until they're well combined. Pour this wet mixture into the dry one and gently stir them together (don't overdo the mixing at this stage or the muffins will be tough). Leave the batter to sit for 1 minute so it thickens up slightly.

4 Divide the mixture evenly between the 10 buttered muffin holes. Sprinkle pepitas and sunflower seeds over the top of each one. Pour about 1 cm of water into the empty holes as this helps stop them overheating, which can cause the muffins around them to burn.

5 Bake for 20–25 minutes (the tops will be quite pointy) or until the muffins spring back when gently pressed or a fine skewer inserted in the middle of one comes out clean. Cool the muffins in the tin on a wire rack for 1 minute, then gently loosen around the sides if they need it and turn them out onto the rack. Leave them to cool and serve them barely warm or at room temperature.

6 Any leftover muffins freeze really well and will keep their fresh flavour for 3–4 weeks.

Honey-toasted muesli muffins

MAKES 11–12 MUFFINS

These are such quick and easy muffins to whip up and lovely for a weekend breakfast or brunch. You may notice that there's not much sugar in the recipe – this is because most toasted muesli is coated with honey already so you don't need to add much more sweetening. I've also made them with gluten-free toasted muesli and spelt flour and they were terrific.

2 cups honey *or* maple-syrup-coated
   toasted muesli
1 cup (150 g) plain flour
2 teaspoons baking powder
½ teaspoon bicarbonate of soda
½ teaspoon salt
½ cup (80 g) natural sultanas

2 eggs
¼ cup (55 g) brown sugar
½ cup (125 ml) light olive oil
1 cup (250 ml) buttermilk
1 teaspoon vanilla extract
coconut chips, pepitas (pumpkin seeds),
   sunflower seeds *and/or* nuts, for topping

1 Preheat your oven to 200°C. Butter a 12-hole muffin tin and set it aside.

2 Put the muesli, flour, baking powder, bicarbonate of soda and salt into a food processor. Whiz them together for about 20 seconds to break up the muesli. Tip the mixture into a bowl and stir in the sultanas.

3 Put the eggs, brown sugar, oil, buttermilk and vanilla extract into the processor and whiz them for 15 seconds so they're thoroughly mixed. Make a well in the middle of the muesli mixture and pour in the egg mixture. Stir them quickly and briefly together until they're just combined; don't worry if there are still a few speckles of flour in the batter; it is better that it's slightly under-mixed than over-mixed, which tends to make the muffins tough. The batter will also seem quite wet but that's fine too.

4 Divide the batter evenly between the muffin holes; I usually end up with 11 – if you do too, just pour a splash of water into the empty hole. Sprinkle the tops with coconut, pepitas, sunflower seeds or some nuts, or a mixture of these.

5 Bake for about 20 minutes or until the muffins are golden and a fine skewer inserted in the middle of one comes out clean. Cool the muffins in the tin on a wire rack for 1 minute, then loosen around the edges if they need it and turn them out onto the rack. Serve them warm or at room temperature with butter, fresh ricotta or cottage cheese.

Crunchy-topped raspberry muffins

MAKES 11–12 MUFFINS

Nearly every Christmas morning I bake a batch of these lovely, buttery muffins and we sit down to them with a bowl of sweet, dark Tasmanian cherries and a big pot of tea. (Actually, that's not quite true – I'm definitely not organised enough to bake them on Christmas morning, however, I do try to make them a few days ahead and freeze them so I can warm them up for breakfast.) They look so pretty and I love the way the tangy little bursts of raspberry contrast beautifully with their tender crumb and crunchy cinnamon-sugar tops – they somehow seem extra-special and are a lovely, festive way to start such a special day.

1½ cups (225 g) plain flour
2 teaspoons baking powder
¼ teaspoon salt
1 teaspoon ground cinnamon
1½ teaspoons finely chopped orange zest
½ cup (110 g) castor sugar
1 egg
125 g unsalted butter, melted and cooled
¼ cup (60 ml) milk
¼ cup (60 ml) sour cream
1 teaspoon vanilla extract
200 g fresh or frozen raspberries
icing sugar (optional), for dusting

CRUNCHY TOPPING
½ cup (110 g) castor sugar
90 g pecans or walnuts
1½ teaspoons ground cinnamon

1 Preheat your oven to 190°C. Lightly butter a 12-hole muffin tin and set it aside.

2 For the crunchy topping, put all the ingredients into a food processor and pulse them together until the nuts are chopped into medium-sized chunky pieces. Tip this mixture into a bowl and set it aside.

3 Put all but 1 tablespoon of the flour into the food processor. Add the baking powder, salt, cinnamon and orange zest and whiz them together for 20 seconds. Transfer the mixture to a large bowl.

4 Put the sugar and egg into the processor and whiz them for 20 seconds. Pour in the butter, milk, sour cream and vanilla extract and process for about 15 seconds or until they're well mixed.

5 Pour the egg mixture over the flour mixture and stir the two gently together (don't overdo the mixing at this stage or the muffins will be tough).

6 Carefully toss the raspberries with the reserved tablespoon of flour so they're coated in a fine, floury film. Using a wooden spoon or spatula, gently mix them through the batter with a few strokes. The batter may get a bit stiff if you're using frozen raspberries but it will be fine. >

7 Divide the batter evenly between the muffin holes; they should each be about three-quarters full (there is usually enough mixture to make 11 muffins). Sprinkle the topping thickly over each one and press it down gently. If you have an empty muffin hole, pour about 1 cm of water into it, as this helps stop the hole overheating, which can cause the muffins around it to burn.

8 Bake for 20–25 minutes or until the muffins are puffed and golden and a fine skewer inserted in the middle of one comes out clean. Cool the muffins in the tin on a wire rack for 3 minutes. Gently ease them out of the tin onto the rack to cool completely. If you like, you can dust them with icing sugar just before serving.

Spicy pumpkin, pecan and maple muffins

MAKES 12

Much favoured for midnight raids in our house (or if truth be known, for a little snackette just about anytime), these moist, golden muffins are really wonderful – light, spicy and tender, but laden with roasted nuts and dried cranberries, which add little bursts of tart sweetness. And they've got lots of good, healthy ingredients in them too – stone-ground wholemeal flour, pumpkin, free-range eggs, maple syrup, buttermilk – you can almost feel them doing you good!

I wanted to give the 'bowl' method for making some of the muffins in this chapter, which I've done here, however, you can just as easily make them in a food processor.

½ small butternut pumpkin, seeded
1 cup (150 g) plain flour
½ cup (80 g) stone-ground wholemeal
 plain flour
1 teaspoon bicarbonate of soda
¾ teaspoon salt
½ teaspoon baking powder
1 teaspoon ground nutmeg
1½ teaspoons ground cinnamon
120 g roasted pecans (see page 80)
120 g dried cranberries (sold as craisins)
 or raisins
2 eggs
½ cup (110 g) brown sugar
½ cup (125 ml) maple syrup
½ cup (125 ml) light olive oil
1½ teaspoons vanilla extract
½ cup (125 ml) buttermilk

TOPPING
¼ cup (55 g) castor sugar
¼ cup (40 g) chopped pecans
1½ teaspoons ground cinnamon

1 Preheat your oven to 200°C. Sit the pumpkin, cut side-down, on a baking paper-lined baking tray. Bake until it is tender; the time will vary a bit depending on its size, but it will probably take 45–60 minutes. When the pumpkin is ready, remove it from the oven and leave it to cool on the tray. When it's cool enough to handle, peel away the skin, scoop the flesh into a bowl and mash it until it's fairly smooth. Measure 1 cup for the muffins, then put the remaining pumpkin in the fridge for another use.

2 Reduce the oven temperature to 180°C. Lightly butter a 12-hole muffin tin and set it aside.

3 Combine the flours, bicarbonate of soda, salt, baking powder, nutmeg and cinnamon in a large bowl and whisk them with a balloon whisk for 1 minute. Add the nuts and cranberries and toss them about to coat them in the flour mixture. Set aside.

4 Lightly whisk the eggs in another bowl, then add the remaining ingredients and the cup of mashed pumpkin. Whisk them together until they're thoroughly mixed.

5 Make a well in the middle of the dry ingredients and pour in the pumpkin mixture. Stir them together until they're just combined; the mixture will be quite loose and sloppy so let it sit for 1 minute to thicken up. Divide the batter among the muffin holes, filling them to the top.

6 For the topping, stir all the ingredients together. Sprinkle the topping mixture thickly over each muffin.

7 Bake for 25–30 minutes or until a skewer inserted in the middle of a muffin comes out clean. Cool the muffins in the tin on a wire rack for a few minutes, then ease them out onto the rack to cool completely. Serve them warm or at room temperature.

Apple, pecan and cinnamon muffins

MAKES 12

For me, there's something Proustian about the aroma of apples and cinnamon baking; just one sniff immediately conjures up the memory of my mum's spicy apple crumble, its top sinking into a slew of warm, buttery apples, with a scoop of vanilla ice-cream melting into a puddle on the side. These apple-laden muffins capture that same evocative fragrance, and if friends visit when I'm baking them they virtually form a queue by the oven waiting for them to come out. True!

The method I've given for making these muffins is the 'bowl' one; however, you can make them in a food processor too. Have a look at the recipe for Crunchy-topped Raspberry Muffins (see pages 112–114) to get the general gist of how to do this.

2 eggs

½ cup (110 g) brown sugar

½ cup (125 ml) light olive oil

½ cup (125 ml) apple juice

1½ teaspoons vanilla extract

2½ cups diced apples (Pink Lady and Fuji are terrific, but Granny Smith will do nicely too) (2–3, depending on their size)

1 cup (160 g) stone-ground wholemeal plain flour

1 cup (150 g) plain flour

3 teaspoons baking powder

½ teaspoon bicarbonate of soda

½ teaspoon salt

1 teaspoon ground cinnamon

½ teaspoon ground nutmeg

¾ cup (90 g) roasted pecans *or* walnuts (see page 80), very coarsely chopped

½ cup (85 g) raisins

CRUNCHY TOPPING

½ cup (110 g) castor sugar

½ cup (70 g) roasted pecans (see page 80), chopped

1½ teaspoons ground cinnamon

1 Preheat your oven to 190°C. Generously butter a 12-hole non-stick muffin tin.

2 In a bowl, thoroughly whisk together the eggs, brown sugar, oil, apple juice and vanilla extract. Gently stir in the diced apples.

3 Put both of the flours, the baking powder, bicarbonate of soda, salt, cinnamon and nutmeg into another larger bowl. Whisk all these together for 1 minute with a balloon whisk. Add the pecans and raisins and toss them about so they're completely coated in the flour mixture.

4 Pour the apple mixture into the flour mixture and stir them together until they're just combined into a very chunky batter; don't overdo the mixing or it can make the muffins tough. Divide the batter equally between the muffin holes; they will be very full.

5 For the crunchy topping, mix together all the ingredients. Sprinkle the topping evenly over each muffin.

6 Bake for about 20 minutes or until the muffins are puffed up and smell positively mouth-watering and a fine skewer inserted in the middle of one comes out clean. Cool the muffins in the tin on a wire rack for 2 minutes. Carefully ease them out and sit them on the rack to cool. They're lovely eaten warm either as is, or with butter or ricotta.

Brown sugar and ginger muffins

MAKES 12 MUFFINS

As a little girl I remember being fascinated with the glazed blue-and-white ceramic ginger jars that my dad would bring home from a trip to the city. They were from China and were beautifully painted with little figures of pretty women standing under blossom trees or on curving bridges holding up parasols to shelter themselves from the sun. However, although I loved the jars themselves, I couldn't believe my father would eat the contents of them! He would spoon out the sticky nuggets of ginger with great relish and try to entice us to eat a little. In my case, it was definitely an acquired taste and it took many, many years for me to start to like and then, eventually, love, the hot, biting sharpness of the ginger in contrast to its honey-like syrup. Of course, now I can't get enough of it and these muffins are the result of my ongoing ginger obsession. You can make them with mild or regular crystallised or glacé ginger, depending on how spicy you like it.

½ cup (80 g) stone-ground wholemeal
    plain flour
1½ cups (225 g) plain flour
1 teaspoon baking powder
1 teaspoon bicarbonate of soda
½ teaspoon salt
16 nuggets crystallised or glacé ginger,
    roughly chopped
120 g roasted hazelnuts *or* pecans
  (see page 80)

½ cup (85 g) raisins *or* natural sultanas
2 eggs
½ cup (110 g) firmly-packed brown sugar
½ cup (125 ml) light olive oil
1 cup (250 ml) buttermilk
1½ teaspoons vanilla extract
slivers of crystallised ginger *or* nuts and
    demerara sugar (optional), for sprinkling

1 Preheat your oven to 195°C. Butter a 12-hole muffin tin and set it aside.

2 Put both of the flours, the baking powder, bicarbonate of soda and salt into a food processor, then whiz them together for 15 seconds. Add the ginger and whiz again until the ginger is in small chunks. Add the nuts and pulse the processor until they're coarsely chopped. Tip the dry mixture into a bowl and stir in the raisins.

3 Put the eggs, brown sugar, oil, buttermilk and vanilla extract into the processor and whiz for about 15 seconds. Pour them into the dry mixture and stir them quickly and briefly until they're just combined. Don't worry if there is the odd speckle of flour – it's better to slightly under-mix the batter, as too vigorous a stir tends to make the muffins tough. Divide the batter evenly between the muffin holes. Gently press some ginger slivers or sliced nuts onto each muffin. You don't have to use the demerara sugar, but if you do, sprinkle a little over each muffin and they'll have lovely crunchy tops.

4 Bake for about 20 minutes or until the muffins are golden and a fine skewer inserted in the middle of one comes out clean. Cool the muffins in the tin on a wire rack for 1 minute, then gently loosen them around the edges if they need it and turn them out onto the rack. Serve them warm or at room temperature with butter.

Date, orange and banana muffins

MAKES 12 MUFFINS

These moist, golden muffins have a lovely, slightly sticky, yet light texture and intense orange flavour. In fact, they're so good that I've been known to pass them off as little dessert puddings. If you want to give this a go, just turn them upside-down, sit half a luscious fresh date on top and spoon a little orange syrup over that – they're fabulous with a scoop of rich cream or ice-cream. And if you're making them for an afternoon tea or kid's party, they look 'wicked', as my niece would say, made in mini-muffin tins and set out in rows on a platter.

1 cup (150 g) plain flour

½ cup (80 g) stone-ground wholemeal
   plain flour

3 teaspoons baking powder

½ teaspoon bicarbonate of soda

½ teaspoon salt

¼ teaspoon ground nutmeg

1 cup (160 g) pitted dates, chopped

1 medium-sized navel orange

2 eggs

½ cup (110 g) brown sugar

½ cup (125 ml) light olive oil

2 medium-sized bananas
   (to yield roughly ½ cup mashed)

½ cup (125 ml) fresh orange juice

1 teaspoon vanilla extract

6 pitted dates, halved, for topping

1 Preheat your oven to 200°C. Butter a 12-hole muffin tin and set it aside.

2 Put both the flours, the baking powder, bicarbonate of soda, salt and nutmeg into a food processor and whiz them together for 15 seconds. Tip the dry mixture into a large bowl and stir in the chopped dates.

3 Thoroughly wash and dry the orange, then chop it into small chunks. Scrape these chunks into the food processor and whiz them for a minute or so until they form a rough-textured purée; you will need to stop the machine a couple of times and scrape down the sides with a rubber spatula as you go.

4 Add the eggs, brown sugar, oil, mashed bananas, orange juice and vanilla extract to the processor and whiz them until the mixture is fairly smooth (it won't be completely smooth as there will be little chunks of orange peel in it).

5 Pour the orange mixture into the dry ingredients and quickly stir them together until they're just combined. As the batter will be quite thin and sloppy, leave it to sit for 1 minute to thicken up so it's easier to scoop. Divide the batter evenly between the muffin holes. Gently press a halved date on top of each muffin.

6 Bake for about 20 minutes or until the muffins are deep golden and a fine skewer inserted in the middle of one comes out clean. Cool the muffins in the tin on a wire rack for 1 minute, then gently loosen them around the edges if they need it and turn them out onto the rack. Serve them warm or at room temperature, either as is or with butter.

Lemon and blueberry muffins

MAKES 12 MUFFINS

It never ceases to delight me that something as simple to make as a muffin can taste so very good. This classic combination of lemon and blueberry is a case in point; they're as easy as all-get-out to make, yet their terrific flavour and texture seems almost disproportionate to the amount of time and effort involved. I love the way the blueberries become almost jammy as they bake and contrast so well with the zing of the lemon and tender, golden crumb. The demerara sugar isn't essential for sprinkling on top; however, it does give the muffins a most satisfying crunch when you bite into them.

1¼ cups (185 g) plain flour
1 cup (160 g) stone-ground wholemeal
  plain flour
3 teaspoons baking powder
½ teaspoon bicarbonate of soda
½ teaspoon salt
2 cups (300 g) fresh *or* frozen blueberries
2 eggs
½ cup (110 g) castor sugar

½ cup (125 ml) light olive oil
½ cup (125 ml) milk
¼ cup (60 ml) sour cream
very finely chopped zest and juice
  of 1 lemon
very finely chopped zest and juice
  of 1 orange
demerara sugar (optional), for sprinkling

1 Preheat your oven to 200°C. Lightly butter a 12-hole muffin tin (or sit paper liners in each hole) and set it aside.

2 Tip the flours, baking powder, bicarbonate of soda and salt into a large bowl. Whisk them together with a balloon whisk for 1 minute so they're thoroughly combined. Add 1¼ cups (190 g) of the blueberries and toss them about gently to coat them in the flour mixture.

3 In a separate bowl, whisk together the eggs, sugar, oil, milk, sour cream, citrus zests and juices. Pour the citrus mixture into the flour mixture and mix them gently and quickly together until they're just combined; the batter will look a bit lumpy which is fine.

4 Divide the batter evenly between the muffin holes. Press a few of the remaining blueberries partly into the top of each muffin and sprinkle them with the demerara sugar, if using.

5 Bake for about 20–25 minutes or until the muffins are golden brown and the tops spring back when gently pressed. Cool the muffins in the tin on a wire rack for 1 minute, then carefully loosen around the edges if necessary and lift them out onto the rack to cool completely.

6 These muffins are lovely served barely warm, either as is, or with butter, ricotta or cottage cheese.

biscuits

Biscuits like a
bit of TLC

Biscuit baking is not an exact science and a lot of that is to do with the vexatious topic of ovens that I mentioned earlier in the book (see page 9). I know it seems like a funny thing to say, but it's a really good idea to get to know (and love) your oven well, so you can bake beautiful biscuits.

SLOW AND STEADY BAKING   I always tend to err on the side of caution when I bake biscuits, as the bottoms 'catch' really quickly and they go from being golden and crisp to burnt in the blink of an eye; that's why the oven temperature for most of these biscuits is usually quite low. It also gives biscuits that are cut thickly a good chance to cook right through and become crisp.

SWAPPING SHELVES   If you're baking more than one tray of biscuits at a time it's always a good idea to swap the shelves they're on halfway through the baking time and to turn the trays around, front-to-back. Both of these things help avoid the 'hot spot' oven syndrome, where certain parts of the oven cook more rapidly than others, so consequently, some of the biscuits on a baking tray will be perfectly golden while others are burnt. It's always so frustrating when this happens, especially after you have lavished so much care on making them.

COOLING BAKING TRAYS IN-BETWEEN BATCHES   This is important to remember: if you're baking batches of biscuits and re-using the baking trays, then you must cool them down between each batch. If you put the cool biscuit dough onto the hot trays, basically it will start to melt before the biscuits have a chance to set, which is all very messy and disappointing. I usually just run the trays under cool water between batches, then dry them off and start again. As far as the baking paper on the trays goes, it can be recycled a number of times, just wipe it if it's a bit 'crummy'.

COOLING OFF   Let your biscuits cool completely before you store them in a jar or tin – by all means eat a couple while they're still warm, but let the rest get quite cool. Otherwise, if even the tiniest bit of residual heat is left in them it causes them to give off steam, especially in a sealed container, which will soften the whole lot.

STORING BISCUITS   Good, tightly sealed glass jars and tins are the secret to keeping biscuits really fresh and crisp, along with storing them in a cool spot. I use clip-seal glass jars (the sort you pick up in the supermarket) as they have a really firm seal with their rubber rings and springy clips. Tins work well too, as long as the lids shut tightly. If the lid seems a bit loose, cover the top of the tin with an over-hanging sheet of baking paper before putting the lid on – this makes for a much tighter fit. Plastic is a bit of a no-no as far as storage goes, as it tends to harbour moisture and it's so frustrating to put crisp biscuits into a plastic container only to find they have softened virtually overnight.

ARE THEY COOKED?   At times, it's difficult to judge if biscuits are completely cooked through. Sometimes, once I've cooled a batch, I find they're not quite as crunchy as they should be. It's absolutely fine to pop them back onto their trays and give them another burst in the oven at the temperature specified in the recipe – usually another five or so minutes does the trick. This is also true if it's very humid and they get a bit soggy. We've had a long, hot summer here and when I tested some of these biscuits the humidity was incredibly high; although the biscuits were crunchy to begin with, if I didn't get them in their jars as soon as they were cool they started to soften, so I did this many times and it worked really well.

Pecan and oat crisps

MAKES ABOUT 50

Pecans are beautiful trees with their delicate lime-green leaves and silvery trunks, and I count myself very fortunate to live in an area where they thrive. Frank, a nearby grower (who is also known as 'The Pecan Man' at my local farmers' market), sells the freshest, sweetest, biggest (they're gi-normous!) pecans that I've ever tasted. Needless to say, I toss handfuls of them into all sorts of things including these lovely, crunchy, somewhat caramel-flavoured biscuits.

2½ cups (375 g) plain flour

¾ teaspoon salt

5 tablespoons rolled oats

60 g pecans, chopped

300 g unsalted butter, at room temperature

180 g soft brown sugar

2 teaspoons vanilla extract

1 Put the flour, salt, oats and pecans into a bowl and whisk them together with a balloon whisk so they're thoroughly combined. Set aside.

2 In another bowl, use an electric mixer on medium speed to beat together the butter, brown sugar and vanilla extract until they're light and fluffy, about 2 minutes. Stop and scrape down the sides of the bowl with a rubber spatula once or twice when you do this. Tip the flour and oat mixture into the butter mixture and use a wooden spoon to stir them together until they form a dough. (I sometimes use the mixer on low to start with and then finish off mixing with the spoon – or better still, I use my hands to squeeze the mixture together as it's quite crumbly.)

3 Lay a large sheet of foil on a bench and cover it with a sheet of baking paper. Divide the dough into thirds. Gently work one piece of the dough briefly to bring it together, then roll it into a log about 5 cm in diameter. Sit the log along one side of the baking paper and roll it up in the paper. Next, roll it in the foil. Twist the ends tightly in opposite directions so you end up with something that looks like a very long bonbon. Do the same with the remaining 2 pieces of dough.

4 If you're baking the biscuits the same day, chill the logs for 2–3 hours until they're firm enough to slice. At this stage, you can also freeze the logs until you need them. They keep well in the freezer for about 5 weeks; just defrost them in the fridge before slicing them.

5 Preheat your oven to 155°C. Cut the logs into 6 mm-thick slices and sit them about 3 cm apart on baking trays lined with baking paper.

6 Bake for 25–28 minutes or until the biscuits are pale golden and somewhat firm when pressed.

7 Remove the biscuits from the oven and leave them to cool on the trays. When they're cold, store them in an airtight container for up to 1 week.

Belinda's polenta and vanilla shortbread

MAKES 45–50

While I was writing this book I would often end up with the fridge, cupboard and freezer full of all sorts of enticing bits and pieces (even my neighbours' cupboards were bulging too as they were often my unofficial taste testers). However, if there happened to be any of these shortbreads in a jar, then I would head for them above and beyond anything else. They may be simple little biscuits but they sneak up on you; they seem quite plain but have a wonderful, old-fashioned, buttery taste and the polenta adds a delicious 'corny' note and slightly gritty texture which I love. Better still; the flavour improves as they age as long as you keep them in an airtight jar.

Try to use really fresh stone-ground polenta in these for a true corn flavour. If you would rather them less 'gritty', substitute half the polenta with rice flour.

270 g plain flour
160 g fine stone-ground yellow polenta (cornmeal) (see page 130)
¾ cup (165 g) castor sugar
⅛ teaspoon baking powder
½ teaspoon salt
250 g cold unsalted butter, cut into small chunks
1 × 70 g egg
1 tablespoon vanilla extract
icing sugar, for dusting

1 Whiz together the flour, polenta, sugar, baking powder and salt in a food processor for 20 seconds. Scatter the butter chunks over the top and process until the mixture resembles medium breadcrumbs.

2 In a small bowl, whisk together the egg and vanilla extract until they're thoroughly mixed. With the processor running, drizzle this egg mixture through the feed tube and process for about 40 seconds, stopping and scraping down the sides of the bowl once or twice with a rubber spatula, until the mixture forms a crumbly but somewhat cohesive mass.

3 Tip this out onto a chopping board and knead it gently, just to bring the mixture together. Divide the dough in half, then roll each half into a log about 5 cm in diameter (you can make them thicker if you like). >

4 Lay a large sheet of foil on a bench and cover it with a sheet of baking paper. Sit one of the logs along one side of the baking paper and roll it up in the paper. Next, roll it in the foil. Twist the ends tightly in opposite directions so you end up with something that looks like a very long bonbon. Do the same with the remaining dough. If the dough seems a little too soft to shape into a log (which can happen in warm weather), chill it for an hour or so to firm it up and then try rolling it again.

5 Chill the logs for at least 3 hours or overnight (you can also freeze them at this stage to use at another time; just defrost them in the fridge before slicing them).

6 When you're ready to bake the biscuits, preheat your oven to 170°C.

7 Cut the logs into 7 mm-thick slices and put them about 2 cm apart on baking trays lined with baking paper.

8 Bake for 20–25 minutes or until the biscuits are pale golden around the edges and feel quite firm when gently pressed. (I usually carefully turn one over to check that the bottom is cooked.) Remove the biscuits from the oven and leave them to cool on the trays. Store in airtight jars for up to 2–3 weeks. Dust them lightly with icing sugar just before serving.

POLENTA FOR BAKING

If possible, when you're baking with polenta (cornmeal), it's best to use the most finely ground you can get. At times, when I haven't had a choice, I've used medium-ground polenta in these biscuits, and although they are still very good, their texture tends to be a bit gritty. Whenever possible, I try to use organic stone-ground polenta.

Brown sugar shortbread

MAKES ABOUT 40 SMALL ROUNDS OR 24 LARGE BARS

Small rituals are terribly important in our lives and when the world all gets too big, I find there's nothing quite like a cup of tea and a homemade biscuit to restore both body and soul. If that biscuit happens to be a finger of shortbread then so much the better, for of all biscuits, shortbread is my favourite. And this melt-in-the-mouth brown sugar one is lovely – very 'short' with a wonderful buttery, vanilla flavour and crunchy sugar topping. For me, everything looks that bit brighter after sitting quietly and enjoying such a simple restorative.

1½ cups (225 g) plain flour

¼ cup (35 g) cornflour

¼ teaspoon salt

250 g unsalted butter, at cool room
   temperature, cut into rough chunks

½ cup (110 g) firmly-packed brown sugar

1½ teaspoons vanilla extract

1 tablespoon white granulated sugar,
   for sprinkling

1 Put the flour, cornflour and salt into a food processor and whiz them together so they're thoroughly mixed. Tip them into a bowl.

2 Put the butter, brown sugar and vanilla extract into the processor and whiz them until the mixture is pale and creamy, about 40 seconds; you may need to stop the machine and scrape down the sides once or twice with a rubber spatula.

3 Add the flour mixture to the butter mixture and pulse the processor in short bursts so they form a dough that just clumps together; try not to overdo this or the shortbread may be a bit tough.

4 Lay a large sheet of foil on a bench and cover it with a sheet of baking paper. Turn the dough out onto a chopping board and roll and pat it with your hands to form it into a round or rectangular-shaped log – if the dough seems too soft, chill it first so it firms up. Sit the log along one side of the baking paper and roll it up in the paper. Next, roll it in the foil. Twist the ends tightly in opposite directions so you end up with something that looks like a very long bonbon. Chill this for at least 4 hours or until it is firm enough to slice. (If you want smaller biscuits, make two separate logs, as one is a bit too long to handle comfortably.)

5 Preheat your oven to 160°C. Cut the log into 8 mm-thick slices and put them about 3–4 cm apart on baking trays lined with baking paper (if you're making large rectangular shortbread, prick each one a couple of times with a fork). Sprinkle the tops with the white sugar.

6 Bake for 25–30 minutes or until the shortbread is golden around the edges and on the bottom. To check, break one in half; it should be virtually cooked through to the centre. Remove the biscuits from the oven and leave them to firm up on their trays for a couple of minutes, then carefully transfer them to a wire rack to cool completely. Store the shortbread in an airtight jar for up to 1 week.

THE LOW-DOWN ON SHORTBREAD

Shortbread bakes most evenly at lower temperatures as the slow heat allows the centre to cook through and be as crunchy as the edges. After the shortbread has cooled, if by any chance you find that it isn't quite as cooked through and crisp as it should be, don't hesitate to reheat the oven and put it back in for a while. It's not always easy to tell when it's ready – I've done this many times and it works a treat.

Anzac biscuits

MAKES 24–30

I've always loved Anzac biscuits. How my mum ever kept up with the rate we ate them, I'll never know. Yet somehow she managed to keep just ahead of our voracious appetites and nimble fingers (that could even whisk them off the baking trays while they were still hot). And even though we burnt our mouths as we ate them, they were worth it and more. I doubt that anyone these days could ever lay claim to the recipe as their own, as there are so many versions and they all tend to use similar ingredients – although some now include fairly exotic additions like wattle seeds and lemon myrtle, while others are studded with chocolate chips. Very good they are too – but for me, it's hard to beat the chewy, oat-laden, golden-syrupy originals.

This recipe makes biscuits that are quite chewy as I like them that way, but if you're one of the 'crisp biscuit' brigade, just use a bit more flour in the mixture and cook them slightly longer.

1 cup (90 g) rolled oats	2 tablespoons golden syrup
(not quick cooking oats)	2 tablespoons boiling water
⅔ cup (50 g) shredded coconut	1½ teaspoons bicarbonate of soda
1 cup (150 g) plain flour	1 teaspoon vanilla extract
¾ cup (165 g) castor sugar	whole blanched almonds (optional),
125 g unsalted butter	for topping

1 Preheat your oven to 160°C. Line a couple of large baking trays with baking paper and set aside. In a large bowl, thoroughly mix together the oats, coconut, flour and sugar.

2 Put the butter and golden syrup into a small saucepan over low heat and warm them, stirring occasionally, until the butter has melted. Remove the pan from the heat. Add the boiling water and bicarbonate of soda and stir them in briefly; just be a bit careful as the mixture froths up. Pour this buttery liquid into the oat mixture along with the vanilla extract. Quickly stir the two together until they're thoroughly combined.

3 Roll the resulting sticky dough into walnut-sized balls, then flatten them slightly and sit them at least 5 cm apart (as they spread quite a bit) on the prepared baking trays. Press an almond, if using, into the top of each biscuit; the almonds are really just a bit of window-dressing to make them look a bit different, so you certainly don't have to use them. Depending on the size of your oven, you may find you need to bake these in batches.

4 Bake for 16–20 minutes or until the biscuits are deep golden brown but still soft, then remove them from the oven. (It's a good idea to rotate the trays from shelf to shelf halfway through the baking time to ensure the biscuits cook evenly.) Leave them to cool on the trays for a few minutes, then carefully transfer them to wire racks to cool completely. They keep well in an airtight container for up to 1 week (I wish – I don't think they have ever lasted that long in my house!).

Dark chocolate chip shortbread

MAKES 20 LARGE SHORTBREAD FINGERS

There's nothing quite like a bit of overkill and combining shortbread with chocolate is a case in point; the combination of buttery shortbread and rich dark chocolate is a made-in-heaven pairing. My Yorkshire friend, Anne, calls this a tray-bake; it's an easy way to make a lot of shortbread very quickly as the dough is just pressed into the tin and doesn't need rolling and cutting. I usually slice it into twenty quite substantial bars; however, you can reduce the size and make about forty shortbread biscuits from it instead.

240 g plain flour

¾ cup (120 g) fine semolina

½ teaspoon salt

180 g good-quality dark chocolate, broken into chunks

300 g unsalted butter, at cool room temperature, chopped

180 g castor sugar

1½ teaspoons vanilla extract

1 Lightly butter a shallow 23 cm × 33 cm baking tin (a Swiss-roll tin is fine) and set it aside.

2 Put the flour, semolina and salt into a food processor and whiz for about 20 seconds. Tip this into a bowl, leaving 1 tablespoon of the mixture behind. Add the chocolate to the processor and pulse to chop it into small chunks, then stir them into the flour mixture.

3 Put the butter, sugar and vanilla extract into the food processor. Whiz them for about 1 minute or until the mixture is light and creamy, stopping and scraping down the sides once or twice with a rubber spatula. Scrape the butter mixture into the flour mixture and stir them together with a strong spatula or spoon just until they're combined. You'll find the dough is quite thick and a bit awkward to mix – I sort of squash it down and slide it with the spoon which seems to work quite well.

4 Scrape the shortbread dough into the prepared tin, then dust your hands lightly with flour and use them to spread the dough out evenly. It's a good idea to roll a tumbler over the top to smooth out any lumps and bumps. Prick the shortbread all over with a fork and chill it in the fridge for 20 minutes.

5 Meanwhile, preheat your oven to 150°C. Bake the shortbread for 45–50 minutes or until it is pale golden around the edges and on top. Remove from the oven and leave it to settle for 2 minutes, then carefully slice it into fingers while it's still hot; I rest a ruler over the top of the tin to help me cut straight lines. Leave it to cool in the tin for 45 minutes, then carefully loosen it with a spatula and transfer the shortbread fingers onto a wire rack to cool completely. The shortbread keeps well in an airtight container for at least 1 week.

Cheese and nigella seed biscuits

MAKES 75–80

Whenever I offer to make something for a get-together, I can almost guarantee that nine times out of ten I'll be asked to bring a plate full of 'those fantastic little cheese biscuits with the chilli'. And they really are terrific – crisp, deliciously cheesy and very straightforward to make. Although I've published the recipe for them once before, in *Belinda Jeffery's 100 Favourite Recipes*, you may not have it and they're just too good not to include in this book. The full recipe makes about eighty biscuits, which may be more than you need. However, the rolls freeze beautifully for one month so you can slice and cook as many biscuits as you like, then put the rest of the rolls in the freezer, so you've always got some back-up supplies of dough on hand. Many times I've been grateful to have them there too.

2 cups (300 g) plain flour
⅓ cup (50 g) self-raising flour
1 teaspoon salt
½ teaspoon dried chilli flakes
½ cup (40 g) freshly grated parmesan
1¾ cups (200 g) grated good-quality tasty *or* cheddar cheese
250 g cold unsalted butter, cut into small chunks
1½–2 tablespoons lemon juice, strained
nigella seeds (see Ingredients page 5) *or* black *or* white sesame seeds, for sprinkling

1 Put the flours, salt and chilli flakes into a food processor and whiz them so they're well combined. Add the parmesan and cheddar and blend together until the cheeses are thoroughly mixed in. Add the butter and process until the mixture resembles coarse breadcrumbs. Drizzle in the lemon juice and let the processor run until a ball of dough forms around the blade; don't be alarmed if this takes a minute or two.

2 Lay a large sheet of foil on a bench and cover it with a sheet of baking paper. Knead half the dough lightly to bring it into a ball, then shape it into a log about the diameter of a 50 cent piece. Sit the log along one side of the baking paper and roll it up in the paper. Next, roll it in the foil. Twist the ends tightly in opposite directions so you end up with something that looks like a very long bonbon. Do the same with the remaining piece of dough. (Or if you would rather, you can divide the mixture into thirds or quarters and make smaller rolls to freeze.) If you're baking the biscuits the same day, chill the logs for 2–3 hours in the fridge until they're firm enough to slice. Or at this stage you can freeze the logs until you need them (they keep well in the freezer for about 5 weeks; just defrost them in the fridge before slicing them).

3 Preheat your oven to 180°C. Cut the logs into 5 mm-thick slices and put them onto baking trays lined with baking paper. Press some nigella seeds or sesame seeds, if using, on top.

4 Bake for 12–15 minutes or until the biscuits are golden. Remove them from the oven and leave them on the trays for 1 minute, then transfer them to a wire rack to cool completely.

Buttery ginger squares

MAKES ABOUT 48

These crisp, buttery biscuits are very much for ginger lovers – what with their double whammy of chewy chunks of crystallised ginger and the warmth of powdered ginger too. Funnily enough, as I write this recipe, I've just come from the kitchen where I've been putting the finishing touches on a batch and I can vouch for the fact that the dough tastes as good raw as it does cooked. I'm a great one for licking spoons and running my finger around bowls of cake and biscuit mixture – for me it's one of the greatest pleasures of baking. It's certainly an act of love when I offer the spoon to someone else rather than licking it clean myself!

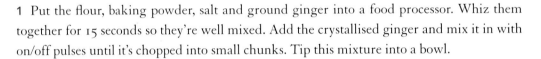

2 cups (300 g) plain flour
¼ teaspoon baking powder
¾ teaspoon salt
2 tablespoons ground ginger
180 g crystallised ginger chunks

250 g unsalted butter, cool but not cold,
    cut into large chunks
⅔ cup (150 g) firmly-packed brown sugar
2 teaspoons vanilla extract
flaked almonds (optional), for decorating

1 Put the flour, baking powder, salt and ground ginger into a food processor. Whiz them together for 15 seconds so they're well mixed. Add the crystallised ginger and mix it in with on/off pulses until it's chopped into small chunks. Tip this mixture into a bowl.

2 Add the butter and brown sugar to the processor. Whiz them together until they're creamy, about 40 seconds. Stop the machine once or twice to scrape down the sides with a rubber spatula. While they're mixing, drizzle the vanilla extract in through the feed tube.

3 Tip the flour mixture back into the processor and combine it with the butter mixture with quick on/off pulses. Do this as rapidly as possible, as too much mixing once the flour is added to the batter can cause the biscuits to toughen when they bake.

4 Scrape the dough, which will be quite soft, out of the processor into a bowl. Cover the bowl with plastic film and put it in the fridge for about 45 minutes so the dough firms up a bit. Divide the dough in two and roll each half into a log 5–6 cm in diameter (you can make them bigger if you like).

5 Lay a large sheet of foil on a bench and cover it with a sheet of baking paper. Sit one of the logs along one side of the baking paper and roll it up in the paper. Next, roll it in the foil. Twist the ends tightly in opposite directions so you end up with something that looks like a very long bonbon. Do the same with the remaining dough. Chill the logs in the fridge for 1 hour or until they're quite firm. Lift the logs of dough out of the fridge and slap them firmly against your bench to straighten the sides, so the biscuits will be square-shaped when you slice them. Return them to the fridge for a couple of hours or overnight. (You can freeze one or both logs at this stage for up to 1 month to use at another time; just defrost them in the fridge before slicing them.) >

6 Cut the logs into 8 mm-thick squares and put them about 3–4 cm apart on large baking trays lined with baking paper. Press a few flaked almonds gently onto the top of each biscuit. Return them to the fridge for 15 minutes. You'll need four trays if you're baking the full quantity at once, or recycle the trays you have, but make sure to cool them between baking each batch; the quickest way is to run them under cold water, then dry them.

7 Meanwhile, preheat your oven to 160°C. Unless you have a fabulous, big oven that will bake all four trays of biscuits evenly in one hit, it's best to bake the biscuits in batches. Sit two trays in the oven and bake the biscuits for 25–30 minutes or until they look a little darker all over, especially around the edges and on the bottom. Halfway through the cooking time, swap the trays around and turn them back-to-front so the biscuits cook evenly. Remove the biscuits from the oven and leave them to firm up on their trays for 5 minutes or so, then carefully transfer them to a wire rack to cool completely. Repeat this process with the remaining squares. Store them in an airtight container in a cool spot for up to 1 week.

'Auntie' Beryl's Mexican wedding biscuits

MAKES ABOUT 45

My mother's dearest friend, who became our surrogate aunt, was called Beryl. She was a very special person – big-hearted, generous to a fault and we loved her dearly. She was also a terrific cook and would ring me up and say, 'Darling, I've just made the most fabulous chocolate cake/biscuit/tart (you name it) and want to give you the recipe. Now have you got a pen?', and off she'd rattle it at a rate of knots while I'd desperately try to keep up the pace. These particular biscuits have a special place in my heart as she made mountains of them for my wedding day. They're delicate and melt-in-your-mouth – I never make a batch without immediately seeing her in my mind's eye, surrounded by a flurry of icing sugar as she made them. I'm afraid you're going to have to get out the electric mixer (hand-held or the whole kit and caboodle, whichever you have) for these, but it's only to beat the butter and sugar for a few minutes.

250 g unsalted butter, at room temperature, cut into large chunks
½ cup (80 g) pure icing sugar, sifted
2½ teaspoons vanilla extract
70 g roasted hazelnuts *or* pecans (see opposite), finely chopped
2 cups (300 g) plain flour, sifted
icing sugar, for coating

1 Preheat your oven to 175°C. Line two or three baking trays with baking paper and set aside.

2 Put the butter, icing sugar and vanilla extract into a bowl and, using an electric mixer, beat them together on medium speed for 5 minutes or until they're light and fluffy. In another bowl, thoroughly mix the nuts and flour together. Tip the nut mixture into the butter mixture and stir them together until they're well combined. I find it's best to do this stirring together with a spoon rather than using the mixer because too much mixing can cause the biscuits to toughen as they bake.

3 Drop heaped teaspoonfuls of the biscuit mixture onto the prepared baking trays, leaving a few centimetres between each one so the biscuits can spread a little as they cook.

4 Bake the biscuits for about 20 minutes. Halfway through the cooking time, rotate the trays so they sit on different shelves and turn each tray around, back to front; it may sound a bit fiddly but this really helps them to cook evenly. After about 18 minutes, start checking the biscuits – they're ready when the tops are speckled with gold and the bottoms are golden brown (lift them carefully to check as they're rather fragile at this stage).

5 While the biscuits are baking, sift a thick layer of icing sugar onto a plate. When the biscuits are ready, remove them from the oven and let them cool for a minute or so on the baking trays. Sit a few biscuits at a time on the icing sugar and sift more icing sugar over the top. Transfer them to a wire rack and leave them to cool.

6 When they're completely cool, carefully stack the biscuits in airtight jars or containers and seal them tightly. They keep well for 2 weeks.

ROASTING YOUR OWN HAZELNUTS

Although you can buy roasted hazelnuts, it's very simple to do yourself and they taste much fresher. Just spread the shelled nuts (they will still have their dark skins), onto a shallow baking tray. Pop the tray in a 180°C oven and roast the nuts for 12–15 minutes or until the skins have darkened and started to split.

When they're ready, remove them from the oven and immediately tip them into a clean tea towel. Bundle the nuts up in the towel and leave them for a few minutes to sweat. Now, rub the nuts together through the tea towel to loosen and remove the skins. Don't worry if they still have some bits of skin clinging stubbornly to them, it's nearly impossible to remove it all (unless you want to go stark raving mad!).

Sally's terrific biscotti

MAKES ABOUT 40

I'm in the fortunate position that friends, knowing what I do, at times pass on their cherished family recipes to me. It's a great privilege as I think they're such treasures, and often the best recipes of all. My good friend and terrific cook, Sally Rourke, scribbled this on the back of a postcard with a note to say that the biscotti were really delicious, incredibly easy to make and her boys were mad about them. Sally and her family were our neighbours some years ago and they became my official taste testers as they all love their food. So, whenever I was trying something out, part of it would make its way next door to get either the thumbs-up or thumbs-down. We had great fun and I found all three boys to be a fantastic barometer for what worked and what didn't.

Consequently, when Sally tells me something is well worth trying, I'm there. And she's dead right with these biscotti – you can make the dough in a matter of minutes and they have a simple, direct coconut and vanilla flavour that is just right for when you want something plain and not-too-sweet (they're low in fat too). But best of all is their texture – they're really crunchy (but not so much so that you think you're going to break a tooth when you bite into one) and just right for dunking.

If you would like a more pronounced coconut flavour and can lay your hands on some coconut extract, add a teaspoon of it to the recipe and reduce the vanilla extract to 1½ teaspoons – it really boosts the coconut flavour.

1½ cups (225 g) plain flour

1½ teaspoons baking powder

½ teaspoon salt

100 g roasted pecans (see page 80), very coarsely chopped

½ cup (35 g) shredded coconut

1 egg

1 egg white

¾ cup (165 g) castor sugar

½ cup (125 ml) light olive oil

2½ teaspoons vanilla extract >

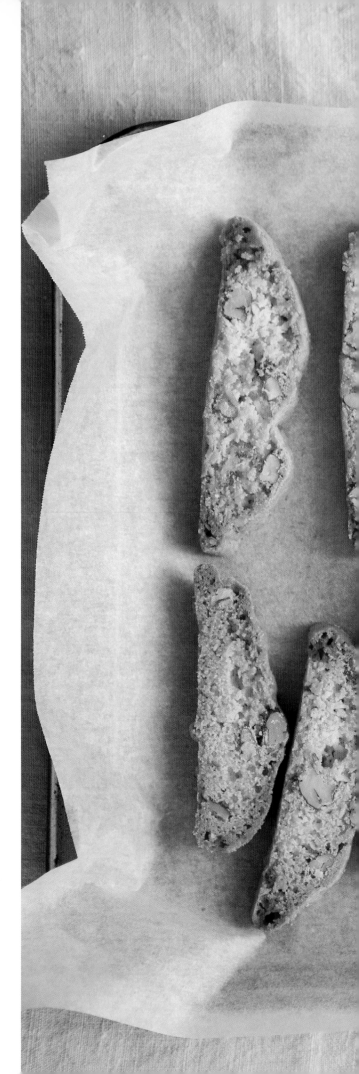

1 Tip the flour, baking powder and salt into a bowl and mix them together with a balloon whisk for 40 seconds. Add the pecans and coconut, then toss everything together so it's well mixed.

2 In a separate bowl, beat together the egg, egg white and sugar with a balloon whisk for about 40 seconds or until they look pale and creamy. Pour in the oil and vanilla extract, and coconut extract, if using, and whisk them in for another 20 seconds or so. Tip the flour and pecan mixture into the egg mixture and stir the two together to form a fairly stiff dough. Cover the bowl tightly with plastic film and put it in the fridge to chill and firm up for at least 6 hours or preferably overnight.

3 When you're ready to bake the biscotti, preheat your oven to 160°C and line a large baking tray with baking paper.

4 Take the dough out of the fridge and divide it in half. Sit one half on a chopping board and sort of squeeze and roll it at the same time (it's a funny description, I know, however, it's the best way I can think of to explain it) into a log about 20 cm long. The squeezing bit is really important, because the nuts tend to clump together here and there and form little air-pockets which cause the biscuits to break as they bake. Don't worry if they do, as you can do an awful lot of rescuing with these. Repeat this process with the remaining dough and sit both logs on the prepared tray, leaving a good gap between them as they spread a bit during the first stage of baking.

5 Bake for about 35 minutes or until the logs are golden brown and resemble two not very high, fat little loaves. Remove from the oven and leave them to cool on the tray for 1 hour. While they're cooling, line a couple more baking trays with baking paper.

6 When the logs have firmed up somewhat but are still slightly warm and a little soft inside, use a sharp knife to cut them on the diagonal into 8 mm–1 cm-thick slices. Hold the logs firmly around the sides as you slice them to help prevent them breaking too much. If some of the slices come apart, when you put them back on the baking trays just gently squeeze them together again as they tend to join up on the second baking.

7 Lay the slices flat on the prepared baking trays. Return them to the oven and bake for about 15–18 minutes or until they're crisp and golden brown.

8 When they're ready, remove the trays from the oven. Leave the biscotti to firm up a little on the trays, then carefully transfer them to wire racks to cool completely. Handle them gently when you do this as they're still a little soft at first. When they're completely cool, store them in airtight containers. Now comes the hard part – the flavour of these is much more pronounced if you can bear to leave them at least a day or so before eating them – sorry! They freeze well too, for up to 3 weeks.

Crunchy peanut butter and sea salt biscuits

MAKES 50–60

One taste of these simple biscuits is like tasting my childhood; I can clearly remember standing on a stool next to my nan, running a finger scrupulously over the beater she had just given me, trying to scrape up every last morsel of rich peanut-filled dough. (I'm quite sure she deliberately left much more dough on the beater than necessary to bring joy to a four-year-old's heart.) Her biscuits were always dense and chunky with peanuts, and my job was to make a criss-cross pattern with a fork across the tops of them.

These particular biscuits are a little different in that they're surprisingly light but still satisfyingly crunchy, with a subtle peanut flavour. The somewhat unusual thing about them is that they have a smattering of crystalline sea salt flakes on top. This really came about by chance as I was making them and thinking how yummy salted peanuts are. One thing led to another and I decided to give it a whirl, and I'm so glad I did because I just love the result – crisp, sweet, nutty biscuits with the surprising tang of the salt. I even put them on my tongue upside-down so the first thing I taste is the salt.

2 cups (300 g) plain flour	⅓ cup (75 g) firmly-packed brown sugar
⅛ teaspoon baking powder	1 teaspoon vanilla extract
½ teaspoon salt	1 egg
180 g unsalted butter, cool but not cold, cut into chunks	110 g crunchy peanut butter
	⅓ cup (50 g) salted peanuts
⅓ cup (75 g) castor sugar	sea salt flakes, for topping

1 Put the flour, baking powder and salt into a food processor and whiz them together for about 10 seconds so they're well combined. Tip them out into a bowl.

2 Put the butter and both sugars into the food processor. Whiz them for 40 seconds, stopping and scraping down the sides once or twice with a rubber spatula, until they're light and creamy. Add the vanilla extract and egg and whiz them in for 10 seconds; the mixture may look a bit curdled, but it will be fine once the flour is added. Scrape the peanut butter into the egg mixture and whiz the machine briefly again so it mixes in. Add the flour mixture to the processor and mix it in with on/off pulses, until it just forms a thick soft dough. (Don't overdo the mixing in of the flour or the biscuits will be a tad tough.)

3 Add the peanuts to the dough and stir them in with a spatula (you might find it easier to do this if you tip the dough out into a bowl and work the nuts in by hand, as it's always a bit awkward in the processor). Scrape the dough out onto a chopping board and divide it in half. >

4 Lay a large sheet of foil on a bench and cover it with a sheet of baking paper. Gently knead one piece of the dough briefly to bring it together, then roll it into a log about 5 cm in diameter. Sit the log on one edge of the baking paper and roll it up in the paper. Next, roll it so it's wrapped in the foil. Twist the ends of the foil tightly in opposite directions so you end up with something that looks like a very long bonbon. Repeat with the remaining dough.

5 If you're baking the biscuits on the same day, chill the logs for 2–3 hours in the fridge until they're firm enough to slice. Or, at this stage, you can freeze the logs until you need them (they keep well in the freezer for about 5 weeks; just defrost them in the fridge before slicing them).

6 Preheat your oven to 150°C. Line some baking trays with baking paper. Unwrap the log (or logs) and cut into 6–7 mm-thick slices. Sit the rounds, about 2 cm apart, on the prepared baking trays. Gently sprinkle a little sea salt onto each one; I'd go fairly lightly on the salt the first time you make them, and then when you've tried them once you can adjust the amount.

7 Bake, in batches if necessary, for 20–25 minutes or until the biscuits are light golden-brown and feel crisp to touch. If your oven cooks a bit unevenly, turn the trays back to front and swap the shelves halfway through the baking time. Remove the trays from the oven and leave the biscuits to cool completely on them. Store the biscuits in an airtight container, where they will keep well for 5–6 days, or freeze them for up to 2 weeks, and when you want, defrost them at room temperature.

MEASURING PEANUT BUTTER
Peanut butter is an awkward thing to measure as it's so sticky and messy. There are two ways to go about it: scoop it out onto a sheet of baking paper and weigh it (you need 110 g for this recipe); or squash it into a measuring jug and check the level on the jug – both work well.

Very crisp lemon thins

MAKES 60–70

These are rather plain-looking little biscuits but they pack the most wonderful lemony punch. They're very thin and really, really crunchy – the sort of things that are just right served with poached fruit. As I write this, white nectarines are in season and we cooked some in a vanilla syrup last night and ate them with a scoop of honey ice-cream and these biscuits. It was such a simple yet perfect finish to a summer dinner and everything looked so delicate and cool too – the rosy pink flush of the nectarines, the pale golden ice-cream and the icing sugar-speckled biscuits. At the risk of stating the blindingly obvious, I should add that these are great with a cup of tea or coffee too.

1½ cups (225 g) plain flour
½ teaspoon baking powder
¼ teaspoon bicarbonate of soda
¼ teaspoon salt
150 g unsalted butter, at cool room temperature
¾ cup (165 g) castor sugar
finely grated zest of 2 large lemons (about 1 packed tablespoon)
¼ cup (60 ml) lemon juice, strained
1 teaspoon vanilla extract
icing sugar, for dusting

1 Put the flour, baking powder, bicarbonate of soda and salt into a food processor. Whiz them together for 10 seconds so they're well mixed, then tip them into a bowl.

2 Put the butter and sugar into the food processor. The butter needs to be firm but pliable – if it's too warm the dough is a bit hard to handle and sticks to your fingers. Whiz them together for 40 seconds or until they're creamy, stopping and scraping down the sides once or twice with a rubber spatula. Sprinkle in the lemon zest, lemon juice and vanilla extract. Mix them together for 10 seconds; occasionally the batter looks a bit curdled at this stage, but don't worry, once you add the flour mixture it comes together again.

3 Tip the flour mixture into the butter mixture and pulse the two together just until they form a soft dough. Try not to overdo this as it causes the biscuits to toughen as they bake.

4 Lift the dough out onto a chopping board. Working quickly, divide the dough in half and gently roll each half into a log about 4 cm in diameter. The dough is very soft and a little awkward to handle at this stage. If it's just too difficult and sticks to your fingers, sit it on a plate and put it in the fridge for a while until it is firm enough to roll easily.

5 Lay a large sheet of foil on a bench and cover it with a sheet of baking paper. Sit one of the logs along one side of the baking paper and roll it up in the paper. Next, roll it in the foil. Twist the ends tightly in opposite directions so you end up with something that looks like a very long bonbon. Repeat with the remaining piece of dough. Chill the logs in the fridge for at least 2 hours or until they're firm enough to slice. (By the way, at this stage you can also freeze one or both of the logs to use further down the track – they keep well in the freezer for up to 6 weeks. Just defrost them in the fridge overnight before you slice and bake them.)

6 About 10 minutes before you want to bake the biscuits, preheat your oven to 170°C. Line two or three baking trays with baking paper (the number of trays depends on how many biscuits you're baking). Cut the logs into 5 mm-thick slices. Sit the rounds on the prepared trays, leaving a 2 cm gap between each one as they spread a little when they cook.

7 Bake for 15–20 minutes or until the biscuits are golden brown around the edges. Unless you have a really reliable oven with no 'hot' spots, it's a good idea, halfway through the cooking time, to swap the shelves the trays are on and turn the trays around back to front, so the biscuits have a chance to bake evenly.

8 Put the baking trays on a wire rack and leave the biscuits to cool on the trays. Once they've completely cooled, store them in airtight jars in a cool spot. They keep well for up to 1 week, although the lemon flavour does become a bit subtler over that time. Or you can freeze them for up to 2 weeks; just bring them to room temperature before eating them.

9 Dust the biscuits lightly with icing sugar just prior to serving.

scones

A light touch and other helpful scone lore

Give me a freshly-baked scone any day – buttery date ones, brilliant orange pumpkin ones or fluffy soda powder puffs laden with jam and cream. I adore them all and will cheerfully choose a scone any day over something more elaborate. They're so very rewarding to bake too, because for such a little amount of work you get such wonderful results. Scones are a terribly good thing to start off with if you're a novice baker, as it's really encouraging to make a batch and see the pleasure that they give other people. It's a real treat – scones tend to make people smile and be happy and I'm convinced that they are good for the soul.

MASTERING THE ART OF SCONE MAKING   I know the list below looks quite long, however, it's all very easy stuff to remember and really will have you making great scones effortlessly.

* Rule number one – and the one to remember even if you forget everything else you read here – is to be careful not to over-mix scone dough. It needs to be mixed quickly and very lightly for feather-weight scones.
* Ideally, use a sturdy baking tray as scones cook at a high temperature and the bottoms can burn if they're on a flimsy tray. Having said this, I don't actually have any really heavy baking trays so I line mine with one or two sheets of baking paper, which works well.
* It helps if ingredients like the butter, eggs and buttermilk or milk are cold as this makes the dough easier to handle, which results in lighter scones.
* Dip whatever you're cutting the scones with, be it a tumbler, scone cutter or knife, into flour as you go to help stop the dough sticking to it.
* When you're cutting out the scones, try to stamp them out and not twist the cutter too much, otherwise they tend to become lopsided as they bake. (I rather like this whimsical look, however, if you're after nice, neat scones this technique helps.)

* Snuggle the scones closely together on the baking tray so they cook almost as a batch rather than individually. This keeps them really moist and helps them rise more evenly. They will more than likely join together, but just gently pull them apart when they're cooked.

* I rather like floury tops on my scones; however, you can make them shiny by lightly brushing the tops of the scones before they're baked with either an egg yolk beaten with 2 teaspoons of water, or for a dull, golden glaze, use a little milk.

* Scones like hot ovens – if the temperature is too low they take longer to cook and consequently tend to dry out.

* They also like to be cosseted, so wrap them in a clean tea towel as soon as they come out of the oven, and let them sit for 5 minutes before serving them. This traps some of the steam in the scones so they stay very moist and fluffy.

* A good thing to know about scones is that they freeze remarkably well. So you can double the recipe that you're making, bake the scones, then freeze half of them. To do this, sit them on a tray lined with freezer wrap and freeze them until they're rock solid. Once frozen, store them in a sealed bag. Just before eating the scones, zap them in a microwave for about 1 minute per scone, then pop them into a 200°C oven for 5–8 minutes.

* Remember, there's a wonderful saying (I'm not sure who said it first) that good scone-makers are good in bed too – if you ever needed encouragement to master the art then there you go!

PATTING OUT SCONE DOUGH

Scones don't rise as much as you might think, so don't pat the dough out too thinly or the scones will be quite flat – it needs to be at least 4–5 cm thick.

Really good cheese scones

MAKES 8 (BUT THE RECIPE CAN EASILY BE DOUBLED)

When I first started out experimenting with savoury scone recipes I really wanted them to have a robust cheese flavour as I found that many of the cheese scones I tried were a bit bland. After making rather a lot of scones (in fact, having scones just about coming out of my ears) I've realised the secret is to use a combination of a good, strong cheddar or tasty cheese and a little parmesan; this gives them just the right amount of 'oomph' and the aroma is mouthwatering as they bake.

These particular scones really do grow on you – one bite and you think, 'Oh, that's rather nice'; two bites, and it's more, 'That's really, really nice' and by the third bite it's, 'Mm-mmm' territory. (In fact, one of my guides to something being really good is if I find myself hiding it in the back of the freezer in the hope that no-one else will notice it, and that's exactly what happens with these.) I tend to serve them with a big bowl of soup in winter, however, it is summer as I write this and I've just split one open, slathered it with mustard mayonnaise and filled it with avocado and tomato. I must say it is exceedingly satisfying and good – and just the thing for somebody who is writing about food and getting very hungry as they do!

1¼ cups (185 g) self-raising flour
½ cup (80 g) stone-ground wholemeal self-raising flour
½ teaspoon salt
½ teaspoon dry mustard powder
freshly ground black pepper, to taste
1¼ cups (150 g) grated good-quality sharp cheese (like cheddar or tasty)
30 g parmesan, grated, plus a little extra, for sprinkling
60 g cold unsalted butter, cut into chunks
½ cup (125 ml) cold milk

FROZEN ASSETS
It probably harks back to my restaurant days, but I don't think I really know how to cook in small quantities. Even now, when I don't have a dining room full of guests to feed, I still tend to cook for a crowd. I think it's partly my nature, and also partly looking after my tummy, as I love to have bits and pieces of delicious things tucked away in the fridge or freezer that I can pull out at times when I suddenly develop a desperate craving for a little morsel of something delicious (or I just don't feel like cooking, or unexpected guests arrive). These scones freeze really well and fluff up beautifully once they're warmed, giving even the simplest meal a comforting air.

1 Preheat your oven to 200°C. Line a baking tray with two layers of baking paper and set it aside.

2 Put both of the flours, the salt, dry mustard and a few grindings of black pepper into a food processor and whiz them for 15 seconds so they're well mixed. Add the cheeses and whirl them in for another 10 seconds or so. Dot the butter chunks over the top of this mixture and whiz them in until the butter is cut into tiny bits.

3 Tip the flour mixture into a bowl and make a well in the middle. Pour the milk into the well and stir it in as best you can – the dough gets quite thick, so I usually ditch the spoon when it becomes unmanageable and use my hands to bring it together. (If you don't have a processor you can make the scones by hand: just sift the dry ingredients together, then rub in the butter with your fingers, stir in the cheese and continue with the recipe.) >

4 Turn the dough out onto a lightly floured board and pat it out so it's 4–5 cm thick. The dough may seem a little stiff and dry, and although it's tempting to add more milk, it's best not to, as the scones are surprisingly moist and fluffy, despite appearances to the contrary at this stage.

5 Dip a scone cutter or tumbler into some flour, then stamp out a scone. Sit the scone on the prepared baking tray. Continue stamping out scones with the remaining dough, flouring the cutter between each one, and sitting them closely together on the tray. Gently knead the scraps of leftover dough together and use it to cut out more scones. Sprinkle a little extra parmesan over the top of each scone to give them a really crunchy top.

6 Bake for 20 minutes or until the scones are golden (prepare to be driven crazy by the tantalising aroma of them baking). When they're ready, transfer them to a wire rack. Cover them with a light cloth and leave them, if you can bear to, until they're just warm, as their flavour is at its best then.

My mum's pumpkin and date scones

MAKES ABOUT 14

I have clear memories of being about four years old and standing on a little stool next to my mum while she made batches of these golden scones. I always loved being in the kitchen with her and she was endlessly patient, letting me help mix, stir, roll and shape all manner of things (in this case turning a blind eye when I smuggled little nuggets of raw dough and dates into my mouth). We would chat away as we went and she would explain to me what she was doing. I remember to this day her telling me that the secret to making good scones was to use the lightest touch possible when you're mixing the dough together – we had no food processor then so everything was mixed by hand and I loved rubbing the flour and butter together, lifting my hands high as she had taught me to help keep the scones light.

Although I whiz these up in a food processor now, every so often I make a batch by hand and am immediately whisked back into that childhood kitchen where I can almost feel and see Cooee, my mum, beside me in her wonderful cinch-waisted '60s polka dot dress – it's a wonderful image.

3 cups (450 g) plain flour
¼ cup (55 g) castor sugar
1 tablespoon baking powder
¾ teaspoon bicarbonate of soda
¾ teaspoon salt
120 g cold unsalted butter, cut into
   small chunks

150 g chopped pitted dates *or* dried
   cherries *or* cranberries (sold as craisins)
1 cup cold cooked mashed pumpkin
   (preferably butternut, but any
   pumpkin will do) (see page 156)
¾ cup (180 ml) buttermilk >

1 Preheat your oven to 200°C. Lightly dust a sturdy baking tray with flour and set it aside. (If you don't have a heavy baking tray, you can use a lightweight one but line it with baking paper so the bottoms of the scones don't burn.)

2 Put the flour, sugar, baking powder, bicarbonate of soda and salt into a food processor and whiz them for about 20 seconds so they're thoroughly mixed. Add the butter chunks and whiz everything again until the mixture resembles coarse breadcrumbs. Tip it into a large bowl. (If you don't have a food processor, it's easy to do this by hand. Just sift the dry ingredients into a large bowl, then whisk them with a balloon whisk for about 1 minute. Use your fingers to rub in the butter chunks, lifting your hands as you do to help aerate the mixture.)

3 Add the dates to the bowl and toss them about to coat them in the floury mixture. Make a well in the middle of the ingredients. Whisk together the pumpkin and buttermilk and pour them into the well. Stir everything together very gently and quickly. Tip the mixture out onto a floured chopping board and knead it lightly a few times just so it comes together – it's pretty sticky. (This mixing and kneading stage is where you have to maintain the proverbial 'light hand' to end up with fluffy, light-as-a-feather scones.)

4 Pat the dough out into a round about 4 cm-thick. Dip a scone cutter or small tumbler into some flour, then stamp out the scones, dipping the cutter into the flour between each one (this helps stop the dough sticking to it). You can also cut the scones into triangles – see the recipe for Wholemeal Date Scones (page 162) for how to do this.

5 Sit the scones closely together on the prepared baking tray. You'll have some scraps of dough left, so gently knead them together and cut out more scones. To finish them you can either dust the tops lightly with flour or brush them sparingly with milk for a dull golden glaze, or with egg yolk beaten with water for a shiny one (if you do this you need 1 yolk to 2 teaspoons of water).

6 Bake the scones for 20 minutes. When they're ready, remove them from the oven and wrap them immediately in a clean tea towel (this helps keep them moist). Let them sit for 5 minutes, then serve the scones with butter.

COOKING BUTTERNUT PUMPKIN FOR USING IN BAKING

Split a butternut pumpkin in half lengthways, scoop out the seeds and place each half (or one half only if the pumpkin is humungous), cut-side down, on a baking tray lined with baking paper. Pop the tray into a preheated 180°C oven and bake the pumpkin until it's very soft when pierced in the thickest part with a fine skewer. It usually takes about 1 hour or so, however, the time varies a bit depending on the size of the pumpkin. When it's done, remove it from the oven and let it cool. Peel away the skin and scoop the pulp into a container. It keeps well in the fridge for about 5 days. You'll probably end up with more than you need for the scones, however, it makes a delicious vegetable dish too – just mash it and heat it with a good nugget of butter, sea salt, freshly ground black pepper and a little nutmeg.

Strawberry jam 'snails'

MAKES 10

The recipe for these whimsical 'snails' appeared in my first book, *Belinda Jeffery's 100 Favourite Recipes* but I felt I couldn't possibly write a chapter on scones and leave it out, as they're so delicious. I always have this sense of delight at the way they puff up and form little whorls and spirals as they bake. There's also something terribly satisfying about making them – it's just plain good fun, and there's precious little of that at times in this world, especially as we grow up and life somehow seems to become more complex and serious. I must admit I tend to gild the lily somewhat when I serve these, and go the whole catastrophe – lashings of cream, extra jam and a big bowlful of fresh strawberries to squish on top.

2 cups (300 g) self-raising flour

pinch salt

1 tablespoon castor sugar

75 g cold unsalted butter, cut into small chunks

¾–1 cup (180–250 ml) milk

1 egg yolk, whisked with 2 teaspoons of water *or* milk (optional)

icing sugar, for dusting

more jam, copious amounts of double thick cream (see Ingredients page 5)
   and fresh strawberries (optional), to serve

STRAWBERRY BUTTER

60 g unsalted butter, at room temperature

¼ cup (80 g) The Best Homemade Strawberry Jam (see page 252)

1 Preheat your oven to 200°C.

2 Put the flour, salt and sugar into a food processor and whiz them together to combine. Add the butter and process the mixture until it resembles fine breadcrumbs, then tip it into a bowl. (You can also do this by hand in a large bowl. Simply rub the butter chunks into the flour mixture with your fingertips.) Pour in the milk and mix it in lightly with a fork; you will have to adjust the milk a little – you need just enough to make a soft, slightly flaky dough.

3 Turn the dough out onto a floured chopping board and knead it gently until it's fairly smooth. Roll the dough (or pat it out with your hands) into a rectangle about 30 cm × 20 cm.

4 For the strawberry butter, put the butter and jam into the food processor and whiz them together until they're thoroughly mixed. Otherwise, just cream them together in a bowl with a wooden spoon. Spread the strawberry butter evenly over the dough. Starting at the long side nearest you, roll the dough up like a jam roll. Use a lightly floured knife to cut the roll into 3 cm-thick slices. (The dough is a bit soft and squashy to cut but I find if you use a serrated knife and a gentle sawing motion it works well.) >

5 Sit the scones, cut side-down, on a baking tray lined with baking paper, leaving a gap between each one to allow them to spread. (If you have the time you can refrigerate the scones at this stage for 1 hour or so before baking them – they seem to hold together better if you do.)

6 Just before putting the scones in the oven, brush around the sides of each one with the egg yolk mixture, if using, to give them a golden glaze. Bake for 15–20 minutes or until the scones are light golden. Take the scones out of the oven, dust them with icing sugar and pop them into a serving basket lined with a clean cloth or tea towel to keep them warm.

7 Serve them straightaway with jam, cream and fresh strawberries.

DIFFERENT FLAVOURED BUTTERS

You can change the flavour of these scones by using different flavoured butters. For caramel scones, spread the dough with a mixture of brown sugar, butter and vanilla extract. Or try it with any other sort of jam – raspberry is rather fab; or just spread the dough with creamed butter and sugar and scatter dried fruit and cinnamon over the top before rolling it up. You can make savoury ones like this too, if you leave out the sugar in the dough and mix in some grated cheddar or parmesan; or slivers of olives or semi-dried tomatoes instead, then flavour the butter with cheese or chutney – they're wonderful with soup.

Lemonade scones

MAKES ABOUT 18

This is a terrific recipe to have up your sleeve, for as long as you have some lemonade on hand you can whip up a batch of scones in a matter of minutes. I know adding lemonade to the dough sounds like a really bizarre thing to do, but I promise you that it actually works remarkably well – the scones are very light and fluffy. The original recipe used regular self-raising flour only, so the texture was fabulous, however, the flavour was a bit dull – but with some stone-ground wholemeal flour and a little sugar the difference is startling (stone-ground wholemeal flour in particular is wonderful in scones because it gives them a really lovely wheat-y flavour). While these are great with the 'usual suspects' that go with scones, my favourite way of all to eat them is to split them and butter them thickly while they're still warm, so the butter slowly melts into them.

2½ cup (375 g) self-raising flour
1 cup (160 g) stone-ground wholemeal
   self-raising flour
⅓ cup (75 g) castor sugar
½ teaspoon salt
100 g dried currants *or* natural sultanas

1 cup (250 ml) cream
1 cup (250 ml) lemonade
plain flour *or* milk, for topping
The Best Homemade Strawberry Jam
   (see page 252) and double thick cream
   (see Ingredients page 5), to serve

1 Preheat your oven to 200°C. Line a baking tray with two layers of baking paper and set it aside.

2 Put both of the flours, the sugar and salt into a large bowl and whisk them with a balloon whisk so they're really well mixed together. Tip in the currants and toss them about so they're well coated in the flour. Make a well in the middle of the flour mixture and pour in the cream and lemonade. Stir everything together with a wooden spoon until it gets a bit too awkward and sticky to stir, then forget about the spoon and use your hands to bring the dough together. Although you have to make sure the dough is mixed, try not to overdo this as scones are better for a light touch.

3 Tip the dough out onto a chopping board and just bring it together. Pat it out into a 5 cm-thick rectangle – no less if you want good, high scones, as I always think little ones somehow look a bit sad and miserable. Dip a scone cutter or tumbler into some flour then stamp out the scones, dipping the cutter into the flour between each one (this helps stop the dough sticking to it).

4 Sit the scones fairly closely together on the prepared tray. You'll have some scraps of dough left, so gently knead them together, pat them out, and cut out more scones from this. (When they bake, the scones from these off-cuts will be a bit lopsided and rather quirky looking as they don't rise as evenly as the others, but I think they look rather lovely, nonetheless.) When they're all done, either dust the tops lightly with flour or brush them with a little milk. >

5 Bake for 20 minutes or until the scones are golden. While they're baking I usually zoom around and get the tea things ready, pile some cream into a bowl and find a pot of strawberry jam – if I'm in luck we will still have some of The Best Homemade Strawberry Jam (see page 252) in the pantry. When the scones are ready, cool them briefly on a wire rack while you make the tea, then bundle them up in a basket lined with a clean cloth or tea towel and sit down and enjoy them.

DIFFERENT FLOUR, DIFFERENT WEATHER, DIFFERENT RESULTS

Baking is a funny business because ingredients react differently depending on the weather, for one thing, and the actual ingredient itself, for another. This philosophising is due to the fact that I notice every time I make these they vary slightly depending on both the humidity and the flours I use.

Yesterday I made a batch and they were moist and high; today, with different flour, they're softer and have a bit of a lean-on, although I hasten to add they're still delicious. I can attest to that, as I have one by me as I'm writing now, and am desperately trying to field the crumbs so they don't drop into my keyboard! All this comes down to the amount of liquid the flour absorbs and that contrary element, the weather. When you've made them once or twice and got a feel for them, then you can adjust the cream very slightly (by a tablespoon or two either way) to get them just right.

Wholemeal date scones

MAKES 8 (BUT THE RECIPE CAN EASILY BE DOUBLED)

You may notice as you read this chapter that a number of the recipes use a mixture of stone-ground wholemeal and plain flour. I generally find that scones made completely with white flour can be a bit bland, but once you add a little stone-ground wholemeal flour they develop an irresistible nutty, wheat-y flavour. These scones are made entirely from stone-ground wholemeal flour, and despite any misgivings you may have about that (and I well understand if you do, as we've all had run-ins with gluggy stone-ground wholemeal cakes and scones), they are well worth a try. They really are very good – thickly studded with dates, yet light and moist.

1⅔ cups (250 g) stone-ground wholemeal
   self-raising flour, plus a little extra,
   for dusting
1 tablespoon castor sugar
100 g cold unsalted butter, cut into
   small chunks

150 g pitted dates
100 ml buttermilk
1 tablespoon honey
good-quality butter, to serve

1 Preheat your oven to 200°C. Line a baking tray with two layers of baking paper and set it aside.

2 Put the flour and sugar into a food processor. Whiz them together for 10 seconds, so they're well combined. Scatter the chunks of butter over the top and whiz them in until the butter is cut into tiny pieces and the mixture looks like breadcrumbs. Add the dates and process them in with on/off pulses of the processor so they're still in big chunks. Tip the mixture into a largish bowl.

3 In another bowl, whisk together the buttermilk and honey (warm the honey briefly if it's really thick so it mixes in properly). Make a well in the middle of the flour mixture and pour in the honeyed buttermilk. Mix everything together to form a soft dough; I start mixing with a spoon, then once it gets a bit too gluggy I ditch the spoon and resort to using my hands for the last bit. (If you don't have a processor you can make the scones by hand. Just sift the dry ingredients together, then rub in the butter with your fingers, chop the dates and mix them in and continue with the recipe.)

4 Lightly knead everything so it comes together, then tip it out onto a floured chopping board. Instead of regular-shaped scones, I often make these into nuggetty little wedges instead. To do this, shape the dough into a longish rectangular sausage, flattening the top a bit so it's about 4–5 cm-thick. Cut the dough into fat little triangles with a floured knife (you'll need to dust the knife with flour a couple of times while you're cutting, to stop the dough sticking to it). Sit the scones closely together on the prepared baking tray and dust them with a little extra flour. You don't have to do this – I do it because I'm really fond of floury tops on my scones, but you can just leave them as is, or brush a little milk over them instead.

5 Bake for about 17 minutes or until the scones are golden and smell lovely and nutty (you'll find these wholemeal scones are a bit darker and will colour more rapidly than their white flour cousins). When they're ready, sit them on a wire rack and cover them with a light cloth. Hard as it is, try to leave them to cool for at least 10 minutes so they're warm but not hot – it's worth the wait because the flavour will be much better then. These really are best of all when they're split and generously (in my case, very generously) buttered while they're still warm.

Fluffy buttermilk scones

MAKES 18–20

It's funny how we all have taste memories. Some years ago we moved to live in the countryside, and not long after that, my cooking started to head in a different direction. I find I cook much more 'farmhouse' and hearty country food now than ever before, and I have to say we, and any visitors, love it. I've also found that afternoon tea is quite a big thing and I quickly had to dust off all my scone recipes as they're considered an essential part of an afternoon tea spread in this neck of the woods.

And that's where taste memory comes in – although my first attempts were perfectly acceptable, to me the scones were somehow lacking, and none really tasted like the ones I remembered from my childhood – until the day I replaced the milk in the recipe with buttermilk and basically all the lights went on! These were the sort of scones my mum used to make – light, fluffy and with that lovely tangy soda flavour. This recipe makes rather a lot of scones (I seem to be cooking in country quantities too!) however, just halve it if you want less.

2 cups (300 g) self-raising flour
2 cups (320 g) stone-ground wholemeal
   self-raising flour
¼ cup (55 g) castor sugar
1 teaspoon salt
160 g cold unsalted butter, cut into
   small chunks

200 g natural sultanas, dried currants
   or chopped dates (optional)
2 cups (500 ml) buttermilk
milk *or* plain flour, for topping
jam and double thick cream
   (see Ingredients page 5), to serve

1 Preheat your oven to 200°C. Dust a sturdy baking tray with flour and set it aside. Or use a lightweight one lined with two layers of baking paper.

2 Put both of the flours, the sugar and salt into a large bowl. Whisk them together with a balloon whisk for 1 minute so they're thoroughly combined and aerated. Scatter the chunks of butter over the top and use your fingers to rub the butter into the flour mixture until it resembles coarse breadcrumbs. (If you like, you can do all of this in a food processor; then just tip the mixture into a big bowl.)

3 Add the dried fruit and toss it about so it's well coated, then make a well in the middle. Pour in the buttermilk and stir it in very lightly until the floury mixture is well moistened. Turn this mixture out onto a floured chopping board and knead it gently until it's just combined. Pat it out into a 4–5 cm-thick round. Dip a scone cutter or small tumbler into some flour, then stamp out the scones, dipping the cutter back into the flour between each one (this helps stop the dough sticking to it). Gently knead together any scraps and cut them again.

4 Sit the scones closely together on the prepared baking tray and either brush the tops with a little milk or dust them very lightly with flour.

5 Bake for 20 minutes or until the scones are golden. Remove them from the oven and immediately wrap them in a clean tea towel. Leave them for 5 minutes, then serve them with lashings of jam and cream.

A scrumptious apple and plum cobbler

SERVES 6

This is a wonderful old-fashioned dessert that always gets rave reviews when I make it (particularly when I go the whole hog and serve it with homemade custard and vanilla ice-cream). I know that strictly speaking this isn't a scone, however, I've made a unilateral decision here (author's privilege, I guess!) and decided that it qualifies for this section because the cobbler topping really is a scone dough in disguise – and besides, it's just too good and too simple to leave out.

In summer I make this with 400 g berries instead of the plums (blackberries, boysenberries or loganberries or a mixture of these are all terrific – and by all means use frozen berries if fresh aren't around). Then in winter I make it using canned plums instead, as I've done here; either way, it's very good.

You can also make rather lovely individual cobblers in small ramekins, or as I did for the photograph, in enamel bowls. This is wonderful served with either rich cream, custard (if it's homemade, better still) and good vanilla ice-cream – or even all of these!

750 g Fuji, Pink Lady *or* Royal Gala apples
1 × 825 g can stoned plums, well drained and coarsely chopped
5 tablespoons castor sugar

COBBLER TOPPING
1 cup (150 g) plain flour
1 teaspoon baking powder
¼ teaspoon bicarbonate of soda
½ teaspoon salt
1 tablespoon castor sugar
45 g cold unsalted butter, cut into small chunks
¾ cup (180 ml) buttermilk
icing sugar, for dusting
double thick cream (see Ingredients page 5), custard and good vanilla ice-cream, to serve

1 Preheat your oven to 200°C. Peel, quarter and core the apples, then slice them thinly. Tip them into a really big bowl and add the plums, then sprinkle the sugar evenly over the top. Gently mix them all together – it's easiest to use your hands for this (especially if using berries as they are so fragile that they tend break up if you use a spoon). Pile the fruit mixture into a lightly buttered medium-sized and fairly deep ovenproof dish (I know it looks as though there is an enormous amount of fruit at this stage but it does cook down considerably). Sit the dish in the oven to start the fruit cooking, while you make the cobbler topping (give the fruit a good 10 minutes before you add the topping). >

2 Meanwhile, for the topping, put the flour, baking powder, bicarbonate of soda, salt and sugar into a food processor. Whiz them together for about 25 seconds or until they're thoroughly mixed. Scatter the butter over the top and whiz it in until the mixture resembles fine breadcrumbs. Tip this into a bowl and pour in the buttermilk. Stir everything together until they combine to form a shaggy sort of mass. (If you don't have a food processor, just whisk the dry ingredients together in a bowl for about 40 seconds. Add the butter and rub it in with your fingertips until it is incorporated, then continue with the recipe.)

3 Carefully remove the dish of fruit from the oven. Dollop big spoonfuls of the topping over the fruit (don't worry about smoothing it down, it's meant to be a bit craggy) then return the dish to the oven.

4 Bake for about 25 minutes or until the topping of the cobbler has risen and is golden brown. Remove the cobbler from the oven and let it cool a little so it's warm, not hot. Tempting as it is to eat it straight away, the fruit is lethally hot and burns your tongue, and the flavour really is better when it has had a chance to cool.

5 I usually dust the cobbler with icing sugar, then bring the dish to the table and serve this family-style, scooping the cobbler into bowls and letting everyone help themselves to the cream, custard and ice-cream.

Kate Llewellyn's mother, Tommy Brinkworth's, prize-winning scones

MAKES ABOUT 15

It gives me such a lot of pleasure to include this recipe here. The first book of Kate's that I read was her unforgettable Blue Mountains memoir, *The Waterlily: A Blue Mountain Diary* (Hudson Publishing). I so loved it that in the ensuing years I sought out as many of her books and poems as I could find. I was very chuffed a few years ago when I received a letter from her saying how much she enjoys cooking, and that she often uses my books.

Since then, we have kept up a regular correspondence and I've had some wonderful meals at her table; despite her protestations to the contrary, she's a really terrific cook and I always come away feeling very cared for. Early on, we discovered that we both have a passion for scones and have discussed their making at some length (you'll either think this is mad or be nodding your head in total understanding about the importance of the ins and outs of scone making!). Therefore, it just seems so fitting that this recipe, which Kate first wrote down when she was thirteen while her mother dictated it to her, should be included here. If you are looking for the original recipe for these scones, it's in Kate's heart-warming book *Playing with Water: A Story of a Garden* (HarperCollins).

3 really heaped cups (approximately 550 g) self-raising flour *or* 2 cups (300 g)
  self-raising flour and 1 cup (160 g) stone-ground wholemeal self-raising flour

½ teaspoon cream of tartar

good pinch salt

2 tablespoons castor sugar (optional)

100 g dried currants (optional)

2 eggs

2 tablespoons pure cream *or* melted butter

1 cup (250 ml) milk, plus a little extra, for dabbing

1 Preheat your oven to 200°C. Line a baking tray with two layers of baking paper and set it aside.

2 Sift the flour, cream of tartar and salt together in a large bowl. Briskly stir in the sugar and currants, if you're using them. In another bowl, beat the eggs and cream or melted butter together until they're well mixed, then whisk in the milk. Make a well in the middle of the flour mixture and pour in this milky liquid. Fold the two together with a blunt knife. (I realise that a knife may seem an odd thing to use for this, however, there's a lot of wisdom in these old scone recipes, and many recommend a knife for mixing the dough, which makes perfect sense as it means it's much harder to overdo the mixing, which can toughen the scones.)

3 Once the ingredients are nearly incorporated, gently bring the dough together with your fingers. (This gentle touch with the dough is really essential for light scones, and Kate says that both her parents stressed to her the importance of 'not toiling with the dough'.) You'll find the dough is sticky which makes it a little awkward to handle, however, it's also what makes the scones so fluffy.

4 Turn the dough out onto a lightly floured chopping board and pat or roll it out into a rectangle about 2.5 cm thick. Fold half the dough up over the other half, then pat it out again so it's 4–5 cm thick; this fold is what helps make the split in the side of the scones. Dip a scone cutter or small tumbler into some flour then stamp out a scone. Sit the scone on the prepared baking tray. Continue stamping out scones (flouring the cutter between each one) and sitting them closely together on the tray, until you can get no more. Gently knead the scraps of leftover dough together and cut out more scones from these. When they're all done, dip your fingers into the extra milk and dab it over the top of the scones.

5 Bake for about 15 minutes or until the scones are golden. Slip them off the tray onto a clean tea towel and wrap the towel up over them. Leave them to cool a little, then serve them with strawberry jam and cream (or as Kate suggests, leave out the sugar and currants and try topping them with smoked salmon, fresh dill and sour cream).

I MUST ADMIT . . .
that I make one small change here and use a mixture of 2 cups regular self-raising flour and 1 cup stone-ground wholemeal self-raising flour. I suspect the flour in many older scone recipes was slightly less refined and had a 'wheatier' flavour than it does now, so I like to add a little stone-ground wholemeal flour to the mix to compensate for this.

Old-fashioned gem scones

MAKES 12 (OR 18 IF USING A MINI-MUFFIN TIN)

IF YOU MAKE THESE IN MINI-MUFFIN TINS . . .
you may need to halve the dates if they're really large, otherwise the batter tends to overflow when you sit them in the middle of each one.

I still use my great-great grandmother's gem scone iron to make these lovely, homely scones. It must be well over a hundred and fifty years old, weighs a tonne and is as solid as a rock – and I suspect it will still be going strong when I'm long gone. I really love using it as it warms my spirit to think that Irena Kathleen (for that was her name) was baking this same recipe with this same iron all those years ago, in such a very different world – I can feel a fine thread winding its way back into the past and binding us together as I bake them.

Although I have seen these gem scone irons for sale in second-hand and junk shops and you can pick them up on the internet, I realise they aren't so common now, but you can successfully use mini-muffin tins instead. I've also heard that they're being made again as there's been quite a resurgence in their popularity. I'm not really surprised as the scones themselves are wonderful – two-bite sized, really moist, with a warm plump date nestling in the centre (and, in my case, eaten with a good dollop of butter melting into them).

¾ cup (110 g) self-raising flour	1 egg
¼ teaspoon salt	½ teaspoon vanilla extract
30 g unsalted butter, at room temperature, plus extra, for the iron	90 ml milk
	12 pitted dates
⅓ cup (75 g) castor sugar	good-quality butter, to serve

1 Sit the gem scone iron on a baking tray (this makes it much easier to manoeuvre as it becomes red-hot after a while). Put it in the oven and preheat the oven to 200°C.

2 Meanwhile, sift the flour and salt together and set them aside. Put the butter and sugar into a bowl and beat them with a wooden spoon or whisk until they're light and fluffy. (You can do this in an electric mixer, but it's such a small amount of mixture that I usually do it by hand. It takes a couple of minutes of vigorous beating with a spoon, and I look on it as a good arm work-out.) Beat in the egg and vanilla extract until they're thoroughly mixed in. Gradually stir in the reserved flour mixture alternately with the milk, mixing it in lightly until the batter is smooth. Leave it to sit for 1–2 minutes while you butter the gem scone iron.

3 Carefully take the iron out of the oven, and while it's hot, use a thick wad of kitchen paper dipped in melted or soft butter to generously butter each hollow. Give the batter a stir, then spoon it into the hollows so they're nearly full. Tuck a date into the centre of each one.

4 Return the iron to the oven and bake for about 10 minutes (if using a mini-muffin tin, it will take about 8 minutes) or until the scones are golden and springy when gently pressed. Remove the scones from the oven and let them settle in the iron for 1 minute, then tumble them out onto a wire rack. Line a small basket or dish with a clean napkin and nestle the scones into this, bringing the napkin up over them to keep them warm.

5 Serve the scones with plenty of butter and cups of good strong tea. They're best eaten freshly-baked and warm as they don't keep well.

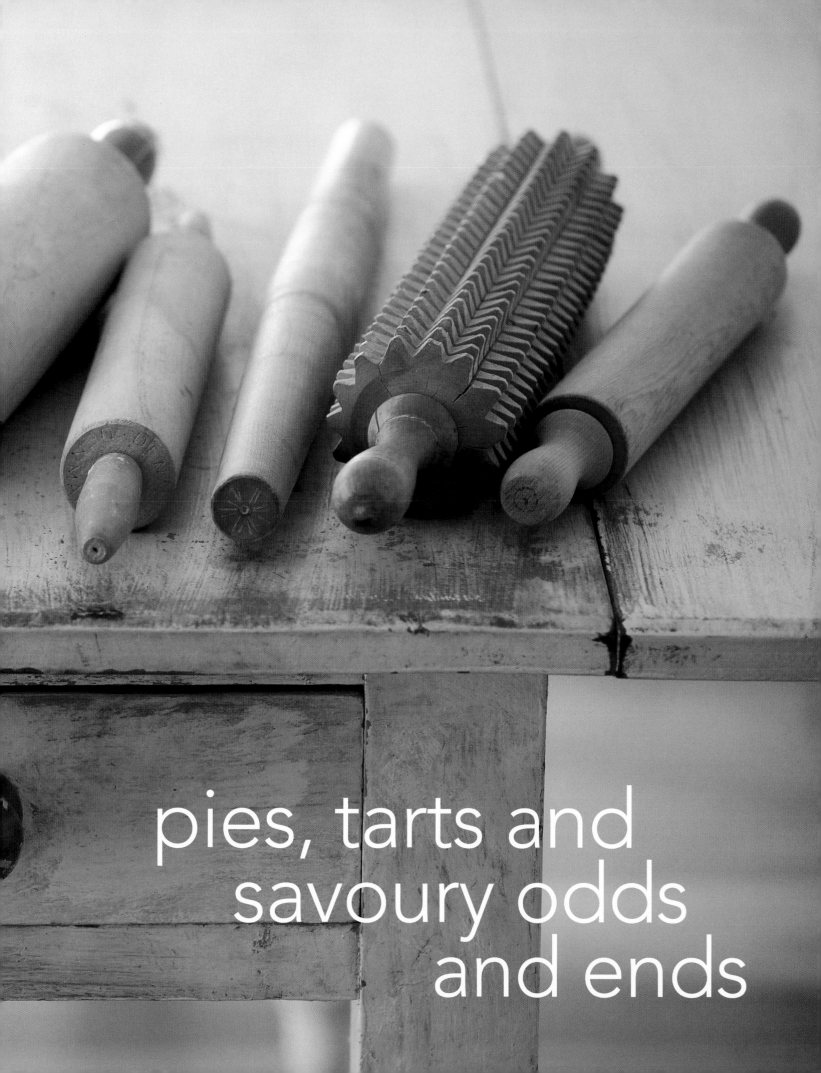

pies, tarts and
savoury odds
and ends

Some little quirks and foibles of making shortcrust pastry

I realise that the mere mention of the word 'pastry' will cause some people to avoid this chapter like the plague. If you're brave enough to read on you'll be pleased to know that, for a start, not all the recipes need you to make pastry – there are some wonderful dishes here that make stunning main courses without you having to even think of picking up a rolling pin. And those that do require 'proper' pastry aren't difficult.

You'll see in the beginning of the chapter that I've given recipes for two simple pastries: one that needs rolling and one that is, blessedly, just pressed into the tin. I know they look a bit long-winded, however, I wanted to make them detailed to help dispel the myth that pastry is difficult to make, and hopefully to help if you're feeling a bit daunted by the prospect of tackling it. For once you've mastered a good shortcrust pastry it's a wonderful thing because it adds so many fantastic dishes to your repertoire. Gorgeous fruit tarts, quiches (although they're considered a bit passé now, a good quiche, deep golden and fragrant with cheese, is a thing of beauty), old-fashioned pies and Italian tortas will all be at your fingertips.

You'll also be relieved to know that I've only dwelt on one type of pastry – a classic shortcrust with a few variations. Although there are many other pastries, this is the one you're most likely to use. Homemade puff pastry is fantastic, but few of us have the time or patience to make it, so I thought I would just stick to the basics.

Most of the recipes here are fairly detailed, but there are just a couple of extra things to keep in mind.

* It's usually much easier to manoeuvre a tart tin if you sit it on a baking tray from the word go, particularly tart tins with removable bases. Otherwise they're quite hard to hold onto and it's all too easy to lift these awkwardly, especially once they're hot, and pop the bottom up when you don't mean to. Believe me, it's hugely disappointing and very messy – been there, done that!

* Shortcrust pastry loves being cool – cool ingredients, cool benchtops, cool weather, cool fingers. They say that really good pastry cooks have cold fingers and I tend to believe it's true (especially so if you're rubbing the butter into the flour by hand, although using a food processor gets around this). The reason for this penchant for coolness is that the warmer the pastry is the softer the butter in it will be, making it more awkward to handle. So if at any stage the pastry starts to feel too soft, just put it in the fridge for a while.

* Shortcrust also likes a rest – and there's a good reason for this. The joy of it is its crisp, short texture and too much working of it and not enough rest makes it tough. As you work the pastry, the gluten in the flour, which is what gives it structure, stretches and becomes quite elastic. Now this elasticity is all well and good when you're making bread dough as you need it to trap in the air bubbles, however, it's not so good when it comes to a very short pastry, for these elastic strands contract when they're heated if they're not given a chance to relax. So what's the meaning of all this when it comes to making shortcrust pastry? Well, for starters, it causes the pastry to be tougher – and worse still, if it's baked too soon after rolling it also causes it to shrink. So if you've ever blind baked a tart shell only to have it shrink down the sides of the tin, this is the reason.

I INVARIABLY END UP WITH ALL SORTS OF PASTRY BRUSHES *in my kitchen drawer, and as much as I love the simple wooden ones, they do get a bit rusty and mucky after a while, and tend to discard their bristles into things (not a good look!). I was recently given a silicone brush to try and I must say it works a treat and avoids the worry of ending up with a mouthful of bristles in your lovingly made tart.*

Good, simple shortcrust pastry

MAKES 1 × 26–28 CM TART SHELL

This is the pastry recipe that I use all the time – it's short and buttery but is one of the easiest pastries I've come across as far as handling goes. There's nothing more frustrating and disheartening than making really buttery pastry only to have it disintegrate and almost dissolve in your hands as you try to roll it. I'm sure experiences like this are the reason that many people say they're terrified of making pastry. This particular shortcrust is a really good compromise as it's robust enough to stand up to a bit of push and pull, but when it's baked it's still crisp and buttery.

I pretty much make it as is for both sweet and savoury tarts and pies, and every so often just do a slight variation on it to suit whatever I happen to be baking – I've listed some of these below to give you an idea of what you can do. By the way, I don't want to sound like a school marm but if you haven't read the introduction to this chapter it's well worthwhile, as it gives you a bit more understanding of the nature of the beast, which always helps.

1½ cups (225 g) plain flour
¼ teaspoon salt

125 g cold unsalted butter,
   cut into small chunks
¼ cup (60 ml) iced water

1 Put the flour and salt into a food processor and whiz them together. Add the butter and whiz everything again until the mixture resembles coarse breadcrumbs. With the processor running, pour in the iced water and process it only until the pastry forms a ball around the blade. The time for this varies a bit depending on the weather – when it's warm it seems to come together faster.

2 Tip the pastry out onto a chopping board and shape it into a ball. Flatten it into a disc and wrap it tightly in plastic film. Chill the pastry in the fridge for about 40 minutes or until its firm but supple enough to roll. If you want to make the pastry ahead, it keeps well in the fridge for up to 3 days, but it will be too firm to roll at this stage, so let it warm up at room temperature until it's pliable. You can also make this a few weeks ahead and freeze it, then just defrost it in the fridge overnight.

VARIATIONS

* *For a slightly sweet pastry, add 2 tablespoons castor sugar and 2 teaspoons finely grated lemon zest to the flour mixture when you're whizzing it.*
* *The addition of just 1 tablespoon fine polenta to the flour gives the pastry a very satisfying crunch and is especially good when you're making Italian-style tarts.*
* *To make enough pastry for a 24 cm pie with a lid, just prepare 1½ times this recipe.*

Pre-baked good, simple shortcrust tart shell

MAKES 1 × 26–28 CM TART SHELL

Blind baking pastry may seem a bit fiddly but there is a point to it; the combination of the pastry being cooked and the egg wash forming a barrier between it and the filling really does help stop it from becoming soggy.

Probably one of the most important things to get the hang of with pastry is knowing when it's at the right stage for rolling – it's not hard to pick this up, however, you may have to make it a few times before you feel entirely comfortable with it. If the dough seems too soft to roll, chill it for a bit longer; if it's hard then let it soften a bit more. The temperature of the room where you're rolling the pastry also makes a difference; pastry is always much easier to handle when the weather is cooler as it softens rapidly in warm weather. Having said that, I live in a near-tropical climate and still make pastry, so there is hope – I just find I have to work quite quickly when I'm rolling it before it gets too warm and soft.

As to the egg wash, it helps seal the pastry by filling in any hairline cracks and forming a lacquer-like layer between the crust and filling. This in turn helps stop the filling leaking into the base and making it soggy.

One of the good things about 'blind baking' is that you can bake the shell in the morning, then fill and finish the tart at night. If you're going to do this, once the shell has cooled, carefully wrap it in the tin with plastic film as this helps stop the pastry softening, especially if the weather is humid.

I should also say that you can freeze the unbaked pastry shell for 3–4 weeks; you just need a bit of freezer space to do it. Once the shell is rolled, rather than chilling it in the fridge, put the whole lot (the tin on the baking tray) into the freezer. When it's frozen solid, carefully cover the pastry with plastic film. It's best baked from frozen – just unwrap and add another 1–2 minutes or so to the initial cooking time.

1 quantity Good, Simple Shortcrust Pastry (see page 177)
egg wash, made from 1 egg yolk beaten with 2 teaspoons water >

1 Make and chill the pastry. On a lightly floured chopping board, roll out the pastry into a large round, about 2 mm thick. Roll the pastry over your rolling pin. Carefully lay it over a 26–28 cm tart tin with a removable base. Use your knuckles to gently press the pastry into the tin, leaving an overhang all around the edge. I usually trim a little pastry off the overhang and keep it in the fridge in case I need to patch up any cracks later on. Put the tart tin on a baking tray (this makes it much easier to manoeuvre when the tin is hot), then chill it in the fridge for 30 minutes or until the pastry is firm.

2 Preheat your oven to 200°C. Completely cover the pastry with a big sheet of foil or baking paper, pressing it gently down into the corners. Spread pastry weights (see page 10), rice or dried beans to a depth of 6 mm all over the base to weigh it down, so the pastry base stays flat while it bakes.

3 Bake for 20 minutes or until the tart shell is nearly set. Take it out of the oven and run a rolling pin over the foil on the top edge to cut off the excess pastry. Return the tin to the oven with the foil and weights still intact and bake the shell for another 8–10 minutes or until the pastry is set. To check, gently pull back the foil – the pastry should be slightly coloured and feel firm and dry.

4 Carefully lift out the foil and weights. If there are any hairline splits or cracks in the pastry now is the time to patch them up. Just press little balls of the reserved pastry into the cracks and spread out gently with your fingers; it's easy to spread because the warmth from the pastry shell softens it.

5 Brush the egg wash over the shell and return it to the oven for another 1–2 minutes or until it has set and the pastry is golden. Take the tart shell out of the oven and leave it to cool in the tin on a wire rack. Once cool, just fill it with whatever filling you are using and continue with the recipe.

Crisp cheese pastry that doesn't need rolling

MAKES 1 × 26 CM TART SHELL

While teaching cooking over the years, I've noticed that one thing that makes people more anxious than anything else in the kitchen is the thought of making pastry. It's probably because there seem to be so many little quirks and foibles associated with it. It's really not hard but I guess it's like most things in life – the more you do it, the more familiar and comfortable you are with it.

This pastry came about as a good compromise for my more uncertain students as it's very easy to make. Just whiz it up in a food processor and press it into the tin, no rolling required – you can hear the sigh of relief when I say this to a class! It also tastes remarkably good: rich, crisp and cheesy.

This tart is particularly delicious with any kind of vegetable filling, and you could also try using it to make the Brie and Pear Tart on page 193.

1½ cups (225 g) plain flour
100 g grated tasty cheese such as cheddar
120 g cool unsalted butter, cut into small chunks
egg wash, made from 1 egg yolk beaten with 2 teaspoons water

1 Put the flour and cheese into a food processor and whiz them quickly together until the cheese is chopped into little pieces. Add the butter and whiz everything again until the mixture either forms a ball around the blade (this can take up to 1 minute) or looks thoroughly mixed and crumbly. The type of cheese you use will determine what happens – a soft textured tasty cheese forms a ball while a firm one is more likely to make a crumbly dough. Tip the pastry onto a chopping board and knead it gently to bring it together.

2 With your fingers, press the pastry evenly over the base and sides of a 26 cm tart tin with a removable base. Take your time with this and try to make sure the sides are evenly covered – if they're too thin they tend to crumble a bit once the shell is baked. Roll a tumbler over the base to smooth it out. Sit the tin on a baking tray and put it in the fridge to chill for at least 20 minutes, or overnight if you want to make it ahead.

3 Depending on how much time you've got you can vary this next bit. When you're flat out, just make the pastry, press it into the tin and once it's chilled, fill and bake the tart. It works well, but the pastry can be a bit soggy as the filling can leak into it. However, if you have a bit more time, it's a good idea to blind bake the pastry as this helps to keep it crisp.

4 To blind bake, preheat your oven to 200°C. Carefully press a big sheet of foil into the prepared shell and sit a 6 mm-thick layer of pastry weights (see page 10), rice or dried beans on top to weigh it down. Put the tin on the baking tray and bake for about 25 minutes or until the pastry is nearly set, then carefully lift out the foil with the weights.

5 Brush the pastry with the egg wash and return it to the oven for another 1–2 minutes or until the glaze sets and is golden. Leave it to cool in the tin on a wire rack. Once cool, just fill it with whatever filling you are using and continue with the recipe.

Zucchini, feta and dill pie

SERVES 6

THIS PIE ALSO MAKES
A TERRIFIC NIBBLE TO
HAVE WITH DRINKS
*Just press more cherry tomatoes
over the top so when you cut it
into little squares you end up
with a tomato half on each one.
Sit a tiny herb leaf on top and
line them up on a platter.*

While this actually started out as a bread, along the way it somehow morphed into more of a pie than anything else. It's very simple and straightforward and makes a remarkably good meal with a platter of sliced ripe tomatoes drizzled with good extra-virgin olive oil and a big bowl of salad greens. More often than not I serve it on a scrubbed wooden board, however, if you want to smarten it up a bit and you happen to have a large square white platter, then sit it on this as it looks really quite swish. It's also handy to know that the recipe doubles well – you just need to bake it for longer in a larger tin.

fine polenta (see page 130), for dusting

700 g zucchini, coarsely grated

5 eggs

½ cup (125 ml) extra-virgin olive oil, plus extra, for brushing

1 cup chopped chives

½ cup chopped dill *or* mint *or* basil

220 g feta

150 g freshly grated parmesan

sea salt and freshly ground black pepper, to taste

1 cup (150 g) self-raising flour

8–12 cherry tomatoes, halved

mint sprigs *or* leaves (optional), to serve

1 Preheat your oven to 180°C. Butter a 22 cm square cake tin and line it with buttered baking paper. Dust the tin with the polenta, tap out the excess and set it aside.

2 Pile the grated zucchini into a large sieve or colander, sit a plate on top to weigh it down a little and leave to drain.

3 Meanwhile, break the eggs into a large bowl and whisk them together. Add the oil, chives and dill, mint or basil and whisk them in.

4 Press down firmly on the plate over the zucchini to squeeze out as much liquid as possible. Stir the grated zucchini into the egg mixture. Crumble in most of the feta (reserving a little for the top of the pie) along with the parmesan, then season to taste with salt and pepper. Add the flour and mix it in until it is combined (I often slip disposable latex gloves on and mix this by hand, as it gets quite thick). Spread the batter into the prepared tin and sprinkle the reserved feta over the top. Gently press the cherry tomato halves, cut-side up, into the surface. >

5 Bake for 45–50 minutes or until the top of the pie is springy when pressed. I discovered on my first attempt at making this that it's a bit hard to know when it's cooked. It seemed ready after 30 minutes but when I took it out and let it cool a little I realised it was still squishy in the centre, so I put it back in the oven for another 15 minutes (thank goodness it's forgiving!). So when you think it's cooked, make sure the top is quite bouncy, and to double-check, insert the tip of a fine knife down into the middle and press the two sides of the cut apart – it should look quite set.

6 Take the pie out of the oven and cool it in the tin for 10–15 minutes. If you're feeling game you can just gently grasp the baking paper and lift the pie out of the tin onto a serving plate, then slide the paper out from underneath. Or, put a wire rack on top and invert the pie onto the rack. Peel away the paper, then sit your serving platter on top of the pie and invert it again onto this. Tidy up any straggly bits and brush the tomatoes with a little extra oil. If you have some herb leaves left, scatter them on top.

7 I think this is best eaten at room temperature when the flavour has had a chance to develop. Leftovers keep really well in the fridge for a couple of days.

Cooee's baked ham and asparagus roll-ups

SERVES 4–6

Although this isn't quite what you might expect to find in a book on baking, I couldn't bear to leave it out as it's very, very good. I always remember my mum cooking it when she had friends coming for lunch. We would go off to school praying that there would be leftovers when we got home – she knew we loved it and I suspect she made extra so we wouldn't be disappointed. It may be somewhat old-fashioned and rich, but it's really more-ish, and so easy to make.

It's never really had a proper name – in my mum, Cooee's, handwritten family cookbook it has the wonderful title of, 'An easy savoury dish for Luncheon or the Evening Meal'. It is one of those recipes where the proportions don't have to be exact so don't worry if you have a few more or less rolls to fit your dish, or need a bit more sour cream or cheese. And fortunately, because it is so flexible, you can easily double or treble the recipe for a crowd. You just need to be aware before making this that it needs to be refrigerated for at least eight hours before baking.

Usually I'm all for using fresh produce wherever possible, but in this case I just can't imagine it would be the same if it were made with fresh asparagus rather than canned. However, that's quite possibly because I have such strong taste memories of it – I've no doubt it would be fine, as would be substituting prosciutto for ham.

When buying the ham, bear in mind that you need enough to cover each slice of bread thinly. If the slices are very large you will probably only need about half the quantity.

12–15 slices white sandwich bread, crusts removed

Dijon mustard, for spreading

12 small, very thin slices ham

1 × 440 g can white asparagus spears, drained

2 tablespoons melted butter

300 ml sour cream

1–2 tablespoons freshly grated parmesan

snipped chives or herb sprigs, to serve

1 Lightly butter a medium-sized gratin dish and set it aside.

2 Lay the bread out on a chopping board. Run a rolling pin over each slice a few times to flatten it out, then spread a little mustard evenly over each one. Arrange a slice of ham on top, cutting it to fit if you need to, and leaving a 1 cm gap at the end furthest away from you (this makes it easier to seal the rolls later). Lay one asparagus spear (or two if they're thin) along the edge of the ham-covered bread nearest you, then roll it up in the bread, pressing down lightly at the far end to seal the roll. Sit the roll in the gratin dish, seam-side down, and continue making the rest of the rolls, tucking them tightly together in the dish as you go. When they're all done, brush the tops lightly with the melted butter.

3 Stir the sour cream to loosen it, then pour it over the rolls and spread it out evenly. Cover the dish tightly with plastic film and refrigerate it for at least 8 hours or preferably overnight.

4 An hour or so before you're ready to bake, remove the dish from the fridge and return it to room temperature.

5 Preheat your oven to 180°C. Uncover the rolls and sprinkle the parmesan over the sour cream.

6 Bake for 30–35 minutes or until the top of the rolls has puffed up a bit and turned a deep golden-brown. As it bakes, the bread becomes more like a thin crêpe wrapping for the asparagus and ham and the sour cream soaks in and forms a crust. It also rises quite dramatically, but unfortunately sinks almost immediately after being removed from the oven, so don't worry when it does this. It mightn't look quite so spectacular, but the taste more than makes up for it.

7 Sprinkle the top with chives or herb sprigs and serve warm.

AS THIS IS SO RICH . . .
it's a good idea to keep anything to go with it simple: a watercress, witlof and orange salad, with its deep mineral flavour and sharp tingle of citrus, works very well, as does a platter of slow-roasted tomatoes. If you're after cooked greens, spears of broccolini tossed in a little olive oil would be rather fabulous too.

A wonderful, easy upside-down tomato and basil 'pie'

SERVES 6

IF YOU'D LIKE TO GET THIS READY AHEAD OF TIME . . .

you can have the tomato part already sitting in the pie dish, and the wet and dry ingredients for the topping ready in separate bowls. All you need to do then is mix them together and spoon the batter over the top, before popping the whole lot into the oven.

This is one of my great stand-bys when I want something really delicious that looks special but doesn't take forever to make. The recipe was in my first cookbook, *Belinda Jeffery's 100 Favourite Recipes* and I've been both astounded and delighted by the number of people who tell me that they make it regularly, and now make their own versions of it too. I'm told by a very good cook that a layer of sautéed onions over the diced tomatoes is particularly delicious; another friend adds slivers of olives and semi-dried tomatoes to the batter.

1 × 800 g can diced tomatoes

1½ cups (225 g) self-raising flour

1 teaspoon salt

1 teaspoon dry mustard powder

100 g parmesan, freshly grated

50 g good cheddar, finely grated

125 g cold unsalted butter, cut into chunks

2 eggs

⅓ cup (80 ml) milk

a couple of shakes of Tabasco sauce

6 medium-sized ripe tomatoes
(preferably Roma), thinly sliced

⅓ cup finely shredded basil

basil leaves, to serve

1 Preheat your oven to 180°C. Butter a shallow 26 cm round ovenproof dish and line the base with buttered baking paper. Set it aside.

2 Pour the canned tomatoes into a sieve over a bowl and leave them to drain. Give them a stir occasionally to make sure as much liquid seeps away as possible.

3 Meanwhile, whiz the flour, salt and mustard together in a food processor. Add the cheeses and whiz again to just mix them in. Scatter the butter chunks over the top and process until the mixture resembles coarse breadcrumbs. (If you don't have a food processor, you can do all this in a bowl and rub the butter in by hand.) Tip the mixture into a bowl.

4 In another bowl, whisk together the eggs, milk and Tabasco sauce. Make a well in the cheese mixture and pour in the egg mixture, then stir together to make a fairly stiff batter.

5 Lay the sliced tomatoes in overlapping circles in the base of the buttered dish so the bottom is completely covered. Spread the drained tomatoes evenly over the top and sprinkle them with the shredded basil. Dollop spoonfuls of the batter over the basil and tomatoes, then, with lightly floured hands, pat it out with your fingers to spread it evenly. (Don't worry if there are a few little gaps – they fill out as the pie cooks.)

6 Bake the pie for 30–35 minutes or until the topping has risen and is golden. (The time will vary a bit depending on how thick your dish is.) Test it by inserting a fine skewer into the topping; if it comes out clean the pie is ready. Remove the pie from the oven and leave it to settle in the dish for 5 minutes before inverting it onto a warm serving platter. Mop up any juices that seep out onto the platter and scatter over some basil leaves.

Ricotta and smoked paprika tart with agrodolce capsicum

SERVES 6–8

For ages I'd been toying around with the idea of making a capsicum and ricotta tart with a little smoked paprika to deepen the flavour. So when I arrived home from the farmers' market yesterday with an armful of beautiful glossy red capsicums, it seemed like the right time to do it.

Well, we had it for dinner last night and it was terrific. I should tell you now that it's a bit more work than other recipes in this book, but it's a wonderful tart and quite a sophisticated way of using capsicum. And, you'll be pleased to know that you can make all the different components ahead of time, which makes everything much easier. The pastry shell can be baked, the capsicum cooked a few days ahead and the ricotta filling made the day before, so when you want it, all you need to do is fill the tart shell and bake it. There are quite a lot of definite flavours happening here so anything served with it is best kept simple – lightly sautéed spinach, slow-roasted tomatoes or just a green salad and loaf of good bread.

1 Pre-baked Good, Simple Shortcrust Tart Shell (see page 179), made in a 28 cm tart tin

AGRODOLCE (SWEET AND SOUR) CAPSICUM
1½ tablespoons extra-virgin olive oil
1 tablespoon pine nuts
1½ tablespoons natural sultanas
2 large red capsicums, seeded and finely chopped
3 teaspoons castor sugar
1 tablespoon red-wine vinegar
½ teaspoon sea salt

RICOTTA FILLING
90 ml cream
1 tablespoon smoked paprika, or to taste
3 eggs
700 g fresh ricotta (a mixture of soft and firm is good)
60 g freshly grated parmesan
2 tablespoons shredded basil
sea salt, to taste
90 g butter, melted and cooled
roasted pine nuts (see page 80), (optional), for topping

1 Sit the tart tin with the shell on a baking tray and set it aside.

2 For the agrodolce capsicum, heat the oil in a large frying pan with a lid over medium heat. Add the pine nuts and cook them, stirring for 1–2 minutes or until they're golden. Add the sultanas and cook them, stirring, for 30 seconds. Toss in the capsicums, sugar, vinegar and salt and quickly mix them together. Reduce the heat to low and let the capsicum bubble gently, covered, for about 20 minutes, stirring occasionally, until the capsicums are tender and glazed. Remove the lid – there should be a tiny bit of syrupy juice left, so if there's more, increase the heat to high and cook for a couple more minutes to evaporate the liquid. Take the pan off the heat and let the mixture cool to room temperature. (You can cook this mixture a few days ahead and keep it in the fridge if you like.)

3 Preheat your oven to 180°C. For the ricotta filling, put the cream into a small saucepan, then add the smoked paprika and thoroughly mix it into the cream. Place the cream over medium heat until it's hot but not boiling, then remove from the heat and leave it to cool and steep a little while you measure everything else.

4 Put the eggs, ricotta and parmesan into a food processor. Whiz them thoroughly together, stopping and scraping down the sides with a rubber spatula once or twice. Add the basil and salt, then pour in the butter and paprika-infused cream and whiz again until the mixture is thick and smooth.

5 Spread the capsicum over the base of the tart shell. Carefully smooth the ricotta mixture over the top, being careful not to disturb the capsicum layer too much. Sprinkle some roasted pine nuts over if liked and press them in gently.

6 Bake the tart for 25–30 minutes or until the filling is set – if you jiggle it gently it will be wobbly/firm (see page 33). Remove the tart from the oven and leave it to cool somewhat as it is at its best when served warm, not hot, so the full flavour has a chance to develop.

7 To serve, carefully remove the sides of the tin and slide the tart onto a platter.

SMOKED PAPRIKA IS PARTICULARLY DELICIOUS . . .

as the peppers the paprika is made from are dried over smouldering oak fires for about 2 weeks before they're cooled and ground. This gives the paprika the most wonderful rich, smoky flavour but it is quite intense so it's a good idea to add a bit less, rather than more, to a dish initially and then go from there, otherwise the flavour can be overwhelming.

A very delicious cheese and apple tart

SERVES 4–6

As kids, when we came home from school I remember us rushing into the kitchen and declaring to Cooee, our mum, that we were 'starving' and couldn't wait for dinner – for we had important things to do, like climb the mulberry tree or build massive sand fortifications on the beach (which was virtually our backyard). Many were the times that she would give us an apple and a good chunk of cheese to see us through. I always loved that combination of the crisp, sweet apple with the salty sharpness of the cheese, so this beautiful golden tart really seemed like an inevitable and classic pairing.

There's no denying that the ingredients are rich, however, it doesn't taste that way – in fact, the filling surprised me when I first made it as it is remarkably light and delicate. A smidgen of nutmeg and curry powder give it a more complex flavour and it's terrific if you play on the apple theme and serve it with something like an apple, watercress and toasted pecan salad.

1 Pre-baked Good, Simple Shortcrust Tart Shell (see page 179), made in a 26 cm tart tin

30 g unsalted butter

4 spring onions (also called shallots *or* green onions), pale parts only, thinly sliced

3 smallish Gala, Pink Lady *or* Fuji apples, peeled, cored and cut into 1 cm chunks

1½ teaspoons curry powder

¼ teaspoon ground nutmeg

4 eggs

1 cup (250 ml) cream *or* thickened cream

¾ cup (175 ml) milk

sea salt and freshly ground black pepper, to taste

350 g cheddar, Gruyère *or* good tasty cheese, grated

1 Sit the tart tin with the shell on a baking tray and set it aside.

2 Preheat your oven to 180°C. Melt the butter in a frying pan over low–medium heat. Add the spring onions and apples and cook, stirring them regularly, for 10 minutes or so until they're golden and have softened. Sprinkle in the curry powder and nutmeg and cook, stirring, for another 1–2 minutes to release their fragrance, then turn off the heat and let the mixture cool a bit.

3 Meanwhile, whisk the eggs to break them up, then whisk in the cream and milk and season to taste with a little salt and pepper. (It's a good idea to check how salty the cheese you're using is before you salt the mixture as you may not need to add any extra salt at all.) >

5 Spread the apple mixture evenly over the base of the tart shell. Sprinkle the grated cheese evenly over this. Give the egg mixture another quick whisk in case it's settled a bit, then drizzle it over the top.

6 Bake the tart for 35–40 minutes or until it's a glorious golden colour and lightly set. To check whether it is ready, insert the tip of a fine knife into the middle and gently press the sides of the cut apart – the filling should be softly set with no liquid running into the cut. Remove from the oven and leave it to cool and settle for at least 10 minutes before serving.

7 To serve the tart, slip off the outer ring of the tin and gently slide it onto a serving plate.

YOU CAN USE ALL SORTS OF CHEESES FOR THIS
More often than not I don't use anything too flash, just a decent tasty cheese, however, for a real treat try it with Heidi Gruyère from Tasmania – its rich, clean, nutty flavour makes a stunning tart as, I imagine, a good fontina would too.

Brie and pear tart

SERVES 6

Over the years I've made many variations of this glorious tart, but this classic rendition with pears is still my favourite. I've also learned that it's very forgiving – in the small country town where I live good fresh ricotta is not the easiest thing to come by, so at various times I've successfully substituted cream cheese or sour cream instead; and the pears have ended up being apples, tomatoes, and in one rather spectacular pairing, beautiful ripe figs. I've also changed the cheeses too – blue cheese, camembert and fontina all make a remarkably good tart. It also works incredibly well when made with the Crisp Cheese Pastry That Doesn't Need Rolling (page 181).

1 Pre-baked Good, Simple Shortcrust Tart Shell (see page 179), made in a 26 cm tart tin
350 g brie, cut into small chunks
150 g fresh ricotta
2 eggs
7 egg yolks
sea salt, to taste
ground nutmeg, to taste
300 ml cream
1 large just-ripe pear, thinly sliced lengthways
butter, for dotting

AS YOU CAN IMAGINE, THIS TART IS RICH . . . so it's good to off-set it with some slightly bitter, nutty greens. A salad of watercress, rocket, witlof, avocado and fine slivers of pear scattered with toasted pecans makes a fabulous partner.

1 Sit the tart tin with the shell on a baking tray and set it aside.

2 Preheat your oven to 180°C. Whiz the brie and ricotta together in a food processor until they're fairly smooth (there will still be little lumps of brie, but that's fine.) Add the eggs and egg yolks and whiz them until combined, stopping and scraping down the sides once or twice with a rubber spatula.

3 Sprinkle in salt and nutmeg to taste (be careful with the nutmeg as it is pretty powerful – what you're after is a gentle hint of spiciness). With the processor running, pour the cream in through the feed tube. Continue whizzing the filling until it's thick and creamy.

4 Pour the filling into the tart shell and gently lie the pear slices, with the narrower ends pointing inwards, in a circle on top of the filling. Dot a little butter onto each pear slice.

5 Bake for 35–40 minutes or until the tart is wobbly/firm (see page 33) when you jiggle it gently and has puffed up and smells unbearably good. Leave it to settle in the tin for 10 minutes or so – you will find it sinks a little as it settles.

6 When you're ready to serve the tart, remove it from the tin and slide it onto a platter. By the way, if you happen to have any leftover tart it reheats remarkably well – just sit it on a baking tray and heat it through in a 180°C oven until it's slightly puffed and the pastry has crisped up again.

Egg, leek and bacon pie

SERVES 6–8

We're a great family of picnickers and can always find a good excuse to break out the picnic rug – it may be for anything from Easter or a friend's birthday to somebody having a new boyfriend who we all want to meet. And everybody has their particular dish that they bring along: 'Auntie' Beryl's Jewish almond cake, Cassie's thyme-roasted chicken – and for me, it's usually a pie of some sort. I've always loved the idea of old-fashioned egg and bacon pies where you break the whole eggs straight into the pastry case, so a few picnics ago I decided to try one – it was terrific and very enthusiastically eaten.

It's based on a traditional recipe which I haven't gussied up too much; although the addition of the leeks and herbs, while not strictly orthodox, is very good. And if you don't give a fig about tradition and want to try something completely different, give it a whirl with smoked salmon instead of bacon – it's scrumptious.

I'm afraid not just any eggs will do for this; they are the crux of this pie so they need to be the best, freshest eggs you can find, for they make all the difference to the final flavour.

1½ quantities Good, Simple Shortcrust Pastry (see page 177)
   or 600 g bought shortcrust pastry
2 large leeks, white part only, well washed and sliced *or* 2 large onions, roughly chopped
8 large rashers bacon, rind removed and finely chopped
¼ cup chopped parsley
1 tablespoon snipped chives
11 fresh free-range *or* organic eggs
½ cup (125 ml) milk *or* cream
ground nutmeg, to taste
freshly ground black pepper, to taste
1 egg yolk, mixed with 1 teaspoon water, to glaze

1 If you are making the pastry, make and chill it.

2 To cook the leeks, put them in a microwave-proof dish, partially cover them with plastic film and microwave on high for 2–3 minutes or until they're just tender (otherwise you can steam them). Leave them to cool.

3 Fry the bacon in a frying pan over medium heat until it is pale golden, then scoop it into a bowl and leave it to cool.

4 Preheat your oven to 190°C. Divide the pastry into two balls – about two-thirds of the quantity for the base and one-third for the lid. Roll the largest ball out thinly on a lightly floured chopping board so it's big enough to completely line a 24 or 26 cm tart tin with a removable base. Put the tart tin on a baking tray and line it with the rolled pastry, gently easing it into the corners and leaving a little pastry hanging over the edge. Roll out the remaining pastry to make a lid, then carefully transfer it to another baking tray and put it in a cool (not cold) spot. >

5 Scatter the cooled leeks and most of the bacon over the base of the pastry case. Sprinkle just over half of the herbs evenly over the top.

6 Break 10 of the eggs, one at a time, into a cup, then slide each one into the pastry case, being careful not to break the yolks; it's no great drama if you do, it just looks nicer if the yolks are whole. Carefully scatter the rest of the bacon and herbs over the top of the eggs.

7 Whisk together the remaining egg and milk or cream and drizzle this over the top. Sprinkle on a little nutmeg and freshly ground black pepper.

8 Dampen the edges of the pastry case with a little water and drape the pastry lid gently on top, letting it settle lightly over the mound of each egg. Using your fingers, press the pastry lid and base together to seal the edges. Use a sharp knife to trim away the overhanging pastry, leaving a 2 cm rim all the way around. Roll this overhanging rim in to form a border for the pie and pinch to seal it tightly.

9 Roll out any pastry scraps and cut them into leaves to decorate the top of the pie – if you mark the veins with a blunt knife they look really lovely. Dampen the bottom of the leaves with a little water, then sit them on top of the pie. Taking care not to pierce the yolks, use a fork to poke holes in the pastry lid to form steam vents so any steam can escape as the pie bakes. Brush the top with the egg yolk and water glaze.

10 Bake for 50–55 minutes or until the pie is golden and smells wonderful. Sit the tin on a wire rack and leave it to cool completely before removing the tart from the tin. It's great served at room temperature or cold and any leftovers keep well in the fridge for 3–4 days.

A WONDERFUL VARIATION ON A THEME
As I mentioned, I also make a rather special version of this pie using 300 g of roughly chopped smoked salmon instead of the bacon. Unlike bacon, there's no need to cook the salmon – you can just scatter it, along with the cooked leeks, into the pastry case. And, if I have a bit of fresh dill on hand, I use it to replace the parsley, as its flavour is so delicious with smoked salmon.

Plum and hazelnut crostata

SERVES 8–10

I know it's a cliché, but in cooking, as in so many things, more often than not, simple is best. Nothing highlights the truth of this more than this rustic tart, which is neither more, nor less, than a short, buttery round of pastry enveloping sticky, intensely fragrant plums and the faintest tantalising whiff of roasted nuts. It's easy to make as it's not meant to look at all perfect – you can shape it in a pizza pan or just make a free-form tart on a baking tray (it may look a bit higgledy-piggledy but for me that only adds to its charm). I should also say that, much to my surprise, the very small bit that was leftover when I first made it held up really well in the fridge for a couple of days; even the pastry was still quite crisp.

> 1 quantity Good, Simple Shortcrust Pastry (see page 177)
> ¼ cup roasted hazelnuts *or* almonds (see page 80), finely chopped
> ½ cup (110 g) castor sugar
> ¼ cup (35 g) plain flour
> 1 teaspoon ground cinnamon
> 1 kg just-ripe plums
> ⅓ cup (110 g) good-quality plum jam (optional)
> double thick cream (see Ingredients page 5), to serve

1 Make and chill the pastry.

2 For the filling, in a small bowl, thoroughly mix together the hazelnuts, ¼ cup (55 g) of the sugar, flour and cinnamon, then set aside. Slice the plums thickly, discarding the stones.

3 Preheat your oven to 200°C. Line the base of a large round pizza pan (about 30–35 cm diameter) or a baking tray with baking paper, then set it aside.

4 On a lightly floured bench, roll the pastry out thinly into a big circle that will completely cover the pizza pan and leave a 5–6 cm overhang all around. Lift the pastry up on your rolling pin and unroll it over the pizza pan. Press it very gently into the sides. >

5 Sprinkle the pastry base evenly with the nut mixture, then sit the plum slices, slightly overlapping, in concentric circles over the top. Sprinkle the remaining sugar over the plums (taste the plums while you're slicing them so you can get an idea of how sweet they are, and how much sugar they may need – it could be a little bit more or less). Fold the overhanging pastry gently in over the plums so it forms a border of pastry. Sprinkle this lightly with a little more sugar.

6 If you are using a baking tray instead, then centre the rolled pastry sheet on the tray. Sprinkle the nut mixture evenly over the pastry, leaving a 5–6 cm border around the edge. Sit the plum slices, slightly overlapping, all over the nut mixture, then sprinkle with sugar. Fold the pastry border over the plums at the edge to form the rim of the crostata, then sprinkle it with a little more sugar.

7 Bake the crostata for about 40 minutes or until the fruit is tender and the crust is golden brown, then transfer it to a wire rack.

8 Just before the crostata is due to come out of the oven, heat the jam, if using, in a small saucepan over low heat until it is melted and just bubbling. Gently brush it over the plums. Leave the crostata to cool in the pan or on the tray.

9 To serve the crostata, slide it carefully onto a large platter. Although it is delicious as is, I think it is even better with a dollop of double thick cream.

Italian pumpkin and mostarda tart

SERVES 8–10

This is an unusual, sophisticated and lovely dessert tart. It's refined and somewhat low-key, with its burnished orange top simply decorated with a scattering of pine nuts. Perhaps the two most unusual things about it are the small amount of polenta in the pastry, which gives it a really satisfying crunch; and the *mostarda* (mustard fruits), which add an elusive 'hot' note to the delicately-spiced filling.

If you haven't encountered mustard fruits before, they're an intriguing northern Italian preserve of large pieces of plump fruit that are cooked in a dense sugar and vinegar syrup spiked with mustard and spices. The flavour is sweet and mildly hot all at once and can be quite addictive. In Italy, they're traditionally served with cotechino, a type of rich pork sausage, and lentils. While it may not be quite so traditional, we often have *mostarda* at Christmas as it's wonderful with ham and turkey.

If you can't find any for the tart, just finely slice some really good glacé fruit instead – it's not quite the same but is still very delicious. I often tend to bake the pumpkin the day before, then leave it in the fridge until I need it.

1 quantity Good, Simple Shortcrust Pastry (made with the polenta variation)
    (see page 177)
600 g piece butternut pumpkin, peeled and seeded
½ cup (110 g) castor sugar
2 tablespoons Amaretto *or* overproof (dark) rum *or* Cognac
1 egg
1 egg yolk
¼ teaspoon ground nutmeg
½ teaspoon ground cinnamon
1½ teaspoons vanilla extract
220 ml thickened cream
2 chunks crystallised ginger, finely sliced
⅓–½ cup Mostarda di Cremona (Italian mustard fruits,
    available from delicatessens), plus 3 teaspoons of syrup
2 tablespoons pine nuts
double thick cream (see Ingredients page 5), to serve

1 Make and chill the pastry, then blind bake it in a 26 cm tart tin with a removable base following the instructions on page 180. Sit the tart tin with the shell on a baking tray and set aside.

2 Preheat your oven to 180°C. Put the pumpkin on a baking tray lined with baking paper. Bake for about 40 minutes or until the pumpkin is tender when you pierce it with a skewer. Leave it to cool, then chop it into chunks, mash it well and chill it if you're not using it straight away.

3 Put the pumpkin, sugar, Amaretto, egg, egg yolk, nutmeg, cinnamon and vanilla extract into a food processor and whiz them together until they're smooth. Pour in the cream and pulse the processor a few times until the mixture is just combined. Using a spatula, stir in the ginger and *mostarda*, including the syrup, then pour the filling into the prepared pastry shell. If the mustard fruits tend to clump in one spot, use the spatula to spread them out a bit more evenly. Scatter some pine nuts over the top.

4 Bake for about 40 minutes or until the tart filling is wobbly/firm (see page 33) when you wiggle the tin gently. Remove it from the oven and leave it to cool in the tin on a wire rack.

5 To serve the tart, carefully slip off the outer ring of the tin, then gently slide it onto a serving platter. I find running a palette knife carefully between the bottom of the tart and the base of the tin as you're doing this helps it to slide off more easily.

6 Serve the tart with a bowl of double thick cream. Occasionally I spike this cream with a little Amaretto and vanilla extract to pick up the mellow almond flavour of the liqueur in the tart.

Simple pear galette

SERVES 8–10

I really don't like mucking about with too many flavours in dishes when I'm cooking and this galette epitomises that ideal. It's one of those classic, magical combinations that is so very much more than the sum of its parts. Basically it's crisp buttery pastry encasing, in this instance, fragrant pears, but it could be any fruit that's in season – apples, peaches, nectarines or plums are all terrific. There's not much more to it than that – just clear, pure flavours that only need the softening touch of good cream to make them perfect.

I like some of the pear slices to have quite dark caramelised edges. If they're a bit pale once the galette is baked, I brush them with a little warmed apricot jam, then cover the pastry border with strips of foil (or it will burn) and slide the tart under a hot grill for a minute or two to caramelise the pears.

The galette keeps quite well so you can bake it a few hours before you need it. I'm always surprised that, even a couple of days after being baked, the pastry is still quite crisp if you store any leftovers in the fridge.

SWEET SHORTCRUST PASTRY
1½ cups (225 g) plain flour
¼ teaspoon salt
2 tablespoons castor sugar
125 g cold unsalted butter, cut into
    small chunks
¼ cup (60 ml) iced water

BISCUIT FILLING
60 g shortbread biscuits, crushed
⅓ cup (75 g) castor sugar
2 tablespoons plain flour
1 teaspoon ground cinnamon
5 just-ripe medium-sized pears
30 g unsalted butter, melted
2 teaspoons vanilla extract
1–2 teaspoons white granulated sugar
apricot jam and icing sugar (optional),
    to serve

1 To make the pastry, put the flour, salt and sugar in a food processor and whiz them together. Add the butter and process until the mixture resembles coarse breadcrumbs. While the processor is running, pour in the iced water, then whiz until the mixture forms a ball of dough around the blade. Remove the dough and bring it gently together, then flatten it into a disc. Wrap it tightly in plastic film and chill for about 40 minutes or until it's firm but pliable enough to roll out. (You can make the pastry a day or two ahead.)

2 Preheat your oven to 210°C. Line a large round pizza pan (about 30–35 cm diameter) with baking paper.

3 For the biscuit filling, in a bowl, mix the crushed biscuits with 2 tablespoons of the sugar, the flour and cinnamon. Peel, quarter and core the pears, then cut each quarter into 5 thin wedges. Put them into a large bowl, then sprinkle them with the remaining sugar, melted butter and vanilla extract. Use your hands to very gently mix them all together.

4 On a lightly floured chopping board, roll the pastry out thinly into a round that will completely cover the pizza pan and leave a 5–6 cm overhang all around. Lift the pastry up on your rolling pin and gently unroll it over the pizza pan, then press it very gently into the sides.

5 Spread the biscuit filling evenly over the base. Scatter the pear slices, higgledy-piggledy, over the top so that they completely cover it (or if you like a neater finish, sit overlapping rings of pear slices over the biscuit mixture). Drizzle any pear juices left in the bowl over the top. Gently fold the overhanging dough back over the fruit to form a pastry border, then sprinkle the white granulated sugar over the pastry.

6 Bake the galette for about 35 minutes or until the pastry is crisp and golden brown. Remove from the oven and cool the galette on the pizza pan.

7 Just before the galette is due to come out of the oven, heat the jam, if using, in a small saucepan over low heat until it is melted and just bubbling. Gently brush it over the pears.

8 Leave the galette to cool for at least 40 minutes so the filling has a chance to firm up. With the help of the baking paper underneath, gently slide the galette onto a serving plate.

9 Dust the galette lightly with icing sugar, if liked, and serve it with rich cream or vanilla ice-cream.

Adding a teaspoon or two of finely grated lemon zest to the pastry dough is particularly good with the pear filling.

slices and bars

A repertoire of slices is a wonderful thing to have

In my teens I remember baking up batch after batch of slices as they were always in demand at school fetes and carnivals. They're wonderful for when you want rather a lot of something as they're usually baked in fairly big slabs, so you get lots of bang for your buck, as it were. I must say that some of the most delicious recipes in this book are here – like the Chocolate and Pecan Higgledy-Piggledys (page 208), My Favourite Toffee and Almond Slice (page 212) and the Raspberry and Coconut Bars (page 220). Of all the things I baked and tested, these got the thumbs up again and again.

I have to confess that there's not much you need to know about making these slices as the recipes are so straightforward and simple. Something I do find, however, is that often slices are easier to cut if they're slightly chilled. This is particularly so for ones that have a nut topping, as if the filling is still soft and warm they tend to tear rather than cut neatly. The other thing I do in the 'cutting department' is to rest a ruler over the top of the tin (or slab of slice if I've removed it from the tin) so I can use it as a guide to cut straight lines, as otherwise mine tend to be all over the place. Something else I've noticed that may help is that if the slice is fairly soft it's better to cut it with a straight-edged knife rather than a serrated one, which can tear the surface.

You may also find, as I do, that some of these make terrific desserts if you dress them up a little, particularly the Luscious Lemon Slice (page 219), Coconut and Caramel Slice (page 222) and the Raspberry and Coconut Bars (page 220). If I'm going to use them for dessert I usually cut them into diamonds or long narrow bars so they look a bit more elegant, and often serve them with some fruit such as berries, or a sauce to tart them up (the Luscious Homemade Caramel Sauce on page 257, is sensational with the Coconut and Caramel Slice).

Chocolate and pecan higgledy-piggledys

MAKES LOTS (DEPENDING ON HOW BIG THE PIECES YOU BREAK THEM INTO ARE)

I'm sometimes a little embarrassed when I'm asked for this recipe as it feels almost like a Clayton's recipe – it's just so easy. I never really know what to call these as they're neither a bar nor a biscuit but fall somewhere in between, as you don't slice it into bars, but snap it into higgledy-piggledy pieces, thus our family name for them. They are perfectly scrumptious, far more so than it would seem from such simple ingredients, and it's very hard to stop at one (which is why I break them into both big and little pieces so I feel as though I'm not overdoing it if I eat two small ones rather than a large one – ah, the psychology of eating!).

It's rare that I mention a brand name in my recipes, but I really have to in this case, as McVitie's Digestive biscuits are by far and away the best to use.

BASE
21 McVitie's Digestive biscuits
   (about 320 g), finely crushed
½ cup (110 g) brown sugar
¼ teaspoon salt
200 g unsalted butter, melted and cooled

TOPPING
300 g good-quality dark chocolate,
   finely chopped
200 g roasted pecans, walnuts *or* almonds
   (see page 80), thinly sliced (or use slivered almonds)

1 Preheat your oven to 180°C. Line a 37 × 25 × 2.5 cm (or thereabouts) baking tray with foil, leaving a 5 cm overhang all around. Press the foil snugly into the corners. Set aside.

2 For the base, in a large bowl, thoroughly mix together the crushed biscuits, brown sugar and salt. Pour in the cooled butter and stir together until the mixture looks like wet sand. Tip the mixture into the prepared tray. Use your hands to spread it evenly over the base of the tray, then press down on it firmly to compact it.

3 Bake the biscuit base for 12–14 minutes or until it's a little darker and smells 'toasty'. Remove from the oven and leave it to settle for 1 minute so it firms up slightly.

4 For the topping, scatter the chocolate all over the top of the base as evenly as you can, then return it to the oven for 1 minute to soften the chocolate. Use a palette knife (one with an off-set handle is ideal), to spread the melted chocolate smoothly over the surface. Sprinkle over the nuts, pressing down on them gently to embed them into the chocolate. Leave the tray to cool on a wire rack for 45 minutes.

5 Pop the tray in the fridge (or freezer, if you're in a hurry) for 20 minutes or so until the biscuit base is firm. Holding onto both ends of the foil, lift the whole slab out of the tray, then carefully peel away the foil from the base. Use your fingers to break the slab into pieces. Layer the pieces between sheets of baking paper in airtight containers.

6 Store the higgledy-piggledys in the fridge, where they'll last well for at least 2 weeks. They can also be frozen for up to 1 month.

Walnut and caramel bars

MAKES 24 SMALL OR 12 LARGE BARS

This is a remarkably quick and simple slice that somehow tastes even better than the sum of its parts – the base is lovely and crunchy and the topping is addictively chewy. I find that when I make these bars I become acutely aware of them sitting in the fridge and I'm convinced they are sending out messages, saying 'eat me, eat me' – so that I seem to be forever trekking to and fro for just another fine sliver!

If you like a gooey, chewy slice, then use dark brown instead of regular brown sugar.

BASE
160 g plain flour
70 g castor sugar
120 g cool unsalted butter, cut into
    small chunks

TOPPING
2 eggs
70 g castor sugar
70 g brown sugar
1 teaspoon vanilla extract
2 tablespoons plain flour
1 teaspoon baking powder
½ teaspoon ground cinnamon
½ teaspoon salt
200 g walnuts *or* pecans, coarsely chopped
icing sugar, for dusting

1 Preheat your oven to 180°C. Butter a 23 cm square cake tin and set aside.

2 For the base, put the flour and sugar into a food processor and whiz them together for 10 seconds. Add the butter and whiz again until the mixture resembles fine breadcrumbs – it will seem a bit dry but that's okay. Tip the mixture into the prepared tin and shake the tin to level it, then press down firmly on the mixture to form an even layer.

3 Bake the base for 20 minutes or until the edges are golden brown. Remove it from the oven and sit it on a wire rack while you make the topping.

4 For the topping, put the eggs, castor sugar, brown sugar and vanilla extract into a large bowl and whisk them until they're well combined. In a smaller bowl, stir together the flour, baking powder, cinnamon and salt, then sift them into the egg mixture. Stir until it is well combined, then mix in the nuts.

5 Scrape the nut mixture evenly over the warm pastry base. Return the tin to the oven and bake for another 20 minutes or until the topping is brown and firm to the touch. Leave the slice to cool in the tin on a wire rack.

6 When the slice is cool, cut it into fingers or squares in the tin. Dust them with icing sugar to serve. Store any leftover bars in an airtight container in the fridge for up to a week (they also freeze well for 2–3 weeks).

Cooee's chewy bran bars

MAKES 16–24 BARS

I grew up eating these bars and I found the handwritten recipe for them in my mum's old cookbook. I love this book as it reminds me so much of her – it's wonderful to see her handwriting and read all the extra little notes and changes she made to recipes as she went along; it must run in the family. I suspect these bars probably came about as a quick and inexpensive way to satisfy the seemingly insatiable appetites we three children had when we arrived home from school. There were nearly always some of them (or something else homemade) for afternoon tea, and contrary as children are, all I longed for were the bought green-iced frog cakes that I was given when I visited my best friend! By the by, there's a little trick to eating these (the sort of thing that kids hone in on) – while they taste great at room temperature, the best way to eat them is cold, straight out of the fridge, when they're chewy, buttery and positively addictive.

CUTTING BARS INTO NICE EVEN PIECES
As I've already mentioned, I'm hopeless at cutting bars into nice even pieces – they usually end up all sorts of different shapes and sizes, which I rather like. However, if I want them to look particularly neat, the only way I can do this is to sit a ruler over the top of the tin and use it as a guide to cut the lines – it works rather well.

1 cup (160 g) stone-ground wholemeal self-raising flour

1 cup (60 g) unprocessed wheat bran

1 cup (220 g) brown sugar

200 g dried fruit, including raisins, sultanas, currants, chopped dried apricots
or whatever you happen to have in the cupboard

250 g unsalted butter, melted and cooled

1 teaspoon vanilla extract

1 Preheat your oven to 180°C. Butter a 30 × 20 × 5 cm slice tin and set it aside.

2 Tip the flour, bran and brown sugar into a large bowl and mix them thoroughly together. Add the dried fruit and toss it about in the mixture. Pour in the melted butter and vanilla extract, then mix everything together. Press this slice mixture firmly into the prepared tin as evenly as you can.

3 Bake for about 25 minutes or until the slice is brown and feels a bit like a firm sponge when you press it. (I know it seems quite soft at this stage, but don't worry, it hardens considerably as it cools.) Leave the slice to cool in the tin on a wire rack for 20–25 minutes or until it's firmed up a bit, then cut it into squares or bars. Once they are completely cool, lever the bars out of the tin. Store them, layered with baking paper, in an airtight container in the fridge. They keep well for a week or so – sadly, ours have never lasted past this length of time so I really can't tell you the exact 'use by' date.

My favourite toffee almond slice

MAKES ABOUT 30–40 PIECES

When I make this I forever think of my mum, Cooee, as caramel and nuts were two of her favourite things. When she no longer cooked, I used to make this and bring it down to her as she had a really sweet tooth and a meal was never complete for her without 'a little something sweet' to finish it off. I can still see her sitting by the window, her lovely, long, elegant fingers reaching for one, then two, and inevitably, three slices of this, and saying, 'Oh, I know I really shouldn't, darling, but . . .' It's such a happy memory. I do love the way that food links us with our past and our loved ones, as I can almost feel her warm and comforting presence standing beside me in the kitchen when I make this.

BASE
250 g unsalted butter, at cool room temperature
1 cup (220 g) castor sugar
2 egg yolks
½ teaspoon vanilla extract
2 cups (300 g) plain flour
½ cup (75 g) self-raising flour
⅓ cup (40 g) custard powder
½ teaspoon salt

TOPPING
1 cup (220 g) brown sugar
2 tablespoons honey
180 g unsalted butter
¼ teaspoon salt
250 g flaked almonds
1 teaspoon vanilla extract

1 Preheat your oven to 180°C. For the base, in a large bowl, beat the butter and sugar on medium speed with an electric mixer for 5 minutes or until they're light and fluffy. Add the egg yolks one at a time, beating well after each one is added, then mix in the vanilla extract. Sift the flours, custard powder and salt into the bowl and mix everything together on low speed until it's well combined. >

2 Scrape the dough into a buttered baking tin (32 × 24 × 5 cm) and pat it out with your hands so it covers the base evenly. Roll a small tumbler over the top to help smooth it out.

3 Bake for 25–30 minutes or until the base is puffed up and golden brown. Meanwhile, about halfway through the cooking time, start preparing the topping. Put the brown sugar, honey, butter and salt in a heavy-based saucepan over low heat. Stir until the butter melts and the sugar dissolves, then stop stirring and simmer the mixture for 10 minutes. Add the almonds and vanilla extract and mix them in well, then take it off the heat and keep warm.

4 When the base is ready, remove it from the oven and leave it to cool for a few minutes. Pour the warm topping over it, working quickly to spread it out evenly otherwise it will start to set and you'll end up battling to get it smooth. Return the slice to the oven and bake for another 12–15 minutes or until the top is slightly bubbly and golden. When it's ready, transfer it to a wire rack to cool.

5 Once the slice is barely warm, gently loosen around the edges and cut it into bars or diamonds. Leave it to cool completely in the tin, then gently lever out the pieces. Store them in airtight containers layered with baking paper. They keep well for about 5 days (or longer if you store them in the fridge), although the base will soften a bit over time. They also freeze well for up to 3 weeks.

DRESSING UP

If you want these for a special occasion, you can make them look rather swish by piping a little melted chocolate over the top of each one. Now, before you start shaking your head and thinking I've gone mad to suggest you even contemplate piping, the sort of piping I'm talking about is really easy. Just melt a little dark chocolate and spoon it into the smallest size of snap-lock bag that you can find. Snip a tiny piece off one corner of the bag so you can squeeze the chocolate through it in a thin line. And now just go for it – zig-zag the chocolate back and forth across the slices, then leave it to set. And, if that still seems too daunting, then just dip a spoon into the melted chocolate and drizzle it over the top.

My mum's pistachio and walnut baklava

MAKES 30–40 SMALL DIAMONDS

This recipe may seem a somewhat unusual addition to this chapter, sitting here as it does amongst the more familiar slices and bars, however, my mum, Cooee, loved to cook, and early on experimented with all sorts of dishes from around the world. For us kids it was fantastic, as we all loved our food and revelled in this culinary journey, which took us from China to Japan, the Middle East and beyond in the space of a few days' meals. I remember arriving home from school the first time she made baklava and being bowled over by the exotic, spicy, honey-sweet fragrance of it baking. And it was such an eye-opener to eat: rich and crunchy with the nuts, subtly spicy and marvellous to bite into as the honey syrup squelched out very satisfyingly as you did. Although mum's original recipe was so smudged and faded that I could barely read it, after some experimenting I think this comes pretty close to the mark.

200–250 g unsalted butter

500 g filo pastry

250 g shelled pistachios, finely chopped

250 g roasted walnuts *or* pecans
   (see page 80), finely chopped

½ cup (110 g) castor sugar

1 teaspoon ground cinnamon

¼ teaspoon ground nutmeg

40 whole cloves (optional)

HONEY SYRUP

1½ cups (330 g) castor sugar

1 cup (250 ml) water

⅓ cup (120 g) clear honey

½ cinnamon stick

finely chopped zest 1 lemon

2 tablespoons lemon juice

finely chopped pistachios (optional),
   for sprinkling

1 Gently melt the butter in a small saucepan over very low heat, then leave it to cool. Once it's cool, use a spoon to skim off any white scum that floats on top, then carefully pour the clear golden liquid that remains into a jug – you'll find there will be some milky-looking sediment underneath this, so try and leave it behind as it's made up of milk solids from the butter and they tend to burn as the baklava bakes.

2 Brush a 32 × 24 × 5 cm baking tin with some of the butter. Cut the filo sheets in half widthways and trim them so they're a similar size to the tin. Cover them with a damp tea towel to keep them pliable and stop them drying out.

3 In a bowl, thoroughly mix together the nuts, sugar, cinnamon and nutmeg. Line the base of the prepared tin with a third of the filo sheets, brushing each sheet very lightly with the melted butter as you go. You may have to slightly overlap the sheets if they don't quite fit the tin, and make sure you press them into the corners and sides too. Sprinkle half the nut mixture evenly over the filo and shake the tin gently to even it out. Repeat the layering with another third of the filo and butter, then top with the remaining nut mixture. Layer the remaining filo over this, brushing it with butter as you go, then brush the top with butter too. If necessary, trim and discard any excess filo from around the sides of the tin with a sharp knife.

4 Put the tin in the fridge for about 20 minutes or so to firm up the baklava so it's easier to score. When it's firm, use a fine sharp knife to score the baklava, right through to the base, into diamonds of whatever size you want. Push a clove, if using, into the centre of each one.

5 Meanwhile, preheat your oven to 180°C. Bake for about 1 hour or until the top of the baklava is deep golden brown. Check it occasionally and cover it loosely with foil if it seems to be browning too quickly.

6 Meanwhile, for the syrup, combine the sugar, water, honey and cinnamon stick in a saucepan over high heat. Stir the mixture until the sugar dissolves, then stop stirring and bring it to the boil. Reduce the heat to very low and simmer the syrup, uncovered, for 20 minutes, skimming off any white foam that floats on the surface. Remove the syrup from the heat, discard the cinnamon stick and stir in the lemon zest and juice. Keep the syrup in a warm spot.

7 When the baklava is ready, remove it from the oven. Cool it on a wire rack for 1 minute, then slowly drizzle the warm syrup evenly over the top. Leave it to cool completely – the flavour is best if the baklava mellows for 12 hours or so before serving.

8 To serve the baklava, cut down through the score marks to loosen the diamonds, then ease them out. You can leave the cloves in (but remember to take them out before eating a piece because the cloves pack a powerful punch), or pull them out and sprinkle the tops with chopped pistachios, if liked.

9 Store the baklava, tightly covered with plastic film, in the baking tin. It keeps well at cool room temperature for about 5 days. It's still fine to eat after that, but tends to dry out a bit. Or you can store it in the fridge for up to 10 days. It becomes a bit firm and chewy from the cold, which I rather like, however, the texture is probably better if it's returned to room temperature before serving.

IF YOUR EXPERIENCE OF BAKLAVA IS OF
SOMETHING TOOTH-ACHINGLY SWEET . . .
and too sticky by half, please don't pass this recipe by; it really is fabulous – neither too sweet nor too cloying. You can also alter the flavour by using different nuts; I quite often use almonds, pecans or macadamias instead.

Luscious lemon slice

MAKES 20–24 MEDIUM-SIZED BARS

I really feel as though I should call this a lemon tart rather than a slice as the gloriously golden, tart-sweet topping is so velvety that more often than not I use it as a dessert rather than something to have with a cup of tea or coffee. Actually that's not true; quite frankly, I'll eat this any way I can, as I'm mad about lemon in sweet things – its sharp edge just has that brilliant way of cutting cleanly through sweet, rich flavours.

BASE
1½ cups (225 g) plain flour
½ cup (80 g) icing sugar, sifted
finely grated zest of ½ lemon
180 g cold unsalted butter, cut into small chunks
½ teaspoon vanilla extract
2 teaspoons iced water

LEMON TOPPING
6 eggs
3 cups (660 g) castor sugar
finely grated zest of 3 lemons
1 cup (250 ml) lemon juice, strained
½ cup (75 g) plain flour
icing sugar, chopped pistachio nuts *or* fresh berries (raspberries
    and/or blueberries are lovely) and cream (optional), to serve

1 Preheat your oven to 180°C. Lightly butter a 32 × 24 × 5 cm baking tin and set it aside.

2 For the base, put the flour, icing sugar and lemon zest into a food processor and whiz them together. Add the butter and process it until the mixture resembles coarse breadcrumbs. With the processor going, add the vanilla extract and iced water and whiz the mixture until it forms a ball around the blade. Take it out and press the dough evenly into the prepared tin. Gently roll a tumbler across the top of the dough to smooth it out. Bake the base for about 18 minutes or until the edges are starting to colour and the top is pale golden.

3 While the base is cooking, make the lemon topping. In a large bowl, beat the eggs and sugar with a balloon whisk until they are well combined; you don't have to beat this like crazy, just make sure it's thoroughly mixed. Whisk in the lemon zest and juice. Sift the flour over the top and whisk it in until the mixture is smooth. Set it aside.

4 When the base is ready, transfer it to a wire rack to cool. Reduce the oven temperature to 150°C. Once the base has cooled for 5 minutes, whisk the filling briefly again, as it will have settled a bit, then pour it over the base. Return the tin to the oven and bake for another 35–40 minutes or until the topping is set. Leave the slice to cool in the tin on a wire rack. >

5 Once the slice is completely cool, use a sharp knife to cut it. I vary the shapes depending on what I'm using it for: I tend to cut narrow bars for everyday; small squares to have with coffee (that's to fool myself I'm only eating a little bit – the trouble is I usually eat three or four of them!); or elongated diamonds if it's for dessert, as they look quite elegant.

6 Just before serving the slice, dust the tops with a little icing sugar and sprinkle them with a few chopped pistachio nuts. If you're making this into a dessert, put one slice on each plate and pile berries up on top so some tumble onto the plate. Dust the berries with a little icing sugar, then serve with a dollop of cream on the side.

7 If you're not using the slice straight away, cover the tin tightly with plastic film and keep it in the fridge for 3–4 days. You'll find the bottom will become a bit soggy as time passes but it still tastes wonderful.

Raspberry and coconut bars

MAKES ABOUT 12 NARROW BARS

I don't know what it is about raspberries, perhaps it's because their season is so fleeting and their flavour so intense, but for me they always make even the simplest dish seem somehow special and luxurious – especially in the case of this scrumptious slice, where the intense tang of the raspberries is the perfect contrast to the lush coconut topping. And it really needs little to transform this into a dessert: just cut slightly narrower bars, which makes them look more elegant, and serve them with extra raspberries and a spoonful of rich cream.

BASE
1 cup (150 g) plain flour
¼ cup (40 g) icing sugar mixture
125 g cool unsalted butter

TOPPING
2 eggs
1 cup (220 g) castor sugar
¼ cup (35 g) plain flour
½ teaspoon baking powder
¼ teaspoon salt
½ teaspoon ground cinnamon
½ cup (40 g) desiccated coconut
1 teaspoon vanilla extract
3 teaspoons lemon juice
150 g fresh *or* defrosted and drained
    frozen raspberries
flaked almonds (optional), for topping
icing sugar, for dusting

1 Preheat your oven to 180°C. Lightly butter a 20 cm square cake tin and set it aside.

2 For the base, tip the flour and icing sugar into a food processor and whiz them together. Add the butter and whiz again until the mixture forms a ball of dough around the blade. You can do this by hand too; just mix the flour and sugar together, then rub in the butter.

3 Press the dough evenly into the base of the prepared tin. I find it often ends up with lots of little indents from my fingers in it, which can make it cook a bit unevenly, so I usually roll a thick tumbler over the top when I've finished; this helps to smooth it out.

4 Bake the base for 25 minutes or until it's golden. Not long before the base is due to come out of the oven, make the topping. In a large bowl, whisk the eggs and sugar together with a balloon whisk until they're well mixed. In a separate bowl, whisk together the flour, baking powder, salt, cinnamon and coconut for about 40 seconds. Add this flour mixture to the egg mixture, along with the vanilla extract and lemon juice. Mix them all thoroughly together until the mixture is smooth (apart from the bits of coconut). Gently fold in the raspberries; do this carefully or they break up and leave crimson streaks in the batter.

5 Pour the topping over the hot base, then sprinkle with the flaked almonds, if using. Return the tin to the oven for 40–45 minutes or until the top is a bit puffy and golden. When it's ready, leave the slice to cool in the tin on a wire rack.

6 You can slice this as soon as it has cooled down – in fact I've often sliced it while it's still warm because I can't bear to wait. However, if you can exercise a bit more restraint than me it's not a bad idea to chill it before slicing as the top is a bit crumbly and it tends to slice more neatly when it's cold. Once it's cold, you can either cut the slice in the tin or loosen it around the edges (make sure you get right down to the bottom of the tin) and carefully turn it out onto a chopping board. Turn it right-way up for slicing. Use a sharp knife to cut it into bars, diamonds or squares; for a nice clean edge to each slice, carefully wipe the blade of the knife clean between each cut.

7 To serve the bars, dust them with icing sugar. Store any leftover bars, layered between sheets of baking paper, in an airtight container in the fridge for a couple of days or in the freezer where they keep well for up to 3 weeks.

IN CASE YOU'RE WONDERING WHY . . .
the base needs to be nearly cooked through and hot when you add the topping, it's because both of these things help stop the topping seeping into it, so when the slice is baked you end up with quite a crisp base. It's a textural thing really, as this crispness is a really satisfying contrast with the smooth richness of the topping.

Coconut and caramel slice

MAKES 24 BARS

Coconut and caramel are an irresistible combination; here they go together in a buttery shortbread base with a luscious caramel and coconut topping that sets with a thin, crisp crust. When the slice is freshly baked the surface is addictively crunchy, however, once chilled it becomes a bit more chewy, but that, in its own way, is very appealing too.

I've tried making this with desiccated coconut, which also works, but the shredded coconut is what gives the bars their terrific macaroon-like texture.

BASE

2¼ cups (335 g) plain flour

½ cup (80 g) icing sugar

250 g cold unsalted butter, cut into
    small chunks

1 teaspoon vanilla extract

TOPPING

3 eggs

2 tablespoons coconut cream, stirred

1 tablespoon milk

2 teaspoons vanilla extract

45 g butter, melted and cooled

1 cup (220 g) firmly-packed brown sugar

½ cup (110 g) castor sugar

1 tablespoon plain flour

1½ cups (105 g) shredded coconut

handful of lightly toasted flaked almonds,
    for topping

icing sugar (optional), to serve

1 Line the bottom and sides of a lightly buttered 32 × 24 × 5 cm slice tin with baking paper, then set aside.

2 For the base, whiz the flour and icing sugar in a food processor. Add the butter and vanilla extract and whiz until the mixture just comes together to form a dough. Press the dough evenly into the bottom of the prepared tin. It tends to look a bit bumpy so I roll a straight-sided tumbler over it to even it out. Chill it in the fridge for 15 minutes; this helps stop it from shrinking when it's baked.

3 Preheat your oven to 180°C. Bake the base for about 25 minutes or until it's golden. Transfer it to a wire rack to cool. Reduce the oven temperature to 150°C.

4 Meanwhile, for the topping, lightly whisk the eggs in a large bowl. Whisk in the coconut cream, milk, vanilla extract and butter. In another bowl, mix together both sugars and the flour (or you can whiz these together in the food processor if you still have it out). Stir the flour mixture into the egg mixture, then add the shredded coconut and mix everything thoroughly. Spoon the topping over the cooled base and sprinkle the almonds evenly over the top. >

5 Bake for about 45 minutes or until the topping is set and golden. Leave the slice to cool in the tin on a wire rack. Once it's cool, slice it into fingers or bars; if you briefly chill it in the fridge first you'll find it cuts more evenly. I use a straight-edged knife for this as a serrated one tends to tear through, rather than cut, the topping – I suspect it's to do with the strands of coconut.

6 Layer the bars between sheets of baking paper in an airtight container. Store them in the fridge, where they keep well for up to 1 week. They also freeze well and will last for up to 3 weeks. When you're ready to eat them, dust the bars with a little icing sugar. They're lovely with a cup of tea or coffee, and when cut slightly larger they make a surprisingly good dessert served with a little cream.

Chocolate, caramel and pecan slice

MAKES 24–30 PIECES

The recipe for this irresistible gooey slice seems to have been around forever – or certainly since condensed milk was invented. I remember making a similar slice to this for our school fete when I was nine years old. I loved it, but then again at that age I loved anything with condensed milk in it. I was one of those kids that could happily spoon the sticky syrup straight out of the tin and into my mouth, much to my mother's dismay. All I can remember now was that it was tooth-achingly sweet – and absolute bliss.

I have made this version slightly more sophisticated with its roasted pecan topping, but you can easily leave that off if you prefer the tried-and-true original.

BASE
180 g unsalted butter, at room temperature
¾ cup (165 g) firmly-packed brown sugar
1 egg yolk
1 teaspoon vanilla extract
1½ cups (225 g) plain flour
¼ teaspoon salt

FILLING
1 × 400 g can sweetened condensed milk
30 g unsalted butter
1½ tablespoons golden syrup
2 teaspoons vanilla extract

TOPPING
360 g good-quality dark chocolate,
  finely chopped or grated
200 g lightly roasted pecans (see page 80)

1 Preheat your oven to 180°C. Butter a 32 × 24 × 5 cm baking tin and set it aside.

2 For the base, in an electric mixer, beat the butter and brown sugar on medium speed for 5 minutes or until they're light and fluffy. (I tried to avoid using the mixer; however, the base just didn't work as well when I made it in the food processor.) Add the egg yolk and vanilla extract and beat them in well. Reduce the speed to low (otherwise you'll end up with flour flying everywhere, as I've learnt the hard way) and add the flour and salt. Mix them in only until they just combine to form a dough.

3 Flour your hands lightly, then press the dough evenly over the base of the prepared tin. Roll a lightly floured tumbler over the top to smooth it out.

4 Bake the base for 15–20 minutes or until it is light brown. Leave the base to cool on a wire rack.

5 For the filling, heat the condensed milk in a small heavy-based saucepan over low heat until it's bubbling. Stir it constantly while you do this as it burns really easily. Continue to cook it, stirring all the time, for 5 minutes or until it thickens a bit. (Don't worry if it is a little lumpy at this stage, I invariably find I have a few brown speckles and lumps in mine but it doesn't affect the finished slice.) Thoroughly mix in the butter, golden syrup and vanilla extract.

6 Pour the warm condensed milk mixture over the base and spread it out evenly with the back of a spoon. Return the tin to the oven and bake for another 12 minutes or until the filling is pale golden and set. Remove it from the oven.

7 For the topping, immediately sprinkle the chocolate over the caramel layer. Use the back of a spoon to spread the chocolate evenly. Return the tin to the oven and bake the slice for another 5 minutes or until the chocolate is soft and melting. Sit the tin on a wire rack and use a palette knife to smooth the melted chocolate evenly over the caramel layer. Press the roasted pecans decoratively into the chocolate, then leave the slice in the tin to set and cool completely.

8 To cut it, carefully loosen the slice around the edges and ease it out onto a chopping board so it sits pecan side-up. Cut the slice into bars or whatever shapes you like with a large, sharp knife. For a really nice clean edge to the bars, so you can see the layers clearly, dip the knife into hot water and wipe the blade dry in between each cut.

9 To store the slice, layer it between sheets of baking paper in an airtight container and put it in the fridge. The slice keeps well for up to 1 week, but it's best to return it to room temperature before eating it, so it has its proper luscious texture.

quick sweet and savoury tea breads and soda breads

These simple breads gladden the heart and warm the soul

Including these appealing, old-fashioned breads and cakes in this book came about because I make them so often and find that everyone just loves them – much more so than an elaborate cake or gateau. They're usually wolfed down, with seconds and thirds nearly always on the agenda (and that's just the sort of thing to gladden a cook's heart). I think it's probably because they have that wonderful homely taste that smacks of cosiness, honesty and simple, good things. It's the kind of baking that, if you were lucky, your gran or mum did, or if not, you wished that they had!

Not all the breads here are sweet by any means. I particularly wanted to include some that were more like 'real' bread but without all the kneading and rising involved, because so many people ask me about making bread but find the prospect of doing it rather daunting, especially the thought of using yeast. I find even the mention of the word 'yeast' in my cooking classes is enough to give most students the heebies!

Baking yeast breads is actually a wonderful thing to do – very therapeutic and utterly satisfying. However, it does need time and patience, and both of those things are in somewhat short supply at times with the way we all seem to whiz about from pillar to post. What I've done instead is include a couple of quick soda bread recipes, which come pretty close to the real thing (especially the dense, richly flavoured Pumpernickel and Polenta Soda Bread on page 237), without all the kneading and rising involved in baking regular loaves.

As to the remaining recipes – they're so simple to make that there's not much I can add about them here. Probably the only thing I should mention is that I've noticed that the majority of loaf tins are dark non-stick ones. As I said earlier (see page 10), these tend to cook considerably more quickly and get hotter than regular tins, so I find breads and tea breads baked in them can dry out a little and form a thicker crust. The best way to counteract this is to line the tin with buttered baking paper and lower the oven temperature by 10–15°C. I know it's a bit of a fiddle, but it makes a huge difference.

Cheese, olive and buttermilk herb bread

MAKES 1 LOAF

This simply made, herb-flecked bread really is very good. Although it doesn't have the robust texture of regular bread, it has a scrumptious cheese flavour and is lovely served with soups; it's also remarkably good toasted when it's a day or two old.

When we get together with friends in winter, we'll often just have a stand-your-spoon-up-in-the-bowl sort of soup, a loaf of this bread and a big green salad. It's a simple but satisfying and ever-so-delicious meal, which we usually round out with a fruit tart or crumble for dessert. I find that it's a relaxed, low-key way to entertain, and it's the little things like homemade bread that make it so special.

2¼ cups (335 g) plain flour

2 teaspoons baking powder

½ teaspoon bicarbonate of soda

1 teaspoon salt

1 teaspoon freshly ground black pepper

½ teaspoon dry mustard powder

60 g freshly grated parmesan

60 g cheddar *or* good tasty cheese, grated

½ cup (75 g) stuffed olives, sliced

¼ cup snipped chives

2 teaspoons thyme leaves *or* 1 teaspoon dried thyme

2 eggs

2½ tablespoons olive oil

1¼ cups (310 ml) buttermilk

egg wash (optional), made from 1 egg yolk beaten with 2 teaspoons water

extra thyme sprigs and sea salt, for topping

1 Preheat your oven to 180°C. Butter a large loaf tin (about 23 × 13 × 6 cm) and either line it with buttered baking paper or dust it with flour, then set it aside.

2 Put the flour, baking powder, bicarbonate of soda, salt, pepper and mustard powder into a large bowl. Whisk them together with a balloon whisk for 1 minute (or you can just sift them into the bowl instead). Add both of the cheeses, the olives, chives and thyme and stir them thoroughly together.

3 In a separate bowl, whisk the eggs, then whisk in the oil and buttermilk until they're well combined. Make a well in the middle of the flour mixture and pour in the buttermilk mixture. Stir together until they form a thick, sticky batter. Scrape this into the prepared tin and smooth it out evenly. If you're using the egg wash, brush it over the top, then sprinkle some small thyme sprigs and sea salt onto the loaf. >

4 Bake for 40–45 minutes or until a fine skewer inserted in the middle of the loaf comes out clean – you can almost tell by the tantalising aroma alone when it's ready. Remove from the oven and leave the loaf in the tin for 5 minutes, then turn it out onto a wire rack, remove the paper and leave it to cool.

5 Like most of the breads in this chapter, it tastes best when it's still barely warm or at room temperature. If you find you have leftover bread, wrap it tightly and store it in the fridge for up to 3 days. When you want to use it, wrap it loosely in foil and heat it gently in a 150°C oven. It is still fine for a few more days after that, but is best sliced and toasted.

THERE ARE SO MANY VARIATIONS YOU CAN MAKE TO THIS RECIPE . . .
I find I invariably flavour it slightly differently every time I bake it. Semi-dried tomatoes or roasted capsicums are just as delicious as olives; the thyme can be replaced with oregano or rosemary; a touch of chilli adds a nice little kick; Gruyère or firm goat's cheese is a welcome change from cheddar; and rather than the thyme and sea salt topping, sesame or nigella seeds are especially good and add a nice crunch.

Zucchini and kumara tea bread

MAKES 2 LOAVES

When we moved to the country I was so chuffed to have the space for a veggie garden that I went a bit mad with the planting and we ended up with zucchini just about coming out of our ears. We ate them every-which-way: with pasta, in frittatas, baked, stuffed, steamed and fried – you name it. Finally, I decided it was time to resort to plan B – a little something sweet. As I have a really soft spot for old-fashioned tea breads, and zucchini makes a really moist loaf, it was inevitable that this recipe was high on my list. It's light, spicy, very easy to make and not too sweet – just perfect spread with a little butter or ricotta and washed down with what's referred to in my family as a 'nice cup of tea'.

By the way, this makes two loaves; one for now and one to freeze for later.

> IF YOU DON'T HAVE A KUMARA LURKING ABOUT IN THE CUPBOARD . . .
> *pumpkin, carrot or parsnip all make good substitutes.*

1¾ cups (260 g) plain flour

1¼ cups (200 g) stone-ground wholemeal plain flour

2½ teaspoons ground cinnamon

1 teaspoon ground nutmeg

2 teaspoons baking powder

1 teaspoon bicarbonate of soda

½ teaspoon salt

250 g roasted pecans *or* walnuts (see page 80)

300 g raisins *or* natural sultanas

1 cup firmly-packed grated zucchini (about 2 medium-sized zucchini)

1 cup firmly-packed grated kumara (about 1 small kumara)

3 eggs

½ cup (110 g) castor sugar

½ cup (110 g) firmly-packed brown sugar

½ cup (125 ml) light olive oil

½ cup (125 ml) buttermilk

2 teaspoons vanilla extract

pecan *or* walnut pieces, for topping

1 Preheat your oven to 180°C. Butter and flour two 21 × 11 × 6 cm loaf tins and set them aside.

2 Put both flours, the cinnamon, nutmeg, baking powder, bicarbonate of soda and salt into a very large bowl and use a balloon whisk to mix them together for 1 minute. Stir in the pecans and raisins so they're coated in the flour mixture. Tip in the grated zucchini and kumara and toss them about to mix them in well; I use my hands for this as it's the easiest way to mix everything together evenly.

3 In another bowl, whisk together the eggs and both sugars with a balloon whisk until they're well mixed. Whisk in the oil, buttermilk and vanilla extract. Pour this mixture into the zucchini mixture and stir them together until they're just combined. Divide the batter evenly between the two tins, sprinkle the tops with nuts and pop the loaves in the oven.

4 Bake for about 50 minutes or until a fine skewer inserted in the middle of the loaves comes out clean. Leave them to settle in their tins on a wire rack for 10 minutes, then turn them out onto the rack to cool completely. One thing that I've noticed with these is that the flavour is better if the loaves are left overnight – not that they get much chance of this in my home!

A funny little pumpkin cornbread

SERVES 4–6

This makes a funny flat, square loaf of 'bread' (if you can call it that – I'm really not quite sure what to call it, as it's quite moist and not at all loaf-shaped). However, I have a real soft spot for it and find I'm forever slicing thin slivers off to nibble on when I make it. The pumpkin and nutmeg give it a rich, spicy flavour and it has a beautiful deep golden hue. If you're trying to avoid wheat you can replace the small amount of flour with fine polenta or rice flour; you'll just find the texture is a little more gritty when you eat it.

It's lovely with soup and it also makes rather fabulous nibbles to have with a drink, if you top small chunks with a dollop of goat's curd, roasted red capsicum and a tiny basil leaf.

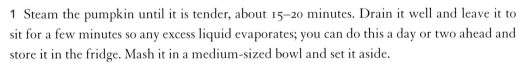

375 g butternut or jap pumpkin, peeled, seeded and cut into 3 cm chunks	½ teaspoon bicarbonate of soda
150 g fine stone-ground yellow polenta, (cornmeal) (see page 130)	¼ teaspoon ground nutmeg
	45 g unsalted butter
1½ tablespoons plain *or* spelt flour (or use rice flour if you want it to be gluten-free)	¾ cup (180 ml) buttermilk
	1 egg, lightly beaten
3 teaspoons baking powder	pepitas (pumpkin seeds), (optional), for topping
1 teaspoon salt	

1 Steam the pumpkin until it is tender, about 15–20 minutes. Drain it well and leave it to sit for a few minutes so any excess liquid evaporates; you can do this a day or two ahead and store it in the fridge. Mash it in a medium-sized bowl and set it aside.

2 Preheat your oven to 200°C. Put the polenta, flour, baking powder, salt, bicarbonate of soda and nutmeg into a bowl and whisk them together for 40 seconds. Set the bowl aside.

3 Put the butter into a 20 cm square non-stick cake tin and pop the tin in the oven for the butter to melt. Thoroughly stir the buttermilk and egg into the mashed pumpkin.

4 Remove the tin from the oven and swirl it around so the sides and base are coated in melted butter. Tip the excess butter into the pumpkin mixture, beating it in as you go. Pour the pumpkin mixture onto the dry ingredients. Mix them lightly together just until everything combines into a 'shaggy' batter. Scrape the batter into the cake tin and give it a shake to smooth the surface. Scatter some pepitas over the top if you're using them.

5 Bake for about 25 minutes or until the bread is light golden and has slightly shrunk from the sides of the tin. Press the middle gently with your finger; if it feels springy it's ready. Remove from the oven and cool the bread in the tin for at least 10 minutes, then turn it out onto a flat plate, invert it again onto a wire rack and leave it to cool a little longer.

6 When you're ready to serve, slice the bread into chunks. It's really at its best warm or at room temperature, however, leftovers keep surprisingly well in the fridge in an airtight container for up to 5 days. Just bring them to room temperature or warm them gently before eating them.

Pumpernickel and polenta soda bread

MAKES 1 SMALL LOAF (RECIPE CAN BE DOUBLED TO MAKE 2 LOAVES)

This dense dark loaf has a rich caraway flavour and just the faintest earthy hint of molasses. I love that it tastes and looks just like a loaf of 'real' rye bread but is remarkably quick to make (it takes less than 20 minutes from when you first think about it until it's in the oven).

Just one thing with this – it's important to be aware that batches of flour vary somewhat in the amount of moisture they absorb. So if the dough seems a bit too sticky when you bring it together, add a little extra plain or rye flour to it, but no more than ¼ cup (35 g).

fine polenta, for dusting

¾ cup (120 g) stone-ground wholemeal plain flour, plus a little extra, for dusting

½ cup (75 g) unbleached plain flour

½ cup (60 g) rye flour

¼ cup (40 g) fine stone-ground yellow polenta (cornmeal) (see page 130)

1½ teaspoons baking powder

½ teaspoon bicarbonate of soda

1 teaspoon sea salt, crushed

1 teaspoon caraway seeds, plus extra, for sprinkling

1⅓ cups (330 ml) buttermilk

1 tablespoon honey

1 tablespoon blackstrap molasses

BLACKSTRAP MOLASSES
This nearly black, treacly syrup isn't used so much nowadays, however, in the past, a spoonful of it was mandatory for children as it is high in minerals, especially iron, calcium, manganese, copper and potassium. It has a robust bittersweet flavour that I find quite addictive; interestingly, if your iron levels are low you may find you actually crave it once you taste it. It's available from health food stores.

1 Preheat your oven to 210°C. Lay a sheet of baking paper on a baking tray and dust the paper with a little polenta.

2 Tip all three flours, the polenta, baking powder, bicarbonate of soda, sea salt and caraway seeds into a large bowl. Whisk them together for a minute or so with a balloon whisk. In a separate bowl, mix together the buttermilk, honey and molasses. (If you gently warm the honey and molasses they will mix into the buttermilk more easily.)

3 Make a well in the middle of the dry ingredients and pour in the buttermilk mixture. I usually start mixing this with a wooden spoon and then resort to using my hands when it gets too sticky. The one thing you don't want is to overdo the mixing as this toughens the bread (which, to be confusing, is the opposite to yeast breads, which require lots of kneading). Bring the dough together so it's soft and sticky, then tip it onto a floured bench. (It's a good idea to have the bench floured before you start – I sometimes forget and end up with dabs of dough on everything I touch as I try to flour the bench after the event!)

4 With floured hands, knead the dough very gently so it just comes together, then shape it into a little football. Sit the 'football' on the prepared baking tray and, with a serrated knife, make 4–5 very shallow slashes diagonally across the top of the dough (if they're too deep the loaf opens out a bit too much while it bakes and is drier than it should be). Sieve a fine dusting of flour over the top and sprinkle with extra caraway seeds.

5 Bake for about 30–35 minutes or until the bottom of the loaf sounds hollow when you tap it with your knuckles. Leave the loaf on a wire rack to cool for about 1 hour before slicing. Unlike many soda breads, leftovers keep well for 1–2 days in a sealed plastic bag.

Spicy pumpkin, pecan and raisin tea bread

MAKES 1 LARGE LOAF

VARIATIONS ON A THEME
You can make lots of different versions of this bread depending on what you have on hand. Carrots or parsnips work just as well as pumpkin; you can replace the raisins with dates or sultanas, ditto the nuts by using other types of nuts such as hazelnuts or almonds. It's a pretty forgiving sort of tea bread so if you want to bump up the quantity of spices that's not a problem.

This loaf is a little unusual as it's made with raw pumpkin rather than cooked. When I think about it, I probably make this dark, sticky bread every second week, as it freezes really well and I love the way the pumpkin gives it such a dense, luscious texture. It has a terrific flavour and is a great mid-morning or afternoon pick-me-up. I tend to make it with spelt flour, however, you can use stone-ground wholemeal flour instead. It is remarkably easy to make once you have everything measured out.

1 cup (160 g) organic spelt flour (see Ingredients page 6) *or* stone-ground wholemeal plain flour

1 cup (220 g) firmly-packed dark brown sugar

1 teaspoon bicarbonate of soda

1½ teaspoons ground cinnamon

½ teaspoon ground ginger (or more, if you like ginger)

½ teaspoon ground nutmeg

1 cup (170 g) raisins

1 cup (140 g) roasted pecans *or* walnuts (see page 80), roughly chopped

1½ cups grated pumpkin (butternut or jap are good, as they are so sweet)

2 eggs

⅓ cup (80 ml) light olive oil

½ cup (125 ml) milk

1½ teaspoons vanilla extract

pepitas (pumpkin seeds) *or* coarsely chopped pecans, for topping

1 Preheat your oven to 180°C. Butter a large non-stick loaf tin (about 23 × 13 × 6 cm) and line the base with buttered baking paper, then dust with flour and set aside.

2 In a large bowl, use a balloon whisk to mix together the flour, brown sugar, bicarbonate of soda, cinnamon, ginger and nutmeg. Do this for a couple of minutes so any lumps in the sugar disappear. Tip in the raisins, pecans and pumpkin and toss them about so they're well-coated in the flour mixture.

3 In a separate bowl, whisk together the eggs, oil, milk and vanilla extract until they're smooth and creamy. Pour this egg mixture into the flour mixture and stir them together until they're well combined. Scrape the batter into the prepared tin, smooth it out and sprinkle pepitas or pecans over the top.

4 Bake for about 1 hour or until a fine skewer inserted in the middle of the loaf comes out clean. Cool the loaf in the tin on a wire rack for 8 minutes, then gently loosen around the sides before turning it out onto the rack to cool completely.

5 You can freeze the loaf whole, but what I usually do is slice it, put freezer wrap between each slice, and then freeze it; it keeps well in the freezer for 3–4 weeks. This way you can just take out a slice or two (or three or four!) as you need them.

Healthy banana and apricot loaf

MAKES 1 LARGE LOAF

When we had our café I tried to keep a balance between offering healthy and not-so-healthy (but all very delicious) cakes, so I was always on the lookout for new ideas and recipes to try. This not-too-sweet loaf became quite a feature on our menu as, despite using stone-ground wholemeal flour and extra wheat bran, it's moist and surprisingly light. Many of our regular customers who wouldn't touch anything labelled 'healthy' with a barge pole, bless them, would make a bee-line for it; although, I must say that on more than one occasion the order would come into the kitchen with a request for 'lashings of butter' to slather over it.

1½ cups (240 g) stone-ground wholemeal self-raising flour
½ teaspoon bicarbonate of soda
1 cup (60 g) unprocessed wheat bran
⅓ cup (75 g) raw sugar
¼ teaspoon salt
½ cup (75 g) chopped dried apricots (dates are particularly good too)
½ cup (70 g) roasted pecans *or* walnuts (see page 80), coarsely chopped
¼ cup (60 ml) milk
125 g unsalted butter, cut into chunks
½ cup (125 ml) buttermilk
1½ teaspoons vanilla extract
2 eggs
3 medium-sized ripe bananas, mashed (about ¾ cup mashed)
extra pecans (optional) and apricot glaze (see page 246), (optional), for topping
ricotta, cottage cheese *or* butter, to serve

1 Preheat your oven to 180°C. Butter a loaf tin (about 23 × 13 × 6 cm) and line the base with buttered baking paper; I usually cut a long strip so it runs up the two narrow ends as well. Dust the tin with flour and set it aside.

2 Put the flour, bicarbonate of soda, bran, sugar and salt into a large bowl and whisk them together with a balloon whisk for about 40 seconds. Add the apricots and pecans and toss them about so they're well coated in the flour mixture. Make a well in the middle of the mixture, then set it aside.

3 Heat the milk in a small saucepan until it's just about to start boiling – you'll see the little bubbles forming around the edge. Take it off the heat and stir in the butter until it's completely melted, then whisk in the buttermilk and vanilla extract.

4 In a separate bowl, lightly whisk the eggs, then pour in the buttermilk mixture, whisking as you pour. Scrape in the mashed banana and whisk it in too. Tip this into the well in the dry ingredients and stir the two together until they're just combined.

5 Scrape the batter into the prepared tin and smooth it out. At this stage I sometimes decorate the top with pecans to make it look a little bit special as otherwise it's quite a plain-looking loaf.

6 Bake for about 45 minutes or until the loaf is golden and a fine skewer inserted in the middle comes out clean. Leave it to settle in the tin for 5 minutes or so, then carefully ease the loaf out of the tin onto a wire rack. Gently pull away the baking paper, sit the loaf so it's right-side up, and leave it to cool completely on a wire rack.

7 If you would like to glaze the loaf, make the apricot glaze following the instructions, then brush it on about 30 minutes before you plan to serve it, so it has a chance to set.

8 In the café we served slices of this with a small pot of ricotta or cottage cheese, but it is also very good served simply with butter. It keeps well in an airtight container in a cool spot for 5 days and it also freezes well for up to 3 weeks. If I'm freezing it I usually slice it first, then layer the slices between sheets of freezer wrap or baking paper in a container so I can pull one or two out as I need them.

Sticky banana, pecan and date loaf

MAKES 1 LARGE LOAF

AS I'VE ALREADY
MENTIONED . . .

*I often make two of these and
freeze one. Rather than leaving
the one destined for the freezer
whole, I usually slice it, then
layer it between sheets of freezer
wrap. The nice thing about doing
this is that you can then just pull
out a slice or two when you need
a little pick-me-up, knowing
that there's plenty left for later.
Well, that's the theory anyhow.
I've rarely known it to last longer
than a week at home – even if
I bury it behind everything else,
it still mysteriously disappears.*

I must admit that the tea breads in this chapter are my most favourite things to bake in this book; I love their simplicity and directness. And obviously I'm not the only one – I can't tell you how many times I've whipped up this irresistible loaf when we've had unexpected visitors and they just demolish it. It has a rich, almost caramel-like flavour that's reminiscent of sticky toffee pudding – I'm not even sure why, it's just the combination of ingredients that does the trick.

With such a response, I've finally learnt to double the recipe when I make it so I have a back-up loaf in the freezer. It keeps remarkably well; some cakes and tea breads tend to lose their fresh flavour quite rapidly when they're frozen, however, not this one – it's great for up to two months and, if anything, just gets better.

1¼ (185 g) cups spelt flour (see Ingredients page 6) or plain flour	1 cup (220 g) castor sugar
1 teaspoon bicarbonate of soda	2 eggs
1 teaspoon ground cinnamon	½ cup (125 ml) light olive oil
½ teaspoon salt	3 very large ripe bananas, mashed (about 310 ml)
120 g roasted walnuts *or* pecans (see page 80), roughly chopped	1½ teaspoons vanilla extract
220 g pitted dates, roughly chopped	sunflower seeds *or* pepitas (pumpkin seeds) *or* both, for topping

1 Preheat your oven to 180°C. Butter a large loaf tin (about 23 × 13 × 6 cm) and dust it with flour. Set aside.

2 Put the flour, bicarbonate of soda, cinnamon and salt into a medium-sized bowl and whisk them together with a balloon whisk for 45 seconds (or you can just sift them into the bowl instead). Add the nuts and dates and toss them about so they're thoroughly coated in the flour mixture.

3 Put the sugar, eggs and oil into another bowl and whisk them together for 1–2 minutes or until they're light and creamy (the mixture is quite thick so your mixing arm will get a bit of a workout!). Add the mashed banana and vanilla extract and whisk them in for another 30 seconds or until the mixture is fairly smooth (don't worry that it's not completely smooth – there will still be some little lumps of banana in it).

4 Stir the dry ingredients into the banana mixture until they form a somewhat sloppy batter. Scrape this into the prepared tin and sprinkle some seeds on top.

5 Bake for about 1 hour or until the top of the loaf is springy and a fine skewer inserted in the middle comes out clean. Cool the loaf in the tin on a wire rack for 10 minutes, before turning it out onto the rack to cool completely. It keeps well in the fridge for about 5 days.

Spicy apple, aniseed and hazelnut tea bread

MAKES 1 LARGE LOAF

I love the flavour of aniseed and it adds such an unusual note to this moist apple-studded loaf. I often make it to munch on through the week, so I don't always do the whole catastrophe with the nuts on top and the glaze, but they do make it look rather lovely if you're baking it for a special morning or afternoon tea.

1 cup (160 g) stone-ground wholemeal
   plain flour
1 cup (150 g) plain flour
¾ cup (165 g) castor sugar
2 teaspoons baking powder
½ teaspoon bicarbonate of soda
½ teaspoon salt
1 teaspoon ground cinnamon
½ teaspoon ground nutmeg
2 teaspoons aniseeds
100 g roasted hazelnuts (see page 139),
   very roughly chopped
120 g natural sultanas
2 eggs
1 cup unsweetened chunky apple sauce *or*
   Quick Apple Sauce (see page 245)
⅓ cup (80 ml) apple juice
½ cup (125 ml) light olive oil
1½ teaspoons vanilla extract
hazelnuts (optional), halved, for topping

APRICOT LEMON GLAZE
½ cup (160 g) apricot jam
juice of 1 small lemon
1 tablespoon water

1 Preheat your oven to 180°C. Butter and flour a large loaf tin (about 23 × 13 × 6 cm), then set it aside.

2 Tip both of the flours, the sugar, baking powder, bicarbonate of soda, salt, cinnamon, nutmeg and aniseed into a large bowl. Whisk them together for 1 minute so they're thoroughly mixed. Scoop about 1 tablespoon of this mixture into a small bowl, then add the chopped nuts and sultanas and toss them so they're well coated in the flour mixture.

3 In a separate bowl, lightly beat the eggs. Pour in the apple sauce, apple juice, oil and vanilla extract and whisk them together. Add this to the flour mixture and stir until they're just combined. Tip in the nuts and sultanas and stir them through. Scrape the batter into the prepared tin. Decorate the top with a closely-packed layer of hazelnut halves, if you're using them. >

4 Bake for about 1–1¼ hours or until a fine skewer inserted in the middle of the loaf comes out clean. The loaf will puff up and crack slightly. Cool the loaf in the tin on a wire rack for 10 minutes, before turning it out onto the rack to cool completely. Leave it to cool top-side up.

5 Glaze the tea bread close to serving time. For the apricot lemon glaze, whisk the ingredients in a small saucepan over medium heat. Bring to the boil and let it bubble, stirring occasionally, for 3–4 minutes or until it's somewhat thickened and syrupy. Brush it over the top of the tea bread and leave it to set.

6 This bread is moist enough to serve plain but it's hard to go past just spreading a bit of butter on each slice. It keeps for 2–3 days at cool room temperature; any leftovers can be frozen for up to 3 weeks.

QUICK APPLE SAUCE
I realise that it's probably unlikely that you have apple sauce lurking about in the fridge, however, if you have some apples on hand you can make it very quickly. Peel, core and chop 2–3 apples (depending on their size), then cook them in the microwave on high until they're soft. Mash them up when they've cooled a bit, and use them instead of the apple sauce.

Prune, date and fig bran loaves

MAKES 2 LOAVES

You find lots of cheap and cheerful recipes like this in cookbooks dating from the late '40s and '50s. Like many of the recipes in those post-war years it was an economical way to use up odds and ends left in the pantry (not to mention any tea left in the tea pot), and was a very good 'filler' for hungry families.

Over time, this one has been somewhat plumped out, as it were, with extra fruit and the addition of a glazed nut topping, but you certainly don't have to do this. The original recipe was only for a single loaf but as it disappears almost immediately – I can't tell you how good a buttered slice is with a cup of tea – I double the recipe in the hope of hanging onto the other to freeze. Although I can't say that my success rate in this department is too high, as someone always manages to sniff it out within a very short space of time.

90 g All Bran breakfast cereal
1 cup (220 g) raw sugar
350 g pitted prunes, very coarsely chopped
300 g pitted dates, very coarsely chopped
250 g moist dried figs (dried currants are
   good too), coarsely chopped
½ cup (175 g) golden syrup
350 ml strained tea, cooled
1 egg, lightly beaten
2⅓ cups (350 g) self-raising flour
100 g almonds (optional), blanched
   or with skins
100 g pecan halves (optional)
butter *or* ricotta (optional), to serve

APRICOT GLAZE

½ cup (160 g) apricot jam *or* conserve
1 tablespoon cold water

1 Tip the All Bran, sugar and dried fruits into a very large bowl. Add the golden syrup and tea, then mix everything together thoroughly. Cover the mixture tightly with plastic film and leave it in a cool spot overnight.

2 The next day, preheat your oven to 165°C. Lightly butter two medium-sized (21 × 11 × 6 cm) loaf tins and line them with baking paper, then set aside.

3 Stir the egg into the dried fruit mixture so it's well combined, then mix in the flour. You'll find that the batter gets very stiff, so make sure you scrape right down to the bottom of the bowl as you mix everything together.

4 Divide the mixture evenly between the two tins and smooth it out. Stud the top of each loaf decoratively with almonds and pecans, if using. This is the sort of job I love when I'm cooking, as it's really creative and you can make all sorts of interesting patterns over the tops of the loaves. Although if you're anything like me and tend to get carried away with the design, you may find you need to use extra nuts.

5 Bake the loaves for about 1¼ hours (the time can vary quite a bit, so it's a good idea to check sooner rather than later, and go from there), or until they're deep golden and a fine skewer inserted in the middle of each one comes out clean. If the loaves start to get a bit too brown early in the piece, just cover them loosely with foil.

6 Cool the loaves in their tins on a wire rack. When they're cool, carefully loosen around the sides and ease them out of the tins. At this stage, you can just slice and serve the loaves as they are, spread with a little butter or ricotta.

7 Otherwise, you can jazz them up a bit with the apricot glaze. I must admit I rarely do this unless I want to make them look extra-special for visitors, but it's a good thing to know how to do, nonetheless. To make the apricot glaze, put the jam and water into a small, heavy-based saucepan over medium–high heat. Bring the mixture to the boil, stirring all the while. Let the mixture boil, stirring it now and then to stop it catching on the bottom, for about 5 minutes or until it thickens and becomes quite syrupy. Take the saucepan off the heat and immediately brush the glaze over the top of the loaves, then leave it to set.

DIVIDING BATTER EVENLY BETWEEN TWO TINS
I don't know about you but I don't have a very good eye for divvying up cake batter between two tins and whenever I do it I invariably end up with one tin much fuller than the other. The best way I've found to get around this is to weigh each tin when I've filled them and then dollop a little batter from one to the other until they're much the same weight.

basics and extras

A few really useful recipes that make all the difference

I always find there are a few extra recipes that don't seem to fit anywhere else in a book, but are terribly important nonetheless. There are only five recipes here – strawberry jam, ganache, a brilliant caramel sauce, chocolate curls and candied citrus zest – yet each is vital as far as I'm concerned. Scones just wouldn't be the same without a dollop of crimson strawberry jam (page 252), and there's nothing quite like the incredible colour and heady fragrance of a homemade one. Ganache (page 256), a sort of shiny dark chocolate icing that flows like satin, can make all the difference between a cake being drop-dead gorgeous and just rather nice. And last, but most definitely not least, comes the best caramel sauce ever (page 257) – rich, so thick you can almost stand a spoon up in it, luscious and perfect to add a final flourish to all sorts of cakes (not to mention what it can do for a scoop of vanilla ice-cream!).

The best homemade strawberry jam

MAKES 4 × 180–200 ML JARS

I really wanted to have a strawberry jam recipe in this book as it's easy to make and tastes so very good. When I read back through the scone chapter I realised I invariably mention serving them with strawberry jam, so it only seemed appropriate to include a recipe here. To me, despite the many beautiful cakes in the world, there really is nothing quite like eating a warm scone with a scoop of your own intensely crimson strawberry jam and a dollop of rich cream.

I promise you this recipe is not hard at all, and I can honestly say that I've never seen, nor tasted, anything quite like a really good homemade strawberry jam either – you just don't get that vibrant colour and deep berry flavour in commercial ones.

There are just a couple of things I should mention before you get started. One is that it's only worth making with really fresh, fragrant berries that aren't battered and bruised. And the other is that, short of adding a setting agent (like powdered pectin), which I don't like doing as you can always taste it, this jam won't set firmly. If the berries are really fresh then you'll get a pretty good gel, however more often than not, it's considerably more runny than its commercial cousins (but much more delicious too). However, as it's best stored in the fridge, I find this helps thicken it a bit.

I've made this recipe for 1 kg berries, but you can just use 500 g if you like and halve the sugar and lemon juice – it will give you a couple of jars. In fact, jams and marmalades in general are much better, clearer and more vibrant when they're made in small batches as you don't risk overcooking the fruit and losing its 'fresh' flavour. I think that's the comment I most often hear, in fact, when people taste this – they can't believe how 'strawberry-ish' it is.

1 kg fresh, fragrant strawberries, hulled (and halved, if large)
1 kg white granulated sugar
juice of 2 large lemons, strained

1 Put the strawberries and sugar into a very large, wide, heavy-based stainless steel or enamel saucepan. (If you don't have a really big pan, it is best to make a smaller quantity of jam, as it rises up when it boils and can spill over the sides of a pan that is too small.) Give the pan a shake so the sugar settles down into the berries. Drizzle the lemon juice over the top, cover the pan and leave it to sit for 1–2 hours.

2 Put the pan over low–medium heat and warm the mixture, stirring gently until the sugar has dissolved. Clip a sugar thermometer to the side of the pan (this isn't essential so don't worry if you don't have one, but it can help if you do). Increase the heat to very high and let the jam boil rapidly, stirring it occasionally to make sure it isn't catching on the bottom, for 15–20 minutes or until it has reached setting point. It's important to be mindful that when jam is close to setting point it bubbles up rather alarmingly in the pan, so you need to keep an eye on it and adjust the temperature a bit so it doesn't boil over (you may well need to do this a few times).

3 There are three good ways to check whether setting point has been reached and I usually do all of them to be on the safe side. First, if you're using a sugar thermometer, check that the temperature has reached 105°C. The next thing to do is to dip a clean wooden spoon into the boiling jam, then lift it up high above the pan and let the jam on it drip back in. What you're hoping to see is those last few drops looking quite thick and syrupy and ideally, running together and joining up then falling as more of a 'sheet' than individual drops (however, long fine 'tails' on them will do nicely!). It is also helpful to spoon a little jam onto an ice-cold saucer and put it in the freezer for a minute or so, then push your finger through it. If the surface wrinkles up a little, it's ready.

4 Keep testing the jam every minute or so, and as soon as it's ready, take it off the heat and let it settle for a few minutes. Ladle it into hot, sterilised glass jars, cover them with a sheet of baking paper to protect them, and leave them to cool completely. When they're ready, remove the paper and seal the jars tightly. Label and date them, then store them in the fridge for up to 4 months.

STERILISING JARS

This jam recipe begs the question of how to sterilise the jars. But just before I go into that, it's important to remember that the jars must be hot when you fill them with the hot jam, otherwise they may crack, so you need to get your timing somewhat in sync with the jam when you sterilise them. There are a few ways to prepare the jars, but the two I mainly use are these:

* *Wash the jars in warm soapy water, rinse them thoroughly then sit them and their lids (as long as the lids aren't plastic or won't melt) on a baking tray. Put the tray with the jars into a cold oven then turn the heat to 125°C. Leave the jars for 25 minutes, then carefully take them out and cover them with a sheet of baking paper until you're ready to use them. (Or you can just switch off the oven and leave them in to stay hot if the jam isn't quite ready.)*
* *The other way, if you have a dishwasher, is to put the jars and their lids through the hottest cycle and leave them in once the cycle has finished, so they stay hot until you fill them. If you find they are a bit damp inside, pop them in a low 120°C oven for a few minutes to dry them out before filling them.*

Chocolate curls

These are something that you may never have considered making yet they're surprisingly simple and fun to do. What I really like about them is that they can dress up a plain cake and make it special, which is wonderful when you're whipping up a birthday or celebration cake and want it to look gorgeous. The important thing to get right is the temperature of the chocolate: if it's too hard it will splinter as you try to curl it; and if it's too soft, it won't want to curl at all. Luckily, both problems are easy to fix.

If you find the chocolate is brittle and splinters just wave a hair dryer set at its lowest temperature over it for a few seconds and try again (or put it in a slightly warmer place and then have another go). And if it's too warm, pop it in the fridge for a minute or so to firm it up enough to roll. I find the first few curls are always a matter of trial and error to get the chocolate 'just so', but once it is they roll effortlessly.

150 g good-quality dark chocolate, chopped into small pieces

1 Put the chocolate in a heatproof bowl and sit it over a saucepan of hot, but not simmering, water. Let the chocolate melt, stirring it occasionally, until there are only a few small lumps remaining. Take it off the heat and stir it vigorously to make sure it's smooth. Pour the chocolate onto a clean, dry smooth work surface – I find a metal scone sheet or acrylic chopping board work well. Using a long palette knife, spread the chocolate thinly across the surface in as uniform a thickness as you can so it will set evenly (ideally it should be about 1 mm or less thick). Leave it to set firmly. If it's a particularly hot day, you may have to put it into the freezer for a minute or so.

2 Once the chocolate is right for rolling, sit the scone sheet or board on your bench and brace the back of it against a wall or something solid (this stops it moving about as you roll the curls). Push a wide scraper (held at roughly a 25-degree angle to the surface of the chocolate) away from you and through the chocolate until a curl forms. Then use the scraper to lift the curl off the board. Repeat this all over the chocolate sheet.

3 Store the curls between layers of baking paper in an airtight container in the freezer. They keep well for a couple of months.

Ganache (shiny chocolate icing)

MAKES ABOUT 1¾ CUPS

Ganache is lovely stuff and terribly easy to make. There are lots of different versions of it and many use cream rather than butter, but basically whatever recipe you make, you end up with a silky, chocolate glaze that forms a gorgeous glossy icing when it's poured over a cake. It's a great thing to have in your repertoire because it makes even the simplest cake look special.

I always make the full quantity of ganache even if I don't need it all as it keeps well in a tightly sealed container in the fridge for at least 3 months. And it's very useful to have on hand if you bake a cake and want to dress it up in a hurry – you can just swoosh some ganache over it and it immediately looks chic and festive.

250 g good-quality dark chocolate, cut into small chunks
125 g unsalted butter, cut into chunks
50 ml water

1 Put the chocolate, butter and water into a medium-sized, heavy-based saucepan over low heat. Let the chocolate and butter melt, stirring the mixture frequently, until the ganache is smooth. (I use a small flat sauce whisk for this, as it gets right into the corners of the pan where the chocolate tends to clump a bit.) The most important thing to keep in mind when you're making ganache is that it mustn't get too hot and boil; if it does, it becomes oily and grainy and there's not much chance of salvaging it. Once it's silky smooth, take it off the heat. Let it cool until it's barely warm and of a thick pouring consistency before using it.

2 Pour any leftover ganache into an airtight container, seal it tightly and store it in the fridge. When you're ready to use it, gently warm it over very low heat, then let it cool to the right consistency.

ENSURING THAT YOUR GANACHE SETS WITH A SHINY SHEEN
Ganache sets beautifully most of the time, however, like all chocolate, it's a bit temperamental in hot, humid weather. This is the norm where I live so I've come up with a few strategies to deal with it. If the ganache just won't set and is still sticky I put the uncovered ganache-coated cake in the fridge for a short time, so the quick burst of chilled air sets it (it can also dull the sheen if it's in too long so you need to keep an eye on it). Having said that, I also find I then need to store such cakes in the fridge, otherwise the ganache is just too soft and awkward to handle.

To store a ganache-coated cake for a few days, just put it, uncovered, in the fridge until the ganache has set, then cover it with plastic film. Before serving the cake, remove the plastic film and return the cake to cool room temperature so the ganache regains its sheen. If it's been in the fridge for a day or two it might not be quite as shiny as it was when originally iced. I must admit I have been known to whiz a hair dryer set on very low across the top of such a cake to restore its lustre – you have to be careful otherwise the ganache will melt, as I discovered on one unforgettable occasion!

Luscious homemade caramel sauce

MAKES ABOUT 2 CUPS

When we were children, on our birthdays and at Christmas time, my mum would bundle us onto a double-decker bus and take us into 'town' for the day. My sister and I would wear our best dresses and shiny black court shoes and feel terribly grown-up. There were certain places that we always visited – the museum, the doll hospital (to have our much-loved dolls fixed), and the David Jones Elizabeth Street store for new shoes (this we adored as the David Jones 'ladies' always made us feel special and would dab little samples of perfume behind our ears). But best of all was the visit to a Cahill's Brass Rail restaurant – an institution in those days. Here, if we were lucky, my lovely mum would have organised a special birthday tea for us, the highlight of which was an ice-cream birthday cake that arrived at the table aglow with candles and accompanied by a group of smiling waiters in long aprons who would sing 'Happy Birthday' – it was an unforgettable treat for a little girl. Invariably, when we left we would buy a carton of their famous caramel sauce to take back with us. And, happy as Larry and full of cake and lemonade, we would fall asleep on the long bus trip home.

Many times over the years I've tried to re-create that sauce and the happy memories that go with it, and although I know nothing will ever taste quite like it (it couldn't possibly), I think this does perhaps come as close as I'll ever get.

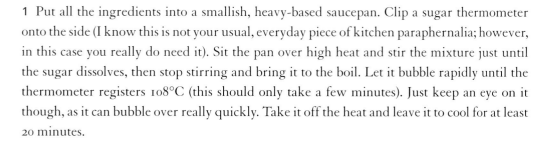

1 cup (250 ml) pure cream

1 cup (220 g) firmly-packed brown sugar

⅓ cup (75 g) castor sugar

¼ cup (60 ml) pure maple syrup

¼ cup (90 g) golden syrup

1 teaspoon vanilla extract

1 Put all the ingredients into a smallish, heavy-based saucepan. Clip a sugar thermometer onto the side (I know this is not your usual, everyday piece of kitchen paraphernalia; however, in this case you really do need it). Sit the pan over high heat and stir the mixture just until the sugar dissolves, then stop stirring and bring it to the boil. Let it bubble rapidly until the thermometer registers 108°C (this should only take a few minutes). Just keep an eye on it though, as it can bubble over really quickly. Take it off the heat and leave it to cool for at least 20 minutes.

2 You can use it warm or store it in the fridge in a tightly sealed container for up to 2 weeks. It tends to separate a little when it's cold, but just give it a good stir and it comes back together.

Candied citrus zest

These delicate strands of sugared zest look lovely strewn over the top of a lemon or orange cake (see A Really Beautiful Orange Cake, page 71). They don't keep all that long (a week at the most in an airtight container and less if it's humid), however, they're very easy to make so I tend to do them as I need them.

3 small lemons
3 small oranges
½ cup (110 g) castor sugar, plus extra, for dusting
½ cup (125 ml) water

1 You only need the brightly-coloured citrus zest for this recipe so keep the peeled fruit for another use. Remove the zest in wide strips from both the lemons and the oranges, making sure there is none of the bitter white pith attached. Slice it into very fine strips (julienne). Drop the strips into a saucepan of boiling water and leave them for 30 seconds, then drain them in a sieve.

2 Put the sugar and water into a medium-sized saucepan. Heat them over high heat, stirring all the while, until the sugar has dissolved; as soon as it has, stop stirring and bring the mixture to the boil. Tip in the drained lemon and orange zest strips and reduce the heat to low so the syrup bubbles gently. Cook the zest strips for 10 minutes, then remove the saucepan from the heat and leave them to cool in the syrup. Once cool, drain them through the sieve again. (You don't need the syrup now either, but as it has such a good, tangy, citrus flavour, it's a shame to throw it out. I usually keep it to drizzle over fruit salad.)

3 When the zest is well drained, tip some castor sugar onto a plate and toss the strips of zest in it so they're coated in the sugar. Lay them onto a sheet of baking paper to set – they don't become brittle but remain pliable. Use them as you need them and store any leftover strips in a small airtight container at room temperature for up to 1 week.

Acknowledgements

I find it hard to know where to begin thanking the many people who have made this book possible, and helped me so much along the way. However, the first thank you should certainly be to my cherished mum, Cooee, for instilling in me such a great love of cooking and for unwittingly starting me down the path of a long and fulfilling career. When your work and the thing you love to do most are one and the same, you can't help but feel very blessed.

To my family, both here and overseas, thank you so much for your unflagging encouragement and love – it's a precious thing and I treasure it.

This book would never have happened without the infectious enthusiasm and warmth of my publisher, Julie Gibbs; your support, as always, has been fantastic. Thank you for your trust, and giving me the opportunity to follow my heart.

In fact, all the 'Penguins' I've worked with have been terrific – Kathleen Gandy, my editor, who so understood what I was trying to do; Alison Cowan, who, when the manuscript finally landed on her desk, wrote me the most encouraging response I could ever have wished for; Ingrid Ohlsson, Executive Editor, and Deborah Brash, Art Director, who were so open and responsive to my ideas and helped shape the final book; Sue Van Velsen in Production, whose quality control was essential; and last, but definitely not least, Debra Billson, the designer of this book, who worked so hard to make it as beautiful as it is. Thank you all; I feel so very proud of what we have achieved.

To my close friend and truly gifted photographer, Rodney Weidland; what a treat working with you on this book has been. Thank you for the care you take, your beautiful photographs and for the happy days we spent working together – it was a special time, helped along with numerous cups of tea and pieces of cake!

It seems so very appropriate with the theme of this book that many of the props come from dear friends and family. There are three people in particular to whom I owe a very heartfelt thank you – Kim Taylor, Julie Gibbs and Don Drinkwater – who sifted and sorted through all their treasured bits and pieces to find much of the lovely linen and rustic kitchenware that makes the photos so special. Combined with family pieces Rodney and I both had, plus others sourced by David Prior, they have added a real depth and richness to these pages.

To my treasured friends, Sue and Mark Kelly, Lizi Beadman, Nick Edmond, Abigail Lewis, Chris Moss, Michelle Hartnett and Richard Kidby, our dear neighbour and number one taste tester – how can I ever thank you enough for your warmth, honesty and encouragement, especially on those days when I started to flag!

A big thank you too, to those lovely friends and colleagues who so willingly passed on recipes in the time-honoured tradition which is so in keeping with the generous spirit of this book. In particular, I would like to thank Barbara Lowery, Kate Llewellyn, Sally Rourke, Karel Moray, Kim Taylor and my 'Auntie' Beryl, whose recipes all appear here. I'd also like to say a very special thank you to Ian McCulloch, a much-loved friend and the most skillful baker I've ever known. Ian, I wish with all my heart that you could see this.

As always, my last and biggest thanks are for my darling Clive – none of this would ever happen without you. Thank you for your love, integrity and never-ending support (and for cleaning up the kitchen time and time again as we photographed this book – I know you got to lick the beaters, but it was a big price to pay!).

STOCKISTS

Art of Wine and Food,
(02) 9363 2817;
www.artwinefood.com.au

The Bay Tree, (02) 9328 1101;
www.thebaytree.com.au

Country Road Homeware,
1800 801 911;
www.countryroad.com.au

Easton Pearson,
(02) 9331 4433;
www.eastonpearson.com

Historic Houses Trust
of New South Wales –
Susannah Place Museum,
(02) 9241 1893;
www.hht.net.au

Le Forge, (02) 9516 3888;
www.leforge.com.au

Mark Conway,
(02) 9360 7806

Peppergreen Trading Co.,
(02) 4877 1122

Index

Page numbers in bold refer to photographs.

agrodolce (sweet and sour) capsicum 188–9
almonds 80
    Almond and lemon syrup cake **56**, 57–8
    Buttery almond and coconut cake
        (gluten-free) **86**, 87
    Classic flourless orange and almond
        (gluten-free) 92, **93**, 94
    My favourite toffee almond slice 212,
        213, 214
Anzac biscuits 132, **133**
apples 51, 97
    Apple, pecan and cinnamon muffins
        116, 117
    Apple and pecan crumble cake 54, **55**
    Apple, rum and raisin cake 58–9
    Kim's delicious apple, pecan and
        cinnamon cake 96–7
    sauce 245
    Scrumptious apple and plum cobbler
        166, **167**, 168
    Spicy apple, aniseed and hazelnut tea
        bread 243, **244**, 245
    Very delicious cheese and apple tart
        190, 191–2
apricots
    glaze 94, 246
    Healthy banana and apricot loaf 240–1
    lemon glaze 243
'Auntie' Beryl's Mexican wedding biscuits
    138–9

bakeware and utensils 9–10
baking times 11
baklava
    My mum's pistachio and walnut baklava
    215, **216**, 217
bananas 51
    Date, orange and banana muffins 119
    Healthy banana and apricot loaf 240–1
    Most fabulous banana cake 73–4
    Sticky banana, pecan and date loaf 242
    Sticky caramel and banana upside-down
        cake 68–9
Barbara Lowery's pecan and macadamia
    panforte **98**, 99–100, **101**
bars
    Chocolate and pecan higgledy-piggledys
        208, **209**

Cooee's chewy bran 211
    dividing evenly 11, 211, 247
    Raspberry and coconut 220–1
    Walnut and caramel 210
Belinda's polenta and vanilla shortbread
    128, 129–30
Best homemade strawberry jam 252–3
biscuits
    Anzac 132, **133**
    'Auntie' Beryl's Mexican wedding 138–9
    baking tips 125–6
    Buttery ginger squares 136, **137**, 138
    Cheese and nigella seed 135
    Crunchy peanut butter and sea salt
        143–4, **145**
    Pecan and oat crisps 127
    Sally's terrific biscotti 140, **141**, 142
    Very crisp lemon thins 146–7
    see also shortbread
Black-bottom cupcakes 22
blackstrap molasses 237
blind baking 179–80
blueberries
    Blueberry and cinnamon crumble cake 62–3
    Lemon and blueberry muffins 120, **121**
breads
    Cheese, olive and buttermilk herb 230,
        231, 232
    Funny little pumpkin cornbread 234, **235**
    Pumpernickel and polenta soda **236**, 237
    see also tea breads
Brie and pear tart 193
Brown sugar and ginger muffins 118
Brown sugar shortbread 131
brownies
    Double chocolate pecan 41
    Marbled mocha 46–7
    Mars Bar 40
    One-pan macadamia and chocolate
        chip 43, **44**, 45
    testing for doneness 17
butter
    flavoured 157, 158
    unsalted 6
buttermilk 5
    Cheese, olive and buttermilk herb bread
        230, **231**, 232
    Fluffy buttermilk scones **164**, 165

butterscotch
    Gooey butterscotch peach cake 64, **65**, 66
Buttery almond and coconut cake
    (gluten-free) **86**, 87
Buttery ginger squares 136, **137**, 138

cakes 17
    Almond and lemon syrup **56**, 57–8
    Apple and pecan crumble 54, **55**
    Apple, rum and raisin 58–9
    baking tips 51–2
    Barbara Lowery's pecan and macadamia
        panforte **98**, 99–100, **101**
    Black-bottom cupcakes 22
    Buttery almond and coconut
        (gluten-free) **86**, 87
    Caramel butter-crunch 88, **89**, 90
    chocolate cakes 15–47
    Chewy coconut macaroon 91–2
    Chocolate and coffee crumble 26–7
    Chocolate and potato 18, **19**
    Classic flourless orange and almond
        (gluten-free) 92, **93**, 94
    cutting in half evenly 73
    Ever-so-easy pear (or plum) and
        hazelnut 95–6
    Flourless Chinese five spice chocolate
        (gluten-free) 32–3
    Flourless chocolate and hazelnut
        (gluten-free) 20–1
    fruit cakes 51–75
    Gooey butterscotch peach 64, **65**, 66
    Kim's delicious apple, pecan and
        cinnamon 96–7
    Most fabulous banana 73–4
    My last-minute Christmas 60, **61**, 62
    nut cakes 79–100
    One-pan mocha cake with coffee bean
        brittle 28, **29**, 30, 31
    Really beautiful orange **70**, 71–2
    Sticky caramel and banana upside-down
        68–9
    Sticky hazelnut chocolate cake with
        coffee syrup 35–6, **37**
    Sticky pineapple, carrot, ginger
        and macadamia 81–2, **83**
    Sticky sour cream, golden syrup
        and ginger 53

Three-nut 84–5
Tropical pineapple crush 74–5
upside-down 64, 68–9
Very quick pear and pecan or walnut 67
White and dark chocolate jaffa swirl 23–4, **25**
'wobbly/firm' 33
Wonderful rich chocolate 34
cake stands 90
cake tins 10, 18, 54, 92
    buttering and flouring 11, 24
Candied citrus zest 258, **259**
caramel
    Caramel butter-crunch cake 88, **89**, 90
    Chocolate, caramel and pecan slice 224–5
    Coconut and caramel slice 222, **223**, 224
    Luscious homemade caramel sauce 257
    Sticky caramel and banana upside-down cake 68–9
    Walnut and caramel bars 210
cardamom 100
cheese
    Brie and pear tart 193
    Cheese and nigella seed biscuits 135
    Cheese, olive and buttermilk herb bread 230, **231**, 232
    Crisp cheese pastry that doesn't need rolling 181
    Dill, ricotta and parmesan muffins **108**, 109
    Polenta, cheese and chilli muffins 106, **107**
    Really good cheese scones 153–4
    Ricotta and smoked paprika tart with agrodolce capsicum 188–9
    Zucchini, feta and dill pie 182, **183**, 184
cheesecake
    Luscious white chocolate 38–9
Chewy coconut macaroon cake 91–2
chocolate 5, 15, 85
    Black-bottom cupcakes 22
    chocolate cakes 15–47
    Chocolate, caramel and pecan slice 224–5
    Chocolate and coffee crumble cake 26–7
    Chocolate curls 254, **255**
    Chocolate and pecan higgledy-piggledys 208, **209**
    Chocolate and potato cake 18, **19**
    Chocolate zig-zags 85
    Dark chocolate chip shortbread 134
    decorations 16–17, 84, 254
    Double chocolate pecan brownies 41
    Flourless Chinese five spice chocolate cake (gluten-free) 32–3

Flourless chocolate and hazelnut cake (gluten-free) 20–1
Ganache (shiny chocolate icing) 256
icing 16
Luscious white chocolate cheesecake 38–9
Marbled mocha brownies 46–7
Mars Bar brownies 40
melting 15–16
One-pan macadamia and chocolate chip brownies 43, **44**, 45
slicing cakes 16
Sticky hazelnut chocolate cake with coffee syrup 35–6, **37**
White and dark chocolate jaffa swirl cake 23–4, **25**
Wonderful rich chocolate cake 34
cinnamon
    Apple, pecan and cinnamon muffins **116**, 117
    Blueberry and cinnamon crumble cake 62–3
    Kim's delicious apple, pecan and cinnamon cake 96–7
Classic flourless orange and almond cake (gluten-free) 92, **93**, 94
cocoa, Dutch-processed 5
coconut
    Buttery almond and coconut cake (gluten-free) **86**, 87
    Chewy coconut macaroon cake 91–2
    Coconut and caramel slice 222, **223**, 224
    Raspberry and coconut bars 220–1
    toasting flakes 91
coffee
    Chocolate and coffee crumble cake 26–7
    Coffee bean brittle **30**, 31
    Marbled mocha brownies 46–7
    One-pan mocha cake with coffee bean brittle 28, **29**, **30**, 31
    syrup 35, 36
Cooee's baked ham and asparagus roll-ups 184–5
Cooee's chewy bran bars 211
cream, double thick 5
Crisp cheese pastry that doesn't need rolling 181
Crunchy peanut butter and sea salt biscuits 143–4, **145**
Crunchy-topped raspberry muffins 112, **113**, 114

Dark chocolate chip shortbread 134

dates
    Date, orange and banana muffins 119
    My mum's pumpkin and date scones 154, **155**, 156
    Old-fashioned gem scones 170, **171**
    Prune, date and fig bran loaves 246–7
    Sticky banana, pecan and date loaf 242
    Sticky sour cream, golden syrup and ginger cake 53
    Wholemeal date scones 162–3
Dill, ricotta and parmesan muffins **108**, 109
Double chocolate pecan brownies 41

eggs 5
    Egg, leek and bacon pie 194, **195**, **196**, 197
Ever-so-easy pear (or plum) and hazelnut 'cake' 95–6

flour 5, 6, 162, 169
Flourless Chinese five spice chocolate cake (gluten-free) 32–3
Flourless chocolate and hazelnut cake (gluten-free) 20–1
Fluffy buttermilk scones **164**, 165
fruit cakes 51–75
Funny little pumpkin cornbread 234, **235**

Ganache (shiny chocolate icing) 256
ginger
    Brown sugar and ginger muffins 118
    Buttery ginger squares 136, **137**, 138
    Sticky pineapple, carrot, ginger and macadamia cake 81–2, **83**
    Sticky sour cream, golden syrup and ginger cake 53
Good, simple shortcrust pastry 177
Gooey butterscotch peach cake 64, **65**, 66
graters, Microplane 10

ham
    Cooee's baked ham and asparagus roll-ups 184–5
hazelnuts 79
    'Auntie' Beryl's Mexican wedding biscuits 138–9
    Ever-so-easy pear (or plum) and hazelnut 'cake' 95–6
    Flourless chocolate and hazelnut cake (gluten-free) 20–1
    Plum and hazelnut crostata 198, **199**, 200
    roasting 139

Spicy apple, aniseed and hazelnut tea bread 243, **244**, 245
Sticky hazelnut chocolate cake with coffee syrup 35–6, **37**
toasted meal 6, 21, 80
Healthy banana and apricot loaf 240–1
honey
    Honey-toasted muesli muffins 111
    Sunflower seed, honey and raisin muffins 110

icing 16, 26
    cream cheese 74–5
    Ganache (shiny chocolate icing) 256
    simple orange 72
ingredients 5–6
Italian pumpkin and mostarda tart 200–1

jam
    Best homemade strawberry jam 252–3
    Strawberry jam 'snails' 157–8, **159**

Kate Llewellyn's mother, Tommy Brinkworth's, prize-winning scones 168–9
Kim's delicious apple, pecan and cinnamon cake 96–7
kumara
    Zucchini and kumara tea bread 233

lemons
    Almond and lemon syrup cake **56**, 57–8
    Candied citrus zest 258, **259**
    Lemon and blueberry muffins 120, **121**
    Luscious lemon slice **218**, 219–20
    Very crisp lemon thins 146–7
Lemonade scones 160, **161**, 162
Luscious homemade caramel sauce 257
Luscious lemon slice **218**, 219–20
Luscious white chocolate cheesecake 38–9

macadamias 79
    Barbara Lowery's pecan and macadamia panforte **98**, 99–100, **101**
    One-pan macadamia and chocolate chip brownies 43, **44**, 45
    Sticky pineapple, carrot, ginger and macadamia cake 81–2, **83**
maple syrup 5
    Spicy pumpkin, pecan and maple muffins 114–15
Marbled mocha brownies 46–7
Mars Bar brownies 40

measuring equipment 9
Most fabulous banana cake 73–4
muffins
    Apple, pecan and cinnamon **116**, 117
    baking tips 105
    Brown sugar and ginger 118
    Crunchy-topped raspberry 112, **113**, 114
    Dill, ricotta and parmesan **108**, 109
    Honey-toasted muesli 111
    Lemon and blueberry 120, **121**
    Polenta, cheese and chilli 106, **107**
    Spicy pumpkin, pecan and maple 114–15
    Sunflower seed, honey and raisin 110
My favourite toffee almond slice 212, **213**, 214
My last-minute Christmas cake 60, **61**, 62
My mum's pistachio and walnut baklava 215, **216**, 217
My mum's pumpkin and date scones 154, **155**, 156

nigella seeds **5**
    Cheese and nigella seed biscuits 135
nutmeg 6
nuts 139
    cakes with nuts 79–100
    Caramel butter-crunch cake 88, **89**, 90
    Crunchy peanut butter and sea salt biscuits 143–4, **145**
    My mum's pistachio and walnut baklava 215, **216**, 217
    Three-nut cake 84–5
    tips 79–80
    Walnut and caramel bars 210
    see also almonds; hazelnuts; macadamias; pecans

Old-fashioned gem scones 170, **171**
One-pan macadamia and chocolate chip brownies 43, **44**, 45
One-pan mocha cake with coffee bean brittle 28, **29**, **30**, 31
oranges
    Candied citrus zest 258, **259**
    Classic flourless orange and almond cake (gluten-free) 92, **93**, 94
    Date, orange and banana muffins 119
    Really beautiful orange cake **70**, 71–2
    Simple orange icing 72
    White and dark chocolate jaffa swirl cake 23–4, **25**
ovens 9, 17, 52

palette knives 10
panforte
    Barbara Lowery's pecan and macadamia panforte **98**, 99–100, **101**
pastry
    blind baking 179–80
    Crisp cheese pastry that doesn't need rolling 181
    Good, simple shortcrust pastry 177
    Pre-baked good, simple shortcrust tart shell **178**, 179–80
    shortcrust tips and variations 175–6, 177
pastry brushes 176
pastry weights 10
peaches 51
    Gooey butterscotch peach cake 64, **65**, 66
peanut butter
    Crunchy peanut butter and sea salt biscuits 143–4, **145**
    measuring 144
pears
    Brie and pear tart 193
    Ever-so-easy pear (or plum) and hazelnut 'cake' 95–6
    Simple pear galette 202–3
    Very quick pear and pecan or walnut cake 67
pecans
    Apple, pecan and cinnamon muffins **116**, 117
    Apple and pecan crumble cake 54, **55**
    Barbara Lowery's pecan and macadamia panforte **98**, 99–100, **101**
    Chocolate, caramel and pecan slice 224–5
    Chocolate and pecan higgledy-piggledys 208, **209**
    Double chocolate pecan brownies 41
    glazed 59, 67
    Pecan and oat crisps 127
    Sally's terrific biscotti 140, **141**, 142
    Spicy pumpkin, pecan and maple muffins 114–15
    Spicy pumpkin, pecan and raisin tea bread 238, **239**
    Sticky banana, pecan and date loaf 242
    Very quick pear and pecan or walnut cake 67
pies *see* tarts and pies
pineapple
    Sticky pineapple, carrot, ginger and macadamia cake 81–2, **83**
    Tropical pineapple crush cake 74–5

plums
    Ever-so-easy pear (or plum) and
        hazelnut 'cake' 95–6
    Plum and hazelnut crostata 198, **199**, 200
    Scrumptious apple and plum cobbler
        166, **167**, 168
polenta 130
    Belinda's polenta and vanilla shortbread
        128, 129–30
    Polenta, cheese and chilli muffins 106, **107**
    Pumpernickel and polenta soda bread
        236, 237
Polenta, cheese and chilli muffins 106, **107**
Pre-baked good, simple shortcrust tart shell
    178, 179–80
Prune, date and fig bran loaves 246–7
Pumpernickel and polenta soda bread
    236, 237
pumpkin
    Funny little pumpkin cornbread 234, **235**
    Italian pumpkin and mostarda tart 200–1
    My mum's pumpkin and date scones 154,
        155, 156
    Spicy pumpkin, pecan and maple muffins
        114–15
    Spicy pumpkin, pecan and raisin tea bread
        238, **239**

raisins
    Apple, rum and raisin cake 58–9
    Spicy pumpkin, pecan and raisin
        tea bread 238, **239**
    Sunflower seed, honey and raisin
        muffins 110
raspberries
    Crunchy-topped raspberry muffins
        112, **113**, 114
    Raspberry and coconut bars 220–1
Really beautiful orange cake **70**, 71–2
Really good cheese scones 153–4
rice paper 5
Ricotta and smoked paprika tart with
    agrodolce capsicum 188–9

Sally's terrific biscotti 140, **141**, 142
scales, digital 9
scones
    baking tips 151–2
    Fluffy buttermilk 164–5
    Kate Llewellyn's mother, Tommy
        Brinkworth's, prize-winning 168–9
    Lemonade 160, **161**, 162

My mum's pumpkin and date 154–6
Old-fashioned gem 170, **171**
Really good cheese 153–4
Strawberry jam 'snails' 157–8, **159**
Wholemeal date 162–3
Scrumptious apple and plum cobbler
    166, **167**, 168
shortbread
    baking tips 131
    Belinda's polenta and vanilla **128**, 129–30
    Brown sugar 131
    Dark chocolate chip 134
shortcrust pastry 175–9
Simple pear galette 202–3
slices 6, 207
    Chocolate, caramel and pecan 224–5
    Coconut and caramel 222, **223**, 224
    Luscious lemon **219**–20
    My favourite toffee almond 212, **213**, 214
    My mum's pistachio and walnut baklava
        215, **216**, 217
smoked paprika 6
    Ricotta and smoked paprika tart with
        agrodolce capsicum 188–9
sour cream 27
spatulas 10
spelt 6
spices 6
Spicy apple, aniseed and hazelnut
    tea bread 243, **244**, 245
Spicy pumpkin, pecan and maple
    muffins 114–15
Spicy pumpkin, pecan and raisin
    tea bread 238, **239**
stainless steel bowls 9
sterilising jars 253
Sticky banana, pecan and date loaf 242
Sticky caramel and banana upside-down
    cake 68–9
Sticky hazelnut chocolate cake with
    coffee syrup 35–6, **37**
Sticky pineapple, carrot, ginger and
    macadamia cake 81–2, **83**
Sticky sour cream, golden syrup and
    ginger cake 53
strawberries
    Best homemade strawberry jam 252–3
    Strawberry jam 'snails' 157–8, **159**
Sunflower seed, honey and raisin muffins 110

tarts and pies
    Brie and pear tart 193

Egg, leek and bacon pie 194, **195**,
    196, 197
Italian pumpkin and mostarda tart 200–1
Plum and hazelnut crostata 198, **199**, 200
Ricotta and smoked paprika tart with
    agrodolce capsicum 188–9
Simple pear galette 202–3
Very delicious cheese and apple tart
    190, 191–2
Wonderful, easy upside-down tomato
    and basil 'pie' 186, **187**
tea breads
    Healthy banana and apricot 240–1
    Prune, date and fig bran 246–7
    Spicy apple, aniseed and hazelnut
        243, **244**, 245
    Spicy pumpkin, pecan and raisin 238–9
    Sticky banana, pecan and date 242
    Zucchini and kumara 233
Three-nut cake 84–5
tomatoes
    Wonderful, easy upside-down tomato
        and basil 'pie' 186, **187**
Tropical pineapple crush cake 74–5

upside-down cakes 64, 68–9
utensils and bakeware 9–10

vanilla 5–6
    Belinda's polenta and vanilla shortbread
        128, 129–30
    Vanilla cream 81
Very crisp lemon thins 146–7
Very delicious cheese and apple tart
    190, 191–2
Very quick pear and pecan or
    walnut cake 67

Walnut and caramel bars 210
washing floury things 11
whisks 9–10
White and dark chocolate jaffa swirl cake
    23–4, **25**
Wholemeal date scones 162–3
Wonderful, easy upside-down tomato
    and basil 'pie' 186, **187**
Wonderful rich chocolate cake 34

zest
    Candied citrus zest 258, **259**
Zucchini, feta and dill pie 182, **183**, 184
Zucchini and kumara tea bread 233

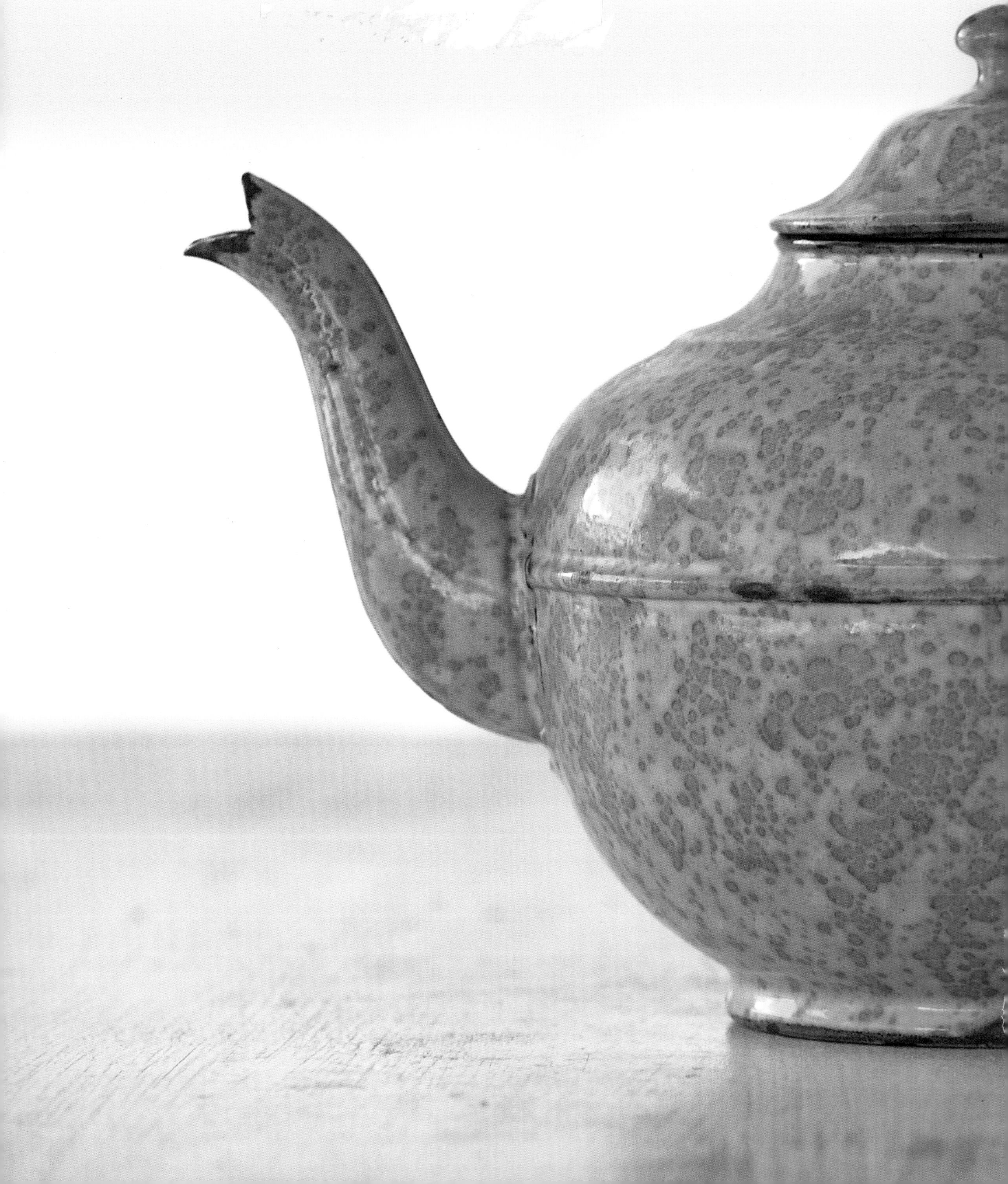